GCSE
Applied Business

Michael Fardon

Chris Nuttall

John Prokopiw

osborne
BOOKS

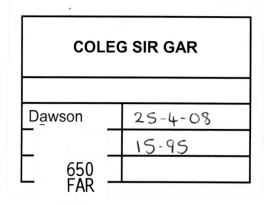
Published by Osborne Books Limited
Unit 1B Everoak Estate
Bromyard Road
Worcester WR2 5HP
Tel 01905 748071
Email books@osbornebooks.co.uk
Website www.osbornebooks.co.uk

Graphic Design by Richard Holt
Cover image courtesy Toyota UK

Printed and bound in Malta by Gutenberg Press Limited

British Library Cataloguing in Publication Data
A catalogue record for this book is available from the British Library

ISBN 978 1872962 320

GCSE
Applied Business

Contents

Unit 1
Investigating business

Unit 2
People and business

Unit 3
Business finance

The authors

Michael Fardon has had extensive teaching experience of vocational business courses at Worcester College of Technology. He now specialises in writing business and financial texts, and was lead writer for the best-selling 'Advanced Business' and 'Intermediate Business' from Osborne Books. He has also worked in a consultancy role for QCA and Edexcel and has been involved in planning and drafting units for vocational business courses.

Chris Nuttall is a freelance lecturer in Business Studies and an established writer for vocational business courses. His publications include 'Business for Intermediate GNVQ' (Collins, 2000) and 'GCSE Business Studies' (Cambridge University Press, 2001).

John Prokopiw is a lecturer in Management and Business Studies at Worcester College of Technology where he is Course Director for the Institute of Personnel and Development programmes. He has been a writer for Osborne Books for a number of years, having contributed the Human Resource Management content for 'Advanced Business' and 'Intermediate Business'.

Acknowledgements

Osborne Books is grateful to a great many people and organisations for helping towards the writing and production of this book.

Particular thanks must go to Adrian Quiney and students of Pershore High School who took part in focus group meetings and advised on the format and design of the book, to Roger Petheram and Carsten Zuntz for reading and advising on the text, to Richard Holt for his designs and production assistance, to Jon Moore for text processing, to Robert Fardon for taking many of the photographs and to Elizabeth Smith for taking the lead role in the Ella Case Study.

Case Studies form an important element of this book and Osborne Books is greatly indebted to a number of businesses who generously donated their time and resources; these include easyJet, McDonald's UK, Richer Sounds, The Royal Bank of Scotland plc, Tesco PLC and Virgin UK Limited.

Osborne Books would also like to thank the following organisations for helping to provide material and illustrations for the book: Amazon.co.uk, Andrew Grant, the Bank of England, Barclays Bank Plc, Biz/ed, Bookcraft, Boots Plc, British Broadcasting Corporation, British Franchise Association, Broadheath Stores, BT, Business Link Hereford & Worcester, Cadbury Schweppes plc, Call Centre Focus, Central Taxis, Central Trains, Checketts News and Food, Co-operative Bank Plc, the Co-operative Group, Cosmoair plc, Department for Work and Pensions, Department of Trade and Industry, Diglis Hotel, Dino's Dial-A-Pizza, easyJet, Equal Opportunities Commission, First Choice Holidays, Halifax Building Society, Harrison Clark, Health and Safety Executive, Highland Water Ltd, HMV, Honda Motor Europe Ltd, HSBC Holdings Plc, the Information Commissioner, Investors in People, Italian Coffee House, Jingos, Jobsite UK (Worldwide) Ltd, Lannies, Lloyds TSB Plc, London Camera Exchange, The Mail on Sunday, Malvern Hills Science Park, MG Rover Group Ltd, Microsoft, Moto, National Shoppers Survey, National Training Awards, National Westminster Bank Plc, Nationwide Building Society, News Team International, Oakstone Classics, One-on-One Fitness Centre, Orange Plc, Peugeot UK, Prontaprint, Robert Hitchins Properties, Roscoe and Crombie Men's and Women's Wear, Royal Mail, Sage Group Plc, Securicor, Simply Gifted, Small Business Service (DTI), Spin UK Ltd, Start-rite Shoes Limited, the Telework Association, Toyota UK, Tramps Nightclub, Transport for London, Unilever UK Limited, Unison, Volvo Car UK Ltd, Whitbread Restaurants, Worcester City Council, Worcestershire Royal Hospital.

A note for teachers

'GCSE Applied Business' has been written as a practical book for a practical course – the vocational 'applied' GCSE offered by the Awarding Bodies, based on common units written by QCA.

This book may seem 'chunkier' than some of the traditional GCSE texts, but the aim has been to make the pages clearer and less cluttered. The design has largely been driven by the opinions of focus groups of teachers and students who have given Osborne Books candid opinions about what they like to see in text book content and design.

'GCSE Applied Business' is divided into three sections reflecting the three units of the course. Each section is divided into short chapters, each with progressive activities, key terms and concise 'nutshell' summaries. The first chapter 'Why start a business?' is not specifically required by the GCSE specification, but has been included to provide a 'jumping off point' for the course. A frequent question posed by the teachers we consulted was, 'How do we start the students off in a stimulating way?' We hope the first chapter solves this problem.

'GCSE Applied Business' provides a number of Case Studies which continue through the chapters and so engage the students' interest, and stimulate learning.

A number of Case Studies are based on real businesses, while some Case Studies are fictitious and are largely unit based: Whittakers PLC, a manufacturer, features in the People and Business unit; Ella, who starts a computer training business, helps to maintain the thread in the Business Finance unit.

Students periodically encounter problems with Business Finance, particularly when it is externally assessed. This book treats this subject in detail, and the author has taken pains to ensure that the publicised assessment requirements of the Awarding Bodies are catered for in the various activities that the students carry out.

A Tutor Pack, containing guidance answers to the Unit 3 activities, together with practice external assessments, is available from Osborne Books (01905 748071).

Osborne Books likes to keep in touch with its customers and would welcome comments of any kind about this book – please write or telephone, or email books@osbornebooks.co.uk.

Michael Fardon
July 2002

Introduction for students

In this introduction we will tell you about the GCSE Applied Business qualification, the assessments you will have to do, and the ways in which this book can help you with your studies.

Applied GCSE Business – a double award

The GCSE in Applied Business is a double award; in other words, it is the equivalent of two GCSEs. Like any other GCSE you will be given a grade at the end of the course, based on an A* to G scale. Because the award is a double award you will receive a qualification which is equivalent to two GCSEs.

Applied GCSE Business – a vocational award

The GCSE in Applied Business is also a vocational award. 'Vocational' means that the qualification is not just a classroom-based study of business, it is 'work related'. This means that you are likely to go on a work placement, visit different businesses and hear talks from visiting speakers. The course will enable you to acquire the knowledge and develop many of the skills that you will need in a business career. This should make it easier for you to get a job.

Assessment of the GCSE

The assessment of your GCSE in Applied Business, like other GCSEs, involves a mix of coursework (known as your 'Portfolio') and external examination. Whichever Examining Board your school or college uses for this GCSE, the assessment will be very much along the same lines.

The GCSE in Applied Business is divided into three units:

Unit 1 Investigating business

This unit investigates different types of business, what they do and how they work. It also looks at all the outside pressures that businesses have to deal with, such as coping with legal requirements and protecting the environment.

This unit is assessed by a Portfolio assignment investigating two different businesses.

Unit 2 People and business

This unit is about people. It involves an investigation into the issues relating to employers and employees, disputes, training, applying for jobs and dealing with customers.

This unit is assessed by a Portfolio assignment investigating one large business.

Unit 3 Business finance

This unit is about money. It deals with financial documents, financial records, making payments, the need to plan and budget and the process of applying for finance.

This unit is assessed by an external practical examination.

How to use the chapters

This textbook is divided into three sections – one for each unit – and each section is divided into chapters. The chapters contain:

- an opening Case Study which sets the scene and introduces the subject, together with a 'point to think about'

- a text with definitions and highlighted key terms

- activities which help you understand the concepts

- a list of key terms at the end of the chapter – useful for notetaking and revision

- a 'nutshell' chapter summary – also useful for notetaking and revision

How to use the Case Studies

There are a number of Case Studies in this book – based on real life situations – which have a story line which continues from chapter to chapter. These help you to see how the areas you study link together.
Here is a description of two of them.

Whittakers PLC (in Unit 2) is a manufacturing company which recruits Sharon onto its staff. The Case Study follows Sharon's  application for the job, her interview, appointment and subsequent training. It also features a labour dispute, a possible dismissal and other workplace problems.

Ella Webster (in Unit 3) sets up a computer training business. She has to plan for her costs and likely income;
she visits the bank to raise finance and to get financial advice.

Using the internet and other resources

The internet is a goldmine for the business student. With the help of search engines such as www.google.co.uk you can log on to the websites of businesses of all sizes, Government departments and Trade Unions.
You can also use business educational websites such as www.bized.ac.uk to search for information.

At the back of this book (page 371) there is a Web Directory of useful websites to help you with your Portfolio investigations.

Good luck with your studies!

Investigating Business

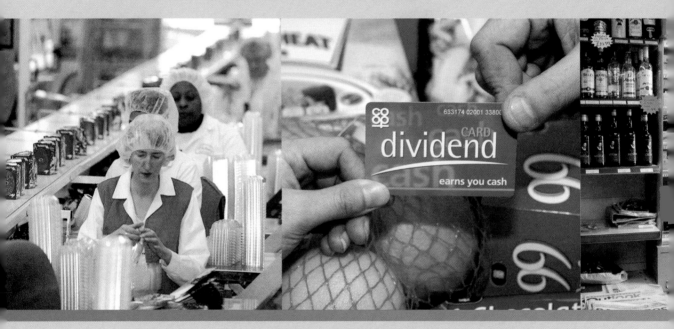

This unit will involve you in investigating a wide range of businesses and studying two in detail. The unit will enable you to find out about:

■ what it is that makes people want to start a business

■ what businesses aim to achieve

■ different types of business

■ the decisions that lead to a business locating in a particular place

■ the different activities involved in business

■ the ways in which businesses communicate and use information and communication technology

■ the threats and pressures that business face and the ways in which they react to them

 Chapters in this Unit...

1

Why start a business?

It's tough out there – but it's worth it!

Running a successful business is hard work. Starting a new successful business is even harder work.

People know about the success stories and the well-known names like Richard Branson and Bill Gates in the present day and Walt Disney and Henry Ford from the past. But nobody knows or cares about the failures and also-rans.

In Business Studies we need to investigate what makes businesses 'tick' and what enables business leaders to create wealth for themselves and for others as well. This is a very human story.

We need to know what a person starting a business is up against – what their goals are and how they achieve them.

In order to do this we have had the help of Julian Richer, founder and Chairman of the 'Richer Sounds' chain of hi-fi stores. This chapter tells his story and also features Stelios Haji-Ioannou, who founded the airline 'easyJet'.

This first chapter sets the concept of 'business' in perspective – a concept we will develop over the chapters that follow.

a point to think about . . .

People who start businesses need to know where they are going – what they are aiming at and what their targets are.

They can either sink or swim!

entrepreneurs

People who start new businesses are often known as **entrepreneurs**.

An entrepreneur is a person who has the idea and energy for starting a business and who is willing to take the risk.

Businesses are certainly risky. Here are some facts:

- 342,000 new businesses started up in the UK in 2001
- 410,000 businesses closed down in the UK in 2001
- 4 out of 10 businesses started in London do not survive for more than three years

We will now look at the Case Study of a success story of a business started in London. We will finish the chapter by examining what exactly is involved in a running a business.

Case Study – Richer Sounds

Julian Richer

In 1978 an unknown nineteen year old, Julian Richer, began piling hi-fi stock into a small unit at London Bridge in which he started selling with the philosophy that customer service meant organising the business for the benefit of the customer, not for the benefit of the managers.

Richer Sounds has now grown to become the UK's largest and most profitable retailer of hi-fi equipment. 47 of its 49 stores are in the United Kingdom, with two in the Republic of Ireland (Cork and Dublin).

The company employs some 350 people and describes itself as 'a big fish in a small pond – we are very good at what we do and we stick to that.'

Richer Sounds has featured in the Guinness Book of Records for the past six years as the company with the highest sales per square foot of any retailer in the world.

Its product range has grown to include budget audio, high-quality reference products, audio-visual home cinema and semi-professional studio equipment. Richer Sounds serves in excess of one million customers per year.

All UK shops are wholly owned by Richer Sounds Plc but shops in Ireland, commencing with the company's Dublin shop in 1993, have so far been organised on a franchise basis.

The company has intentionally positioned its British Isles outlets so that 'every city with a catchment population of over 250,000, within half an hour's drive, has access to a Richer Sounds outlet.'

Julian Richer has made the transition from poor school performer to the building from scratch of a £100m plus group of businesses.

www.richersounds.com

Activity 1.1 – Richer Sounds

Read through the Case Study on the previous page and then answer the questions below.

1 How old was Julian Richer when he set up his first store?
How many stores does Richer Sounds now have?

2 What achievement of the Richer Sounds chain of stores features in the Guiness Book of Records?

3 How many customers does Richer Sounds serve each year?

4 What was Julian Richer's business philosophy when he first started – customers first or managers first? Do you agree with this way of thinking?

5 Richer Sounds is set up as a company but its stores in Ireland are 'organised on a franchise basis'. What does this mean? Can you think of any other organisations that run franchises?

6 What do you think are the main business aims of Richer Sounds?

internal decisions made by a business

Entrepreneurs who start businesses must have energy and ideas. In reading and thinking about Richer Sounds you will already have an idea of how it has become a successful business:

it has decided on an area of activity . . .

It is a hi-fi retailer – it piles its merchandise high and sells it at very competitive prices.

it knows where it is going to operate . . .

It has stores in the UK and the European Union (The Republic of Ireland).

it has defined aims . . .

The business knows where it is going:

- it wants to be profitable
- it wants to expand its sales
- it wants to increase the number of its stores
- it wants to benefit its customers

It is important to note that the company also exists for the benefit of its staff, providing them with many perks including the use of holiday homes free of charge.

it has decided on its ownership . . .

Richer Sounds Plc trades as a company – its owners are shareholders (there is more about this on page 51). Some of its stores are franchises. This means (as you will know if you have done the question on page 14) that some stores are operated by individuals as independent businesses, but using the Richer Sounds name (and paying for it).

outside pressures on the business

Businesses do not exist in a vacuum – they have to deal with individuals, organisations, and the Government.

Many of these 'outside pressures' can get in the way of what businesses are trying to achieve. Businesses have to react to them. Study the diagram below. It shows what drives a business forward – its internal decisions – but it also explains some of the outside pressures it has to deal with. These outside pressures are also illustrated in the Case Study on the next page.

questions a business has to ask

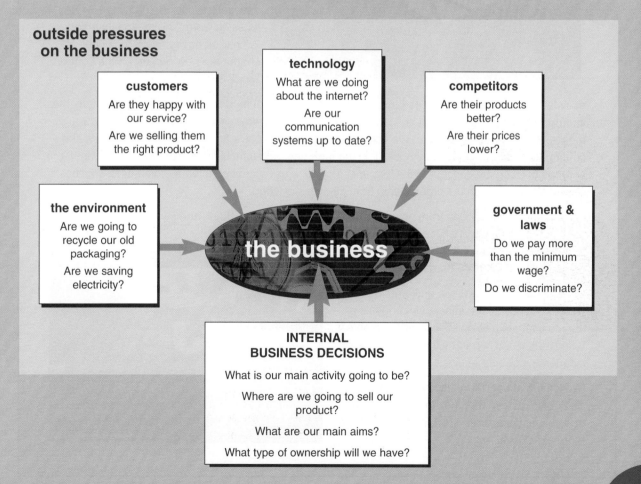

outside pressures on the business

customers
Are they happy with our service?
Are we selling them the right product?

technology
What are we doing about the internet?
Are our communication systems up to date?

competitors
Are their products better?
Are their prices lower?

the environment
Are we going to recycle our old packaging?
Are we saving electricity?

the business

government & laws
Do we pay more than the minimum wage?
Do we discriminate?

INTERNAL BUSINESS DECISIONS
What is our main activity going to be?
Where are we going to sell our product?
What are our main aims?
What type of ownership will we have?

Case Study – Stelios and easyJet

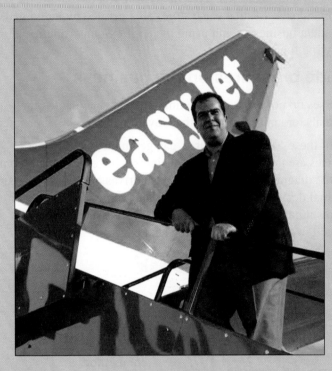

easyJet is one of Europe's leading low-cost airlines.

easyJet was founded in 1995 by the entrepreneur Stelios Haji-Ioannou, who has also founded other 'easy' businesses such easyCar (car hire) and easyinternetCafé. Stelios will remain group Chairman until 2003.

The airline started with a fleet of two Boeing 737s flying from Luton to Glasgow and Edinburgh. The airline now offers over 40 routes from 16 European destinations with a fleet of 30 Boeing 737s.

easyJet's profits in 2001 were £40m, its sales were £357m, and it carried 7.7 million passengers. easyJet shares are now quoted on the London Stock Exchange.

easyJet has managed to keep its fares low through the use of modern technology – particularly the internet. The airline sold its first online fare in April 1998 and now sells 90% of its business through the internet. easyJet does not issue tickets – passengers receive an email with travel details and a confirmation number when they book. The management and administration of the company is carried out using the concept of the 'paperless office' – using central servers (computers) which can be accessed from the organisation from all over the world.

easyJet faces competition from other low-cost operators such as Buzz and Ryanair, but there is plenty of room for expansion as more and more travellers choose the low-cost option at the expense of full-price carriers.

What about airlines and the environment? Concerns such as the effect of jet engines on the atmosphere and noise levels of aircraft are being addressed in part by the introduction of cleaner and quieter engines.

Customers are certainly happy with easyJet. Their only gripe is with the Government's tax on air flight departures which makes travelling more expensive!

www.easyjet.com

Activity 1.2 – outside pressures on easyJet

Read the Case Study on the previous page and answer these questions.

1   What do you think is the main benefit to easyJet's customers of flying with the airline?

2   Who are easyJet's main competitors?

3   Do you think easyJet sees these competitors as a major threat? If not, why not?

4   How has easyJet made the most of information technology?

5   What are the main benefits to easyJet customers of its use of information technology?

6   In what way has the Government intervened with airlines to make travelling more expensive? Can airlines such as easyJet do anything about this?

7   Discuss the ways in which air travel can affect the environment by way of atmospheric and noise pollution. What is being done about it?

8   Discuss the benefits to the business of Stelios starting up other 'easy' companies in the Group such as car hire and internet cafés.

Nutshell summary

- Businesses are normally started by entrepreneurs who are the driving force behind the business.

- Entrepreneurs understand the nature of the risks they are taking. Many businesses do not succeed.

- A business has to take a number of internal decisions:
  - what its main activities are going to be
  - what its aims are
  - where it is going to operate
  - what form of ownership it is going to adopt

- A business is also affected by a number of external pressures which have an effect on the way it develops and operates. These include:
  - the views and attitudes of its customers
  - the strength of its competitors
  - its reaction to the challenges of technology
  - Government regulations and laws
  - the need to protect the environment

Key terms

Entrepreneur
A person who has the idea and energy for starting a business and who is willing to take risks.

Company
A business owned by shareholders.

Franchise
A business run by one or more individuals, but paying to trade under a well-known name.

Internal decisions
Decisions made by the entrepreneur which decide the way the business will operate.

External pressures
Outside factors which decide how the business will operate.

2

Business activities

Who wants to be a millionaire?

Nic was 17 and had already left school. He didn't get very good grades, but one thing he was good at was working with computers and writing computer programs and games. He had been working as a sales assistant at a computer store for six months when he heard that his uncle had won a lot of money on the Lottery. Nic could not believe his luck when his uncle offered him £50,000 capital to start his own business. His uncle said 'I always like to support the family. You can pay me back when you can – when the business starts to produce a profit.'

Nic had to think hard about his new business as so many ideas flooded into his mind . . .

He could live at home and write computer programs all day.

He could buy in components and build computers systems to sell to other businesses.

He could set up as a technician to sort out computer problems and failures.

He could set up an on-line mail order business for computer products such as games.

The problem was deciding on the right product. What was it to be?

a point to think about . . .

It is all very well having the enthusiasm and energy to take on a business, but you have to decide on the right product that people want and that will make you a profit.

products, goods and services

As you will see from the Case Study above, you can carry out a wide variety of activities in business. These activities provide the **products** of the business.

The products of a business include making goods and providing a service.

But what are goods and services?

Goods are items which you can touch and use.

Goods include items like clothes, cans of drink, CDs, computers.

Services are things that other people do for you.

Services include things such as haircuts, selling goods in a shop, giving expert advice.

In your investigation of businesses you will see that there are many different products made available to provide people with what they want. These are the activities of business.

When you compile your Portfolio you will have to describe and analyse the activities carried out by your two chosen businesses. You will need to know how these activities can be classified in a number of different ways – these are shown on the next few pages.

producing raw goods

The first step in the making of many products is the extraction of raw materials.

This page, for example, started off as a tree, probably cut down somewhere in Scandinavia.

Look at the examples below.

food production

Much of the food we consume is extracted in raw form from natural resources.

For example:

- meat and milk from animals
- grain and fruit produced by farms
- fish from the sea and fish farms

The yellow field on the left is oil seed rape, a crop used for making cooking oil.

extraction of raw materials

Many of the products we use are made up from raw materials which have been extracted from natural resources.

For example:

- wood and paper from forestry
- stone and gravel from quarries
- metal and coal from mines
- petroleum from oilfields (as on the right)

manufacturing processes

Many of the products extracted in raw form are then used in the manufacturing process.

Manufacturing can be for:

- **consumer goods** – items such as food and clothes which are kept for a limited period of time

- **capital goods** – items which are kept for a longer period; for most people these include equipment such as microwaves and fridges, for businesses they include machinery and equipment

manufacturing of goods

consumer goods

making chocolate at Cadbury's – a favourite consumer good which does not last for long

capital goods

making machinery – an item kept for a long time and used by businesses

providing services

Many businesses are set up to provide a service. Services can involve many activities – selling goods in shops or providing a benefit such as a holiday or a train trip.

selling goods

Once goods have been manufactured they can be distributed and sold from a variety of outlets – the **retailers**:

- supermarkets

- small independent shops

- mail order companies

- on-line shops on the internet

Some goods pass from the manufacturer to the retailer through a specialist **wholesaler** who will keep stocks of goods that retailers need. For example a fruit wholesaler or a book wholesaler. This book may have passed through a wholesaler.

service businesses – the selling process

store shopping – a service from HMV

online shopping – a service from amazon.co.uk

providing client and customer services

Many services do not involve goods at all. They provide a benefit to clients and customers. Examples include:

■ membership services – health clubs, gyms, sports clubs

■ financial services – bank accounts, insurance

■ personal services – doctors, dentists, haircuts, body piercing

service businesses – client and customer services

gym membership

financial services

health care

industrial sectors

As we have just seen, businesses can be classified according to what they do. Your study of business sometimes requires you to classify a business into one of three **industrial sectors** . . .

primary sector – extracting natural resources

This involves the extracting of natural resources, ie raw materials for use in the manufacturing process. Examples of primary production are mining, farming, market gardening, fishing and forestry.

secondary sector – manufacturing products

This is the next stage of production; it involves the processing of raw materials into the manufactured product: fruit into pies or juice, wood into chipboard, metal into cars, and so on.

tertiary sector – providing services

This third classification involves a business providing a service rather than a manufactured item; examples include catering, shops, insurance, travel, and advertising.

Activity 2.1 – investigating business activity

1   What types of possible business activity can you identify in the Case Study on page 18? State whether they involve extracting raw materials, manufacturing or services.

2   Into which industrial sector would you classify the following businesses? Primary, secondary or tertiary?

(a)	a rubber plantation	**(b)**	a supermarket	**(c)**	a car manufacturer
(d)	a fruit grower	**(e)**	a tyre manufacturer	**(f)**	a travel agent
(g)	an airline	**(h)**	a restaurant	**(i)**	a catering firm

3   What links can you identify between any of these businesses which make them depend on each other?

4   Your Portfolio requires you to choose two contrasting businesses to investigate. One of the areas of difference is likely to be the type of activity they carry out.

To help you make your choice, carry out a 'brainstorming exercise' with your fellow students and make lists between you of:

■   businesses that extract natural resources

■   businesses that manufacture goods

■   businesses that provide services

Use resources such as Yellow Pages and local knowledge.
Try an internet 'key word' search to identify suitable businesses that have useful websites.

the chain of production

As we have seen, businesses depend on each other. From the last Activity you will have seen that . . .

- ■ **extractors of raw materials** and natural resources (primary sector) supply . . .
- ■ **manufacturers** (secondary sector) who produce goods for . . .
- ■ **service providers** such as shops (tertiary sector) to sell

This **chain of production** can be clearly illustrated in the car industry:

the chain of production – Honda cars

primary sector

iron ore extracted from the ground is made into sheet steel

secondary sector

the sheet steel is used on a Honda car production line

tertiary sector

the Honda car is sold by the dealer

Activity 2.2 – the chain of production

1　Identify the two chains of production which are likely to be set up between the following businesses:

home furnishing store　　　　　**fish farm**　　　　　**supermarket chain**

timber company　　　　　**food processing company**　　　　　**furniture manufacturer**

2　Draw two flow diagrams with boxes and arrows (like the one shown above) illustrating your answers.

Include on your diagrams a description of the activity of each business and the industrial sector to which the business belongs.

Use the wording on the diagram on this page as a guide.

changes in business activities

In this chapter we have seen that the main classifications of businesses are by **industrial sector** – using natural resources (primary sector), manufacturing (secondary sector) and service businesses (tertiary sector) – in other words they are classified by what the businesses **do**.

Because of the way that factors affecting businesses are constantly changing, the 'mix' of businesses never stands still.

Factors affecting businesses in the UK include:

- the amount of money people have available to spend
- the type of products people like to buy or are encouraged by advertising to buy
- the fact that some raw materials from abroad are cheaper than raw material produced in the UK
- the fact that some businesses find it cheaper to manufacture goods abroad because wage costs can be lower overseas

Some types of business will therefore do well and increase in number and other types will struggle and decline.
In general, recent trends have been:

- an increase in the number of service businesses (tertiary sector)
- a decline in the manufacturing industries (secondary sector)
- a decline in agriculture, forestry and fishing (primary sector)

Carry out the Activity that follows and you will see exactly what these trends are.

Activity 2.3 – changes in business activities

The table on the next page sets out statistics showing the trend in different types of business activity over the years 1997 to 2000. Study the figures and answer the questions below.

1 What is the trend in businesses which are engaged in agriculture, forestry and fishing?

2 What is the trend in businesses which are engaged in manufacturing?

3 What is the trend in businesses which are engaged in retail, wholesale and repairs?

4 Draw up a multiple bar chart showing these trends. Use an ICT package if you can.

5 What do these trends tell you about the way in which business activity is changing? What reasons can you think of for these changes?

6 Provide examples from the area in which you live which show that these trends might be continuing.

trends in types of business activity

type of business	1997 businesses	1997 employed	2000 businesses	2000 employed
Agriculture, forestry and fishing	220,865	532,000	190,390	467,000
Manufacturing	332,210	4,466,000	332,085	4,191,000
Retail and wholesale services	526,395	4,269,000	536,040	4,509,000

Source: Small Business Service (DTI)

Nutshell summary

- Businesses can carry out a wide variety of activities, selling goods or services (or both) – these are the products of a business.

- Business activities can be classified into three main areas:
  - extracting raw materials and growing food
  - manufacturing raw materials into finished products
  - selling the goods or providing a service

  These three main areas are known as the primary, secondary and tertiary sectors of industry.

- These three areas of business link together in what is known as the chain of production.

- The three areas of business activity are subject to trends brought about by outside forces such as availability of money to spend, and the cost of producing goods in the UK.

- The basic trends for business activity in the UK are currently:
  - extracting raw materials (primary sector) – declining
  - manufacturing (secondary sector) – declining
  - providing services (tertiary sector) – rising

Key terms

Goods
Items made by a business.

Services
Things that people do for you.

Products
Goods or services provided by businesses.

Consumer goods
Goods which are made to be kept for a limited period.

Capital goods
Goods which are made to be kept in the long term.

Primary sector
Businesses that extract raw materials.

Secondary sector
Businesses that manufacture.

Tertiary sector
Businesses that provide services.

3

Business aims and objectives

The McDonald's story

The McDonald's fast food concept was formulated by Mac and Dick McDonald in California in 1954. The first restaurant was opened in 1955 near Chicago by Ray Kroc, who then became the driving force behind the McDonald's chain of fast food outlets.

McDonald's came to the UK in 1974 with the opening of the 3,000th McDonald's in Woolwich, South London. The rest, as they say, is history.

Here are some facts about what McDonald's currently does:

- McDonald's now serves over 45 million customers every day
- McDonald's worldwide sales are around £10,000,000,000 a year and its profits £2,350,000,000
- McDonald's was named Waste-wise Partner for the Year by the US Environmental Protection Agency
- Ronald McDonald Children's Charities has given more than £210,000,000 to charities for sick and disadvantaged children

a point to think about . . .

McDonald's has come a long way, but what are the aims of this well-known business? What is it trying to do? What is it trying to achieve?

www.mcdonalds.co.uk

business aims and objectives

Ray Kroc, who started McDonald's in 1955, would probably have been amazed by the size of the business today. He would, in 1955, have had a number of **aims** and **objectives** in getting the business off the ground. Before discussing these, we need to look at what precisely we mean when we use these words:

an aim is what you set out to do

an objective is a target you want to achieve

For example, a business **aim** is to make a profit.

A business **objective** is to make a profit of over £100,000 next year.

In this chapter we will look at business aims and objectives in a number of businesses.

business aims

To get an idea of business aims, look again at the McDonald's story and compare the likely aims of Ray Kroc in 1955 with the aims of McDonald's today. This will give you a good idea of how aims vary from one business to another.

business aims

1955: First McDonald's restaurant

Like any person starting out in business Ray Kroc would have worked hard to:

■ survive in business for his first year

■ sell as many meals as possible

■ make a profit

■ concentrate on selling to the local community

McDonald's in the 21st century

McDonald's is now a worldwide business with many aims to achieve:

■ to expand and beat the worldwide competition

■ to maximise sales and profit

■ to help charities

■ to be environmentally friendly

It is obvious from this that the first restaurant was a small local business which had to work hard to survive its first year. McDonald's today is a different story: it continues to expand and has the resources to give to charity and to take trouble over its environmental policy.

When you are investigating businesses for your Portfolio you should try to identify the aims that the two businesses have adopted. This could be your checklist:

■ to operate on a small scale locally or on a wider national or international basis

■ to make a profit and expand

■ to maximise its sales and beat the competition

■ to survive

■ to provide a quality product

■ to help or work for charity

■ to help sustain the environment

We will give examples of these aims in the next few pages.

what is the scope of the business?

Many businesses are set up as local businesses: eg corner shops and taxi firms. Some businesses may have the potential – like the original McDonald's – to expand nationally or internationally. But there will always be the place for a local business.

Activity 3.1 – local, national or international?

the local shop

This local shop stands on a busy main road. It attracts its customers from the estates in the immediate area and also from passing traffic. It sells a wide variety of products: newspapers, periodicals, food and drink. It also has a Post Office counter inside and has recently started a video and DVD hire service. The counter staff are very friendly and know quite a few of the customers by name.

Tesco

Tesco originated in 1919 as a grocery business in London's East End markets.

It has now grown to a large chain of 'value-for-money' stores within the UK.

Tesco also operates stores in Eastern Europe, Thailand and Malaysia.

Shoppers who cannot get to a Tesco store can log on to its home shopping service, Tesco Direct.

questions

1 What are the likely aims of the owner of a 'local' business?

2 What are the likely aims of a business which has a national or international presence?

3 Suggest a way in which a local business could achieve national or even international sales.

financial success – aiming for profit and expansion

Profit is measured as

the income of a business from sales minus its running costs

For many businesses making profits is an important aim.

holiday price wars

It provides a reward for the owners of the business and helps the business to have the money to expand its operations.

maximising sales and beating competitors

Making a profit is not the same as selling as many products as possible. The reason for this is that many businesses need to beat the competition. Businesses which sell popular products such as holidays and food often cut prices to get more sales. They may take part in what are known as 'price wars.' But cut prices can mean reduced profits. Often the business owner has to decide which is the more important aim: higher sales or higher profits?

running a business – a game of survival

British Airways route to survival

by Tina Carver, Transport Correspondent

British Airways has cut its fares and cut back on 'extras' such as in-flight meals in order to compete with the low-price airlines.

In order to reduce its costs the airline has cut staff by 23%, routes by 24% and its fleet of planes by 14%.

The budget airlines were said to have been "not at all worried" by this development.

Survival for the new business is critical. Most new businesses are owned by just one person and that person will often depend on the business for living expenses.

More established businesses can also be threatened – often by competitors – and survival has to become a main aim if jobs are to be safeguarded and investors are not to lose money.

A survival plan means a business may have to cut back on its services and in some cases cut its prices too, as in the case of British Airways seen in the newspaper article shown here.

a quality product

providing a quality product

For some businesses the quality of its products is a prime aim.

Quality is becoming more and more part of manufacturing and of service provision. 'Quality Control' will test actual products on a regular basis. 'Quality Assurance' is a way of thinking within a business which relates everything the organisation does to quality.

It should also be noted that there are certain 'prestige' businesses which offer goods and services of superior quality at superior prices. People who can afford these will always buy them.

Examples include exclusive hotels, executive cars and luxury holidays.

corporate social responsibility – helping charity

Businesses support charities by sponsoring events or by giving donations. Not many businesses could claim that this was a main aim – they will want to make the profits first. Charitable giving takes place because it gives the business a 'caring' profile in the eyes of the public. It forms part of what is known as **corporate social responsibility**.

The Ronald McDonald Children's Charities, for example, provides accommodation to families of very sick children and donates equipment for children with special needs.

the need to protect the atmosphere

corporate social responsibility – going green

There is increasing evidence that the earth's resources are being depleted and damaged by business on a worldwide scale. Not only are resources running out, but pollution is damaging the balance of gases in the atmosphere, leading to global warming. These trends directly result from worldwide industrial processes. Businesses are under increasing pressure from governments and pressure groups such as Greenpeace to carry out a policy of **sustainability**. This means adopting objectives such as:

■ cutting down on pollution

■ not wasting natural resources

■ using recycled materials wherever possible

■ using energy efficiently

Businesses like to be seen to be helping to save the environment. If they are thought to be socially responsible, consumers are more likely to think the better of them and therefore more likely to buy their products. Also, savings on the use of resources such as energy use can also mean savings on cost; this directly helps to boost profits.

A business which has recently donated to 'green' causes is HSBC, a leading bank.

HSBC beats 'green' records

by Ivor Pound, Financial Correspondent

HSBC, the banking giant has announced what is thought to be a record charitable donation to 'green' causes.

The bank has donated £35m to three environmental charities which include the Worldwide Fund for Nature. The money will go towards scientific training, river conservation and developing a gene bank of endangered plant species.

mission statements

A business will often set out its main aims in a 'Mission Statement'. It may also include a view of how it sees itself in what is known as the business 'vision'.

When you are investigating businesses for your Portfolio and trying to choose two for special study, you should try to obtain their Mission Statements. Businesses sometimes put them in their annual reports or on their website – accessed in the 'about us' section or possibly from a FAQ ('Frequently Asked Questions') button.

Activity 3.2 – aims and Mission Statements

McDonald's vision is to be the UK's best quick service restaurant experience. This will be achieved through five strategies: Development, Our People, Restaurant Excellence, Operating Structure, and The Brand.

Development

Lead the Quick Service Restaurant market by a programme of site development and profitable restaurant openings.

Our People

Achieve a competitive advantage through people who are high calibre, effective, well motivated and feel part of the McDonald's team in delivering the company's goals.

Restaurant Excellence

Focus on consistent delivery of quality, service and cleanliness through excellence in our restaurants.

Operating Structure

Optimise restaurant performance through the selection of the most appropriate operating, management and ownership structures.

The Brand

Continue to build the relationship between McDonald's and our customers in order to be a genuine part of the fabric of British society.

Source: Biz/ed

1   List the business aims you can identify in the McDonald's Mission Statement and explain how McDonald's hopes to achieve them. Are there any aims that are missing from this Statement?

2   Obtain a copy, if you can, of the Mission Statements of the two businesses you are investigating for your Portfolio. Identify the business aims contained in them and write notes on how the businesses hope to achieve them.

meeting business objectives

an aim is what you set out to do

an objective is a target you want to achieve

We have already seen what aims a business will have in mind. The business will also set **objectives** – targets and challenges – so that it can realistically achieve those aims. Objectives can be set for areas such as sales, profit, customer service and environmental sustainability.

some examples of objectives

Many objectives relate to sales and financial performance because profit and competitive position are important business aims, for example:

■ the business will increase sales by 30% in the next year

■ the business will increase profits by 10% in the next year

■ the business will take 10% of its competitors' market share in the next year

quality targets – customer services

Most businesses set quality targets, often as part of their 'Quality Assurance'. Many public services, railway operating companies for example, set targets for reliability and punctuality as part of their 'Customer Charter'. Performance against these targets is monitored carefully and regularly published.

An extract from the London Underground Charter is shown below.

Improving Service

Our commitment

London Underground aims to deliver the best possible service for all its customers. You want a quick, frequent and reliable train service, a safe, clean and welcoming station environment with up-to-date information and helpful, courteous staff. This means a continuous, demanding programme of improvements to meet rising expectations.

Our targets

To drive and measure these improvements, performance targets covering many aspects of our service have been agreed with Government as part of the Citizen's Charter programme. If you would like to know more, please contact our Customer Service Centre.

environmental targets

As businesses become more aware of the need for sustainability (preserving the environment), the setting of environmental targets has become more common.

The Co-operative Bank, for example, has set a number of environmental targets and has published its success rate . . .

recycling of at least 15% of steel and aluminium cans purchased

recycling of at least 15% of plastic cups purchased

recycling of 100% of fluorescent tubes

reduction in the use of paper by 10%

recycling of 30% of paper used

have the objectives been met?

There is little point in setting objectives if the business does not bother to check if the targets have been met and measure how successful it has been in meeting its objectives.

If it has not been successful, it will have to ask why it has fallen short of its targets and it should take action, either by changing the objective or by taking other action within the business to make sure it meets the target in the future.

Activity 3.3 – meeting objectives

1 Investigate and comment on examples of reports of how public service targets (objectives) have been met, for example published statements of the punctuality of railway services.

2 Obtain details of the objectives of the two businesses you are investigating for your Portfolio. If this is not possible, write down examples of the type of objectives you think the businesses might set. If the opportunity arises, discuss these with people from each business.

Nutshell summary

■ Businesses need to adopt a number of aims which will direct the way in which they develop and operate.

■ Business aims cover a wide area of subjects including:

- where the business will operate

- to make a profit and expand and to survive

- to maximise sales and to beat the competition

- to provide a quality product

- to be socially responsible, ie to help charities and help sustain the environment

■ Businesses also need to set objectives – targets – which will enable them to achieve their aims.

■ Businesses need to take action if their objectives are not met.

Key terms

Aim
What a business sets out to achieve.

Objective
A target which helps a business achieve an aim.

Corporate Social Responsibility
The business aims of helping charities and preserving the environment (sustainability).

Mission Statement
A formal statement setting out the aims of a business.

4

Business location

'Webdreams' – the big move

Ed Thomas is employed by a computer software company 'Softworks' in London. His speciality is website design and he has built up for his employer a list of clients all over the UK and also in Europe.

He is tired of the long daily commute and is thinking of setting up his own website consultancy in an area which is cheaper and where he does not have to spend so long commuting. His partner Elise wants to go and live in the country and keep chickens. She has seen a cottage for sale in Norfolk on a property website. Ed says to her . . .

'This is all very well, but there are a lot of things I will have to think about, for example:

- how do I know I am going to be able to get the skilled design and ICT staff I need?

- how much will I have to pay them?

- am I going to be able to get hold of all the computer kit and servicing I need?

- how am I going to keep in touch with my customers?

- are there any Government grants to help me?

- will I like Norfolk – isn't it rather flat?

a point to think about . . .

Choosing a location for a business can be a very complicated decision involving many factors. Sometimes the decision is made for you – you have to be near your customers. Sometimes it is a personal decision.

choosing a location

What makes a business decide to set up in a certain location?

Many businesses are already based in a particular location; **history and tradition** say that is where they should be. Any expansion or relocation may well be in the same area, because that is where the workforce lives and the commercial contacts have been established.

Also, the decision may be a **personal** one: the owner of a business may well want to set up in a certain location because he or she happens to like it or be familiar with it!

The owner of a business like Ed's 'Webdreams' will need to ask a number of questions when deciding to set up in a particular location.

These factors, as we have seen in the Case Study, include:

- the availability of skilled labour in the area and the cost of that labour
- the cost of moving into and running premises and the availability of Government grants and incentives to help with those costs
- the need to be near the source of raw materials or to customers

Study the diagram below. It illustrates all the questions and factors that you will need to consider in relation to the two businesses you will be investigating for your Portfolio.

In the remainder of the chapter we will look at how some of the questions and factors affect a variety of businesses.

questions a business has to ask about location

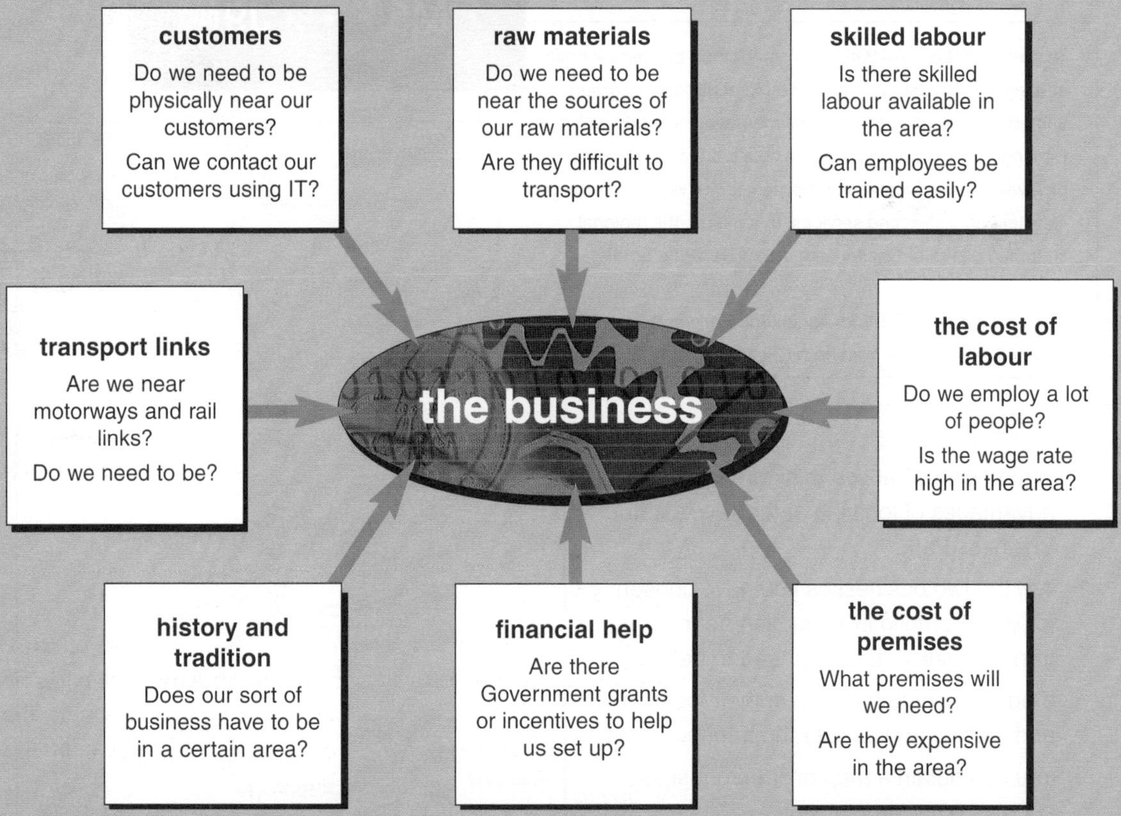

customers
Do we need to be physically near our customers?
Can we contact our customers using IT?

raw materials
Do we need to be near the sources of our raw materials?
Are they difficult to transport?

skilled labour
Is there skilled labour available in the area?
Can employees be trained easily?

transport links
Are we near motorways and rail links?
Do we need to be?

the business

the cost of labour
Do we employ a lot of people?
Is the wage rate high in the area?

history and tradition
Does our sort of business have to be in a certain area?

financial help
Are there Government grants or incentives to help us set up?

the cost of premises
What premises will we need?
Are they expensive in the area?

bottled at source

do we need to be near to natural resources?

If a business is dependent on **natural resources**, it is likely to be sited near to the source of the materials it needs. Brick manufacturers, for example, concentrate in areas where suitable clay is to be found. Scotch whisky is highly dependent on the peaty quality of Scottish water and is therefore distilled on site in Scotland. Businesses that bottle mineral water will clearly want to be near the springs.

transport links with customers and suppliers

Some businesses need access to the transport system – major motorways, airports, railway stations; this is particularly important if the business has a large and active salesforce travelling in the UK and overseas.

 # Activity 4.1 – location and transport links

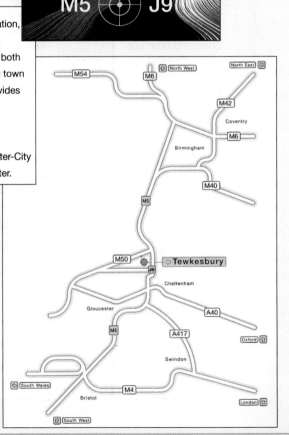

Tewkesbury Business Park is an established business location, strategically located alongside the M5 at Junction 9 giving immediate access to the national motorway network, with both Birmingham and Bristol within an hour's drive. The historic town of Tewkesbury is located immediately to the west and provides excellent amenities and services. In addition, the regional shopping centre of Cheltenham is 9 miles to the South.

Rail links are provided from Ashchurch Parkway (1 mile) Inter-City services are available from both Cheltenham and Gloucester.

questions

1   Write down what you think are the transport advantages of locating at the Tewkesbury Business Park.

2   Are the two businesses you have chosen for your Portfolio investigation near to transport links? Do they need to be?

If possible, obtain a map of their location and identify and assess the transport links.

You can obtain a map online from sites such as www.streetmap.co.uk

the Toyota plant near Derby

do we need to be near the customers?

Some businesses do not need to be 'near' their markets, because their markets do not have a definite geographical location.

Car manufacturers, for example, distribute to dealers throughout the UK and abroad. They are free to locate where skilled labour and government grants are available.

Toyota manufactures some of its cars in Burnaston near Derby, but its customers are to be found throughout the UK.

Mail order companies and internet shops such as amazon.co.uk can also locate where they like – their customers place orders by phone and online and all they have to do is to ship the goods from their warehouses.

a local High Street fast food outlet

Some markets, however, have a very precise geographical location – this is particularly true of service industries.

A small business such as a kiosk that sells sandwiches and drinks must be situated in the area that it serves.

Skilled people such as plumbers and electricians also need to be near their customers.

Similarly, some specialised financial services businesses need to be in financial centres such as the City of London where their customers are.

Activity 4.2 – location and customers

1   Look at the two pictures of businesses shown in the pictures on this page.

   Where are they located?

   How important is it that they are near to their customers?

   Write down the reasons for your answer in both cases.

2   Choose six local businesses and find out why they have chosen their particular location in relation to their customers.

3   Find out if the businesses you have chosen for your Portfolio investigation are near to their customers or whether their chosen location does not need to be near their customers.

   Explain the reason for their location in both cases.

what is the cost of labour?

It is easier to recruit employees in some parts of the country than in others. This may affect the choice of where to set up business. Generally speaking, wages are higher in urban areas and in the South East, reflecting the higher costs of living in those areas.

If a business is labour intensive (in other words, if it employs many people), some businesses may be attracted to areas where labour is cheaper. Of course this choice may not always exist – a business may have to set up in a particular part of the country because that is where the owners live, or where there are natural resources, or customers.

Activity 4.3 – the cost of labour

Average weekly full-time earnings in the UK regions		
	male £	female £
North East	373	280
North West	413	313
Yorkshire & Humberside	390	297
East Midlands	402	308
West Midlands	418	314
East of England	493	358
London	578	450
South East	518	369
South West	448	314
Wales	385	294
Scotland	420	323
Northern Ireland	349	313

Source: Labour Force Survey

This table shows how much, on average, male and female full-time employees earn (before tax) in the different regions of the UK.

1   Take five different regions, including your own region and the highest and lowest figures, and draw up a bar chart showing the average weekly earnings. Include both the male and the female earnings on your chart. How does your region compare?

2   In what ways do these statistics affect the choice of location made by the two businesses you are investigating for your Portfolio? Does the cost of labour affect them at all?

3   Why do you think the average wage for males and females is so different?
    Do you think that this affects the two businesses you are investigating?

the skills factor

Some businesses need a labour force with particular skills – for example:

- scientific skills for research companies
- engineering skills for car manufacture
- financial skills for financial centres

The availability of these skills in the local area is therefore another important factor.

Certain areas are well-known for particular skills: for example, the Cambridge area and the M4 'corridor' for computer technology. Businesses are therefore attracted to certain areas because of the skills that exist there.

In the Case Study below you will see how the technological skills available from Government defence projects in Malvern in the West Midlands are used to attract new businesses to the area.

Case Study – locating where the skills are

The Malvern Hills Science Park is a purpose-built complex suitable for office and laboratory use.

The skills available locally are those developed by QinetiQ (formerly the government-run Defence Evaluation and Research Agency).

QinetiQ has had a hand in innovations such as radar, liquid crystal flat panel displays and the technology used in thermal imaging cameras.

The Malvern Hills Science Park is located immediately adjacent to the QinetiQ site in Malvern. Situated in an area of outstanding natural beauty at the foot of the Malvern Hills, the Science Park is at the heart of a region of emerging technology-based companies.

It has excellent road and rail links to the Midlands, London, Wales and the North and is conveniently situated for Birmingham International and London Heathrow airports.

By Road:

M5 and M50	20 minutes
London Heathrow	2 hours
Birmingham International Airport	1 hour 15 minutes
Oxford	1 hour 20 minutes

By Rail:

Great Malvern - London (direct)	2 hours 15 minutes
Great Malvern - Birmingham New Street	1 hour

government help towards costs

Businesses setting up have to pay substantial costs: premises, equipment and research and development costs.

Businesses are helped by the UK Government and the European Union (EU). Businesses setting up in what are known as **Assisted Areas** receive assistance from both in the form of grants and incentives. The English areas are shown on the map on this page.

Help for new businesses is also available from local authorities.

Any business starting up or relocating will obviously find it advantageous to set up in an Assisted Area. Car manufacturers have been greatly helped in this way.

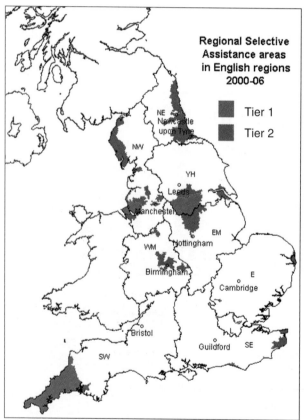

Regional Selective Assistance areas in English regions 2000-06

█ Tier 1
█ Tier 2

The English Assisted Areas
(source: DTI)

UK Government assistance

The UK Government provides financial help – **Regional Selective Assistance** – to businesses setting up in areas which have traditionally had lower earnings levels and higher unemployment. This assistance – grants, cheap rents, free and subsidised advice – is administered through the Department of Trade and Industry, normally referred to as the DTI.

The areas in dark grey on the map are the Tier 1 areas, which are the areas of greatest need and include Cornwall, Merseyside, South Yorkshire. Tier 1 also includes West Wales and the Welsh Valleys and all of Northern Ireland (not shown on this map).

The areas in red are Tier 2 areas and are local areas of need. They do not qualify for grants as high as those in Tier 1. A large part of western Scotland is a Tier 2 area (not shown on the map).

Further details can be obtained from your local office of the Department of Trade and Industry (or the Welsh Office in Cardiff and the Scottish Office in Glasgow.)

Details can also be obtained from the DTI website: www.dti.gov.uk which also contains much useful business information.

European Union assistance

Financial assistance is also available from the EU in the form of the European Structural Fund. This fund works on a similar tier system to the one shown above, and the areas covered are more or less the same.

Activity 4.4 – where to locate?

Businesses may take any of the following factors into consideration when locating their operations:

- being near their customers
- being in an area with skilled labour
- being in an area with good transport links

- being near the source of raw materials
- being in an area with low wage costs
- being in an area which is traditionally home to that type of business

- being in an area in which government grants and incentives are available

1 Which <u>one</u> of the these factors will be <u>most</u> important to

    (a)   a gold mine

    (b)   a business with a very large unskilled labour force

    (c)   a sandwich bar

    (d)   a computer development company

    (e)   a road haulage company

    (f)   a business that needs cash to invest in premises

    (g)   a National newspaper

2 Which of the the factors listed above affect the two businesses you are investigating for your Portfolio? Make a list for each and say in each case how the factors affect the two businesses.

Nutshell summary

- Businesses need to take a number of factors into consideration when locating. These factors include:

   - history and tradition

   - being near the customers

   - being near the source of raw materials

   - being in an area with skilled labour

   - being in an area with low wage costs

   - being where the transport links are good

   - being in an area where Government help is available

- The decision to locate may also be affected by personal reasons such as familiarity with an area.

Key terms

Natural resources
Resources from the earth or sea which are used or extracted by business.

Labour
The supply of people who work in business.

Assisted Area
Areas which receive financial assistance from the Government.

5 Owning a small business

Rashid's taxi business

Rashid is a delivery driver who is thinking of starting a taxi business.

He can buy a second-hand diesel cab. To publicise his business he intends to advertise in the local paper and to wait for customers outside the train station and the clubs in the town.

His friend, Jake, is also interested in running a taxi and wants to know if he can go into business with Rashid. He says 'it will be better if there are the two of us – we can have more time off if we need it and we can share some costs.'

Rashid is not so sure about what this will involve, as he prefers to do his own thing. He asks:

'Won't it make it more complicated if I go into business with my friend?'

'What do we do about a trading name?'

'What happens if we fall out – we always tend to fight like cat and dog?'

'How do we share the profit we make?'

'What happens if he runs into financial difficulties and we go bust?'

a point to think about . . .

Going into business as an individual can be risky but can be very profitable. Going into business with someone else can lead to problems, unless, of course, you like and trust that person.

types of business

In this chapter you will be introduced to the different forms of business by Case Studies within Activities – 'snapshots' of people in business, showing the way their businesses are set up, and the way in which they operate.

This chapter looks at individuals in business. These businesses may be small businesses. It may be that for your Portfolio you will concentrate on larger businesses. Remember, however, that large businesses always start off as small businesses.

sole trader

a definition

A sole trader is an individual who has set up in business. The sole trader owns, controls and is the business.

The majority of businesses in the UK are sole traders – they include shopkeepers, taxi drivers, decorators, accountants, artists – a very wide range of occupations. As you see, they are usually small businesses.

Why do people become sole traders? Because they are their own boss – they own and control the business, and are entitled to all the profit it may make.

But there are financial risks involved. A sole trader will have to provide the money for the business, or raise that money with a bank loan or borrow from friends and family. Just as a sole trader takes all the profit, he or she takes full responsibility for any losses which the business makes.

sole traders and unlimited liability

In the eyes of the law a sole trader is an individual who has to pay all the debts of the business. If the business fails, the sole trader may have to sell his or her personal belongings or be taken to court and made a bankrupt.

Being responsible for all your business debts is known as **unlimited liability.** It is something a person starting in business has to think carefully about – is it worth risking your own house if things go wrong?

examples of sole traders

a trading name?

If you are a sole trader you can use your own name, or make up a trading name. You do not have to register a trading name, but you may find yourself in court if you use someone else's name. You cannot, for instance, get away with opening a shop and calling it 'Marks & Spencer' or 'Next'! If you look through the adverts in Yellow Pages you will get a good idea of the names used in different trades.

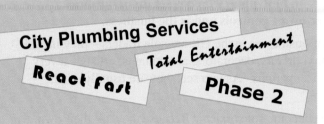

Take mobile discos or plumbing, for example. The names on the left are all in use.

the documentation

Starting as a sole trader is very simple as there is little paperwork to be done. You do not have to draw up any rulebooks or business agreements as you are the only person involved. Once you have decided on a name you will need to get business cards and stationery such as letterheads and invoices printed.

Now compare the advantages and disadvantages of being a sole trader . . .

advantages and disadvantages of being a sole trader

disadvantages

it is risky

you work long hours

you need to be an expert at everything

you cannot afford to be ill

you do not get much holiday

it is less easy to raise money

you have unlimited liability for all business debts

advantages

freedom – being your own boss

less form-filling

you do not have to share the profit with anyone else

it is easier to set up the business in the first place

Case Study – Julie Evans, sole trader

Julie Evans has recently started work as a self-employed fish seller.

She has invested savings of £5,000 into equipment and a van. She has also borrowed £3,000 from the bank to help pay for her van.

Julie has always been keen to be her own boss, and intends to work hard to make a success of the business and make a healthy profit.

She does realise, however, that she could lose her possessions if the business fails.

She is confident that she will succeed. She has set up a contract with a fish wholesaler at a fish market twenty miles away.

She has arranged to sell her fish at local markets and will also sell fish direct from her van in her local area.

She has called her business 'Fresh Fish Today' and is advertising her fish in the local paper and by driving around the neighbourhood in her van.

Activity 5.1 – why be a sole trader?

1   State four advantages to Julie of setting up as a sole trader.

2   State four disadvantages to Julie of setting up as a sole trader.

3   A friend of Julie who has been studying on a business course at the local College says to Julie, 'your main problem is that you will have unlimited liability for your business.'
    Explain what Julie's friend means by this statement.

4   Julie's fish business is obviously a small business. What other larger businesses in the area are likely to sell fish? What advantages does Julie have over these businesses?

5   Julie will need to draw up certain documents before she can start trading. Design a business card and a newspaper 'small ad' for Julie. Use a computer package if you can.
    Make up Julie's address, telephone number and email address.

partnership

In the Case Study at the beginning of this chapter Rashid was thinking about going into business with Jake. If the two of them did go ahead together, the business would become a **partnership**.

a definition

A partnership is a group of individuals working together in business with the aim of making a profit.

Many businesses in the UK are partnerships – they include doctors, dentists and solicitors. Partnerships are owned by all the partners. Partnerships can normally raise more money than sole trader businesses – simply because there are more people to contribute. The day-to-day running of the partnership is normally shared out among the partners – they share control. They also share profits (and losses).

trading names

A partnership – often known as a 'firm' – can either trade in the name of the partners, or under a suitable trading name. For example if M Smith & T Ahmed set up a glazing business, they could call themselves 'Smith and Ahmed & Co.' or adopt a more catchy name such as 'Classy Glass'.

The trading name and the names of the partners will have to be set out on the business stationery: letterheads, business cards, invoices.

G & F PLUMBING

**installation
repairs
maintenance**
**• boilers • central heating • gas fires
• cookers • bathroom installations**
Gary and Fred Horton
01899 526111 mobile 07765 762975

a plumbing partnership

partnerships and unlimited liability

A partnership is easy to set up. Partnerships are regulated in law by the Partnership Act 1890 and also by any written Partnership Agreement which has been drawn up. These between them set out:

■ the money put in by each partner (the 'capital')

■ the money taken out by each partner (the share of profits – or any loss)

■ what to do if the partners disagree (it does happen!)

In law each partner is liable for all the debts of the partnership.

Partners
David R. Harrison
N.G. Hill
Jonathan Brew
Keith Mills
Andrew Caldicott
Andrew M. James
Guy C. Salter
Rod Thomas
Dawn E. Oliver
Robert Sprake
J.H.T. Hooke
Brenda V. Spain
Consultants
S. Driver White

a partnership of solicitors

Like the sole trader a partner has **unlimited liability**. This means that if one partner runs up a big debt, each or all of the other partners could be asked to pay all of it off. In a partnership, like marriage, you clearly have to be careful when you take on a partner!

advantages and disadvantages of being a partner

advantages

more money can be raised – there are more people

shared responsibility

more expertise (skills) will be available

cover is available for illness and holidays

disadvantages

disagreements can occur

profits have to be shared out

less freedom – you have to consult others

each partner has unlimited liability for all the dealings of the partnership

each partner has unlimited liability for all partnership debts

Case Study – forming a partnership

Solomon King and John Maisey are both solicitors working in commercial law firms in Liverpool city centre.

They both earn over £50,000 a year but are tired of the pressures of working in large organisations. They wish to leave their salaried positions and join forces to create a new legal partnership which they will call King & Maisey & Co. This will be set up in Ormskirk, outside Liverpool.

They have some savings to provide start-up costs. They also arrange a bank loan to provide the extra finance that they will need. As lawyers they know the need for a Partnership Agreement.

They have agreed the following:

- they will contribute £50,000 capital each
- they will share profits equally
- if there is any dispute, an official Arbitrator can be appointed to sort things out

Set out below are extracts from the Partnership Agreement. Note that the Partnership Agreement will be a great deal longer than the extracts shown here; it will deal with issues such as the bank they use and what happens when they want to stop working as partners.

PARTNERSHIP AGREEMENT

MADE on 30 June 2003

BETWEEN Solomon King of 45 Park Gardens, Ormskirk

AND John Maisey of Flat 7, Parkway Mansions, Maghull

IT IS HEREBY AGREED AS FOLLOWS

extracts now follow . . .

1. Solomon King and John Maisey will become and remain partners for a period of five years from the date of this Agreement.

2. The Partners shall practise in partnership in the firm name of King & Maisey & Co at the address Equity House, 191, High Street, Ormskirk.

3. The initial capital of the partnership shall be in the sum of £100,000, to be contributed by the partners equally.

4. The partners shall be entitled to the net profits arising from the business in equal shares, or such other shares as may from time to time be agreed by the partners.

5. Each partner shall be entitled to five weeks holiday in each year.

6. Should any dispute arise at any time between the partners with regard to this agreement or in respect of the rights, duties and liabilities of the partners in the conduct of partnership business, then an independent Arbitrator shall be appointed. The ruling of the independent Arbitrator shall be accepted by both Partners.

Signed by
Solomon King of 45 Park Gardens, Ormskirk

Solomon King

in the presence of Henry Purcell, 45 Melody Gardens, Birkenhead

Henry Purcell

Signed by
John Maisey of Flat 7, Parkway Mansions, Maghull

John Maisey

in the presence of Henry Purcell, 45 Melody Gardens, Birkenhead

Henry Purcell

Activity 5.2 – being a partner

Answer the questions below.

1   What is the investment made by each partner in the new business?

2   How will the partners share the profits?

3   What is the liability of Solomon for partnership debts run up by John?

4   What is the liability of John for partnership deals – for example an agreement to rent some computer equipment – set up by Solomon?

5   What could happen if there was a dispute between the two which they could not sort out?

6   What advantages does a forming a partnership have over running a sole trader business?

7   Read again the taxi business Case Study on page 42.
    What are the disadvantages to Rashid of going into business with his friend?
    What would you advise him to do? Write down the reasons for your suggestions.

Nutshell summary

- Small businesses are normally set up for the first time as sole trader or partnership businesses.

- A sole trader is a single individual in business on his or her own. The sole trader takes all the risk in the business and may have to work long and hard hours. The sole trader, however, takes all the profit once expenses and tax have been paid.

- A sole trader has unlimited liability for the debts of the business. This means that the sole trader has full responsibility for paying the business debts, and if the business does badly will have to repay the debts from his or her personal belongings.

- A partnership is a group of individuals working together in business with the aim of making a profit. Partners have unlimited liability for all the debts of the partnership.

- A written Partnership Agreement is often drawn up to set out the rights and duties of the partners and what to do if there is a partnership dispute.

Key terms

Sole trader
An individual who has set up in business on his or her own.

Unlimited liability
Being responsible for paying all the debts of your business – even to the extent of selling your personal possessions.

Partnership
A group of individuals working together in business with the aim of making a profit.

Partnership Agreement
A written agreement setting out the rights of individual partners in a partnership.

Partnership Act
The law which sets out the rights of individual partners if there is no Partnership Agreement.

6
Ownership of larger businesses

Millennium Insurance – three's company

Helen, Tom and Cas work together in an insurance broking partnership 'Millennium Insurance'.

All three partners have contributed an equal amount of capital and they share profits equally. They employ five staff and have been very successful at setting up insurance for businesses of all sizes. They want to expand and need to raise more money. They have been to a meeting with their accountant, Jacqui, and have asked her about forming a limited company. She has been enthusiastic about the idea:

'You will save tax if you form a limited company – tax rates are lower than for individuals.

You will each become directors of the new company.

Your partnership capital will be turned into shares. You can receive a salary and commission and take your share of profits as dividends.

You will no longer have unlimited liability. If you run into financial difficulties, your company may cease trading but your own personal possessions will be safe from the people who are owed money – you have limited liability.

The paperwork is fairly easy to deal with – I can look after it for you.'

a point to think about . . .

Expanding a business always involves decisions, but there is always professional help around to point you in the right direction. If you look around you, most of the largest businesses are companies.

businesses for your Portfolio

It is likely that the businesses that you will have to choose for your Portfolio investigation will not be sole traders or partnerships but will be larger businesses. This is because you will find it easier to get information from larger businesses – from websites and from publicity departments. Larger businesses also have a more defined structure in the form of separate departments, and their financial details are more likely to be made available to the public. Smaller businesses may be less ready to give you the information you need.

limited company

A limited company is a business which is owned by shareholders and run by directors.

shareholders

A limited company is set up in a very different way from a sole trader and a partnership business. The owners are the shareholders who have invested money in the company in return for shares and a 'share' of profits in the form of dividends.

directors

The company employs directors (headed by the Managing Director or Chief Executive) to control the management of its business. Very often the directors own shares in the company.

who is responsible for company debts?

Shareholders are not responsible for all the company's debts. The most money they can lose is the amount they have invested – this arrangement is known as **limited liability** and is quite different from the **unlimited liability** of the sole traders and partners in the previous chapter. Study the diagram below.

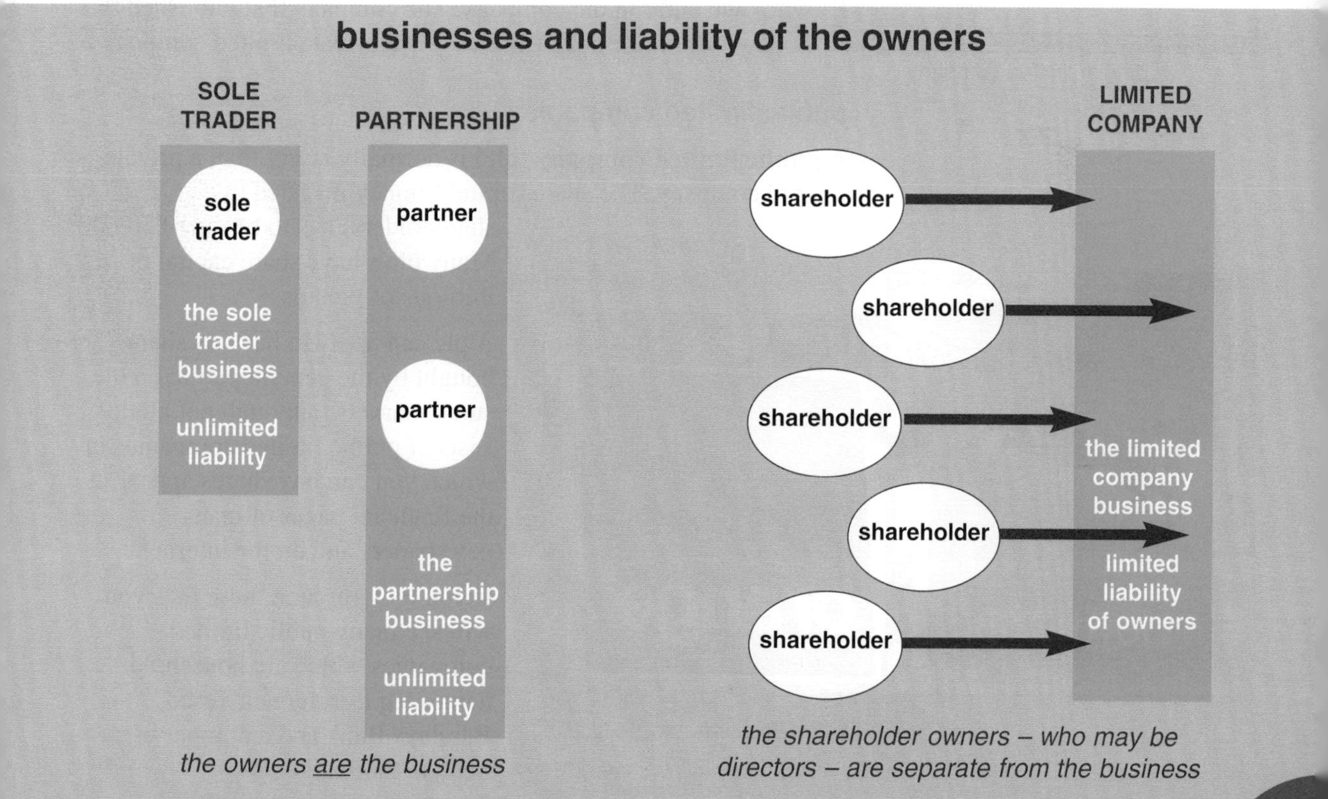

businesses and liability of the owners

SOLE TRADER

PARTNERSHIP

LIMITED COMPANY

sole trader

the sole trader business

unlimited liability

partner

partner

the partnership business

unlimited liability

the owners <u>are</u> the business

shareholder

shareholder

shareholder

shareholder

shareholder

the limited company business

limited liability of owners

the shareholder owners – who may be directors – are separate from the business

private companies and public companies

If you look at the names of the limited companies you are investigating, you will see that they can be followed by the letters – 'Ltd' and 'plc':

R T Designs **Ltd**

J Sainsbury **plc**

The first name is followed by 'Ltd', sometimes spelt out in full as 'Limited' – this is a **private limited company**. The second name is followed by 'plc' – this stands for **public limited company**.

Both private and public limited companies are set up as limited companies. The main difference is normally one of size, and who can buy the shares.

private limited companies

a private limited company

Private limited companies are generally smaller than public limited companies. Common examples are family businesses such as garages, builders, shops, local coach companies. The shares are not available for sale to the general public and are normally owned by the people who run the company – for example the family members in the case of a family business. These shareholders are often also the directors of the company who own and run the company. The company that published this book – Osborne Books Limited – is a private limited company.

public limited companies

A **public limited company** (plc) is normally larger than a private limited company. The share capital (money invested by shareholders) has to be over £50,000. Many plc's have share capital of millions of pounds.

A plc can apply to have its shares bought by the general public on the stock markets (although not all do). Lists of public limited companies in which you can buy shares appear in the financial pages of many newspapers and on the internet.

If you look through these lists you will see many public limited companies which are household names, eg Eurotunnel, Tesco, Barclays Bank and a number of League football teams.

some well-known public limited companies

who controls limited companies?

Shareholders own a limited company and appoint **directors** to control the management of the company and plan for its future. In the case of a private limited company, the shareholders often are the directors, and so the shareholders can be said to control the company. The chief director is the Managing Director. In the case of a public limited company the shareholders can only speak and vote at company meetings (often only once a year) and it is the directors who control the company.

documentation

Small businesses such as sole traders and partnerships require relatively little in the way of paperwork. Setting up a limited company, on the other hand, requires a fair amount of 'red tape'. Companies are regulated by Companies House, a government-owned agency. All companies have to register with Companies House and are issued with the company equivalent of a birth certificate – the Certificate of Incorporation. In addition, a company will also need two further documents:

- the Memorandum of Association – which states what the company can do
- the Articles of Association – the internal 'rulebook' for the directors

company documentation

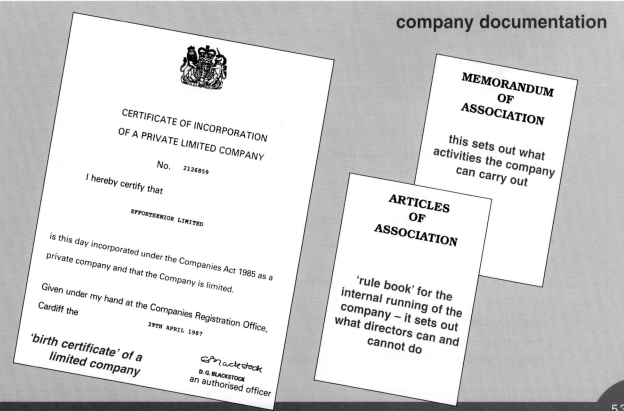

CERTIFICATE OF INCORPORATION OF A PRIVATE LIMITED COMPANY

No. 2126859

I hereby certify that

EFFORTSENIOR LIMITED

is this day incorporated under the Companies Act 1985 as a private company and that the Company is limited.

Given under my hand at the Companies Registration Office, Cardiff the

29TH APRIL 1987

'birth certificate' of a limited company

D. G. BLACKSTOCK
an authorised officer

MEMORANDUM OF ASSOCIATION

this sets out what activities the company can carry out

ARTICLES OF ASSOCIATION

'rule book' for the internal running of the company – it sets out what directors can and cannot do

Activity 6.1 – limited companies

Read through the two short Case Studies and answer the questions that follow.

Foodworld Limited is a limited company which runs a speciality food store in the town. The business is run by the Oliver family who also own all the shares in the company.

Jim Oliver is the Managing Director – he deals with most of the food buying and the finance. His wife Anna is the Sales Director and she is in charge of running the shop and organising all the advertising.

The company makes good profits: last year its takings from the shop were £400,000 and the profits were £80,000. The two directors each took a £20,000 dividend out of these profits, leaving £40,000 in the company.

Tesco Plc is a leading supermarket in the UK with around 700 stores. It also has over 200 stores outside the UK and an internet shopping business – Tesco Direct.

Tesco is also a leading seller of organic food and aims to provide value for money for its customers.

Tesco's annual sales figure in 2001 was £22,773 million and its profit for the same year was £1,070 million.

From this profit the company was able to pay out £340 million in dividends to its shareholders.

questions

1 What form of business is Foodworld Limited and who owns it?

2 Would you be able to buy the shares of Foodworld Limited?

3 How much of the profits did the directors of Foodworld Limited receive as dividends?

4 What form of business is Tesco Plc?

5 Who owns Tesco Plc?

6 What are the sales and profit figures for Tesco and Foodworld? Draw up the figures in the form of a table.

7 Can you buy the shares of Tesco Plc?

8 How much do the shares of Tesco Plc cost? Find out from the newspapers or the financial pages on the internet (try the financial pages of www.yahoo.co.uk).

co-operatives

The word '**co-operative**' refers to two types of business:

- a retail Co-operative Society – which sell goods and services to the public

- co-operative – a group of people 'clubbing' together to produce goods or to provide a service

retail Co-operative Societies – the background

Retail Co-operative Societies date back to 1844 when a group of Rochdale weavers, suffering from the effects of high food prices and low pay, set up a society to buy food wholesale, ie at the same price as it was sold to the shops. This food was then sold to the members at prices lower than the shop prices, and the profits distributed to the members in what was known as a dividend, the level of which depended on the amount of food they had bought.

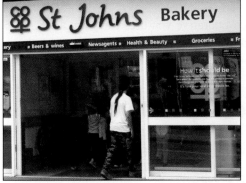

a Co-op store

These self-help co-operatives grew in number during the nineteenth century, but declined in the later twentieth century, largely because of competition from the 'big name' retailers such as Tesco, Sainsbury and Asda.

the Co-op today

A well-known example of a retail co-operative is the Co-operative Group. This collection of companies is generally known as 'the Co-op'. It operates a wide range of businesses, including over 1,000 food stores, the insurance company CIS, the Co-operative Bank (including internet banking), the UK's largest funeral business, car dealerships, travel services and farming. Visit the informative website www.co-op.co.uk for full details of this group of companies.

a Co-op dividend card

who owns the Co-op?

A retail Co-operative Society is owned by its members. You can become a member by filling in a form obtainable from your local Co-op store and buying a share, normally for £1.

As a member you have voting rights (one vote per member) and can obtain discounts at the Society's retail shops and the use of other facilities such as funeral services.

other types of co-operative

The word 'co-operative' also applies to other co-operative businesses. At the time of writing there are around two thousand co-operatives.

owned by a farmers' co-operative

trading co-operatives

Groups of individuals, such as farmers, who do not have the resources in terms of capital and time to carry out their own promotion, selling and distribution, may 'club' together to store and distribute their produce. They may also set up co-operative ventures to purchase machinery and equipment.

workers co-operatives

A workers co-operative may often be found where the management of a business is not succeeding and a shut-down is proposed. The workers step in, with the consent of the management, and take over the ownership and running of the business with the aim of 'making a go of it' and at the same time safeguarding their jobs.

co-operatives on the internet

For an up-to-date view of co-operative ventures carry out a UK search on the internet through www.google.co.uk or other search engine using the word 'co-operative'.

Activity 6.2 – investigating co-operatives

1   What is the cost and the benefit of owning a share in the Co-op Group?

2   What different activities are carried out by the Co-op Group?

3   Identify two other co-operative businesses through investigation – for example by carrying out a search on the internet. What type of co-operatives are they and how do they compare with the Co-op Group in terms of types of activity and the involvement of the members?

some McDonald's are franchises

franchise

Suppose that you wanted to set up in business on your own as a sole trader, but wanted to use a household name such as McDonald's or Bodyshop. The answer is to set up a **franchise** operation.

A franchise is the situation where an individual – the franchisee – in return for a fee can set up in business using the name, equipment and training provided by a franchisor business such as McDonald's.

Franchises can be set up as individual shops (eg Clarks Shoes), or as services (eg Dyno-rod). Franchises can also be set up within department stores as a separate small 'department'.

For full information, comprehensive listings of franchisors and links to websites, visit the useful site www.british-franchise.org.

The illustration below shows the way Prontaprint, a well-known name in the 'quick print' business, promotes its business idea to people interested in taking up a franchise.

Prontaprint!
■ DIGITAL DESIGN PRINT COPY

REDUCING THE RISK

Starting a new business is daunting. Starting a business which is based upon an established and successful formula is much less so.
A Prontaprint franchise offers the opportunity to enter into an exciting and rewarding market, offering customers a proven high quality product with unparalleled levels of service. As part of an established and highly successful nationwide network of modern business service centres, the risks associated with a typical new business are significantly reduced.

Businesses still working after 3-years

60% New start-up

94% Franchise

SOURCE: BFA Guide to Franchising

To summarise:

The Print-on-Demand Market
■ Is dynamic and poised for significant UK, European and global growth.
■ Is developing based upon a regional, national and international "distribute and print" model, which will be satisfied by an integrated and high quality Print-on-Demand network. Prontaprint is that network.

Prontaprint
■ Is part of the largest Print-on-Demand network in the world, with a strategic alliance with the US-based Sir Speedy and its affiliates, covering the USA, South America, Australia, South East Asia, Canada and Europe.
■ Offers expert business planning to assist new franchisees achieve business objectives.
■ Provides close links with major clearing banks for investment assistance.

Network Support Centre providing:
■ Intensive induction training.
■ Training in key services; digital design, print, copying, sales and marketing and IT.
■ Structured support from field-based Business Development Managers.
■ New Franchisee Support Team for on-site, hands-on assistance.
■ On-going training and support programme.
■ Expert assistance from technical, IT and purchasing teams.
■ Legal and estates advice.
■ Centralised Prontaprint brand marketing.

advantages of a franchise

■ you are going into a business which has been tried and tested in the marketplace

■ you are more likely to be able to raise money from a bank for a franchise

■ you should receive training and be provided with the necessary equipment

disadvantages of a franchise

■ the cost of the fee for going into the franchise

■ a proportion of your takings also go to the franchisor (the person you buy the franchise name from)

■ you cannot change the business just as you wish – if you run a Burger King it has to be the same as all the other Burger Kings

Activity 6.3 – investigating franchises

1   List three advantages of setting up a franchise business.

2   List three disadvantages of setting up a franchise business.

3   Study the table shown below and answer the question that follows.

franchises in the UK – who does what? – some examples	
business	*numbers of businesses*
Building services	1080
Catering and hotels	3675
Cleaning services	1775
Direct selling	3995
Parcels and taxis	1520
Quick Printing	600
Retailing	4785
Vehicle services	2035

What types of businesses are franchises, on the whole?

Do they manufacture a product or do they provide a service? Why do you think this is the

public sector businesses

private and public sectors

Businesses are either:

■ private sector businesses or

■ public sector businesses

The **private sector** includes businesses which are directly or indirectly owned by private individuals. Most businesses in the UK are in the private sector. They include all the businesses covered so far in the last two chapters, from sole traders to large companies.

Public sector organisations, on the other hand, are directly or indirectly controlled by the government. They include:

■ Public Corporations

■ Local Authority enterprises

public corporations

Public Corporations are set up by Act of Parliament, and owned and financed by the State, for example the Post Office (part of Royal Mail), the Bank of England and the BBC.

Public corporations are run by a Board of Management headed by a chairperson appointed by the Government. There used to be more

public corporations, but in the 1980s and 1990s a number of them were **privatised**. In other words they were sold off to the public by the government, which turned them into public limited companies, enabling the public to buy their shares. BT and British Airways are examples of privatisations.

Public Private Partnerships (PPP)

In recent years there has been a Government-led initiative in which private sector companies have been encouraged to provide resources and improve public sector businesses.

The idea is that the private sector raises the money for projects and the government then leases (rents) them. Examples include the upgrade of the London Underground, refitting of prisons and barracks and the building of hospitals. This initiative was started as the **Private Finance Initiative** (PFI) although new projects are now known as **Public Private Partnerships** (PPP).

The Case Study which follows shows how private sector companies have financed the building of a new hospital on a PFI basis.

 ## Case Study – Worcestershire Royal Hospital

The new £95m Worcestershire Royal Hospital offers a modern, high-quality environment and incorporates nine operating theatres, a large Accident and Emergency Department and Critical Care Unit, and specialist radiology and scanning facilities in 38,000 square metres of space. It provides around 550 beds.

Worcestershire Royal Hospital is one of the biggest Private Finance Initiative (PFI) projects ever undertaken in the health sector and has been built in partnership with a PFI consortium under the overall title of Catalyst Healthcare (Worcester) plc.

Catalyst – whose shareholders are developers Bovis Lend Lease, service group ISS, Bank of Scotland and Societe Generale – has financed the building and will lease it to the Trust for 30 years.

The Trust is responsible for all clinical services and medical staff and will pay a fixed monthly fee to Catalyst to cover the 'mortgage' on the hospital as well as maintenance and all equipment and support services.

Around 300 porters, cleaners and caterers, generally described as 'hotel services' are transferring to ISS Mediclean, which will also run the laundry, security, car parking, reception and switchboard services.

local authority enterprises

'Local Authority' is a term applied to local governing councils which operate both in county and in city areas. Local Authorities look after a wide range of services. These include education, environmental health, planning, refuse collection, social services, transport, fire services, libraries and leisure facilities.
They finance these services from three main sources:

- Central Government grants
- local taxation (the Council Tax)
- income from local authority enterprises (businesses)

Local authority enterprises include a wide variety of businesses, including, for example:

- leisure – swimming pools, sports centres, golf courses
- transport – local bus services
- car parks
- local lotteries

Many local authority services are provided by private sector firms, on the same principles as the PFI/PPP projects described on the previous page.

local authority enterprises

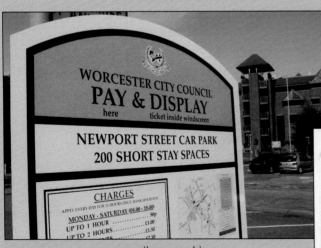

council car parking

contracted out refuse collection

Activity 6.4 – public sector businesses

1   In preparation for your Portfolio investigation, choose a large public sector organisation such as the BBC (www.bbc.co.uk) and find out:

   (a)   who owns it and who is responsible for it

   (b)   who runs it

   (c)   how it is financed

2   Identify one of your local authority facilities, such as a leisure centre, and find out:

   (a)   who the outside contractors are and what type of business they are (eg limited company)

   (b)   the range of services provided within the facility.

Nutshell summary

■ It is likely that you will have to choose two larger businesses for your Portfolio investigations.

■ The most common form of larger organisation is the limited company, which has the advantage over a partnership that its owners have limited liability for business debts.

■ Limited companies are owned by shareholders and run by directors. Shareholders receive dividends as a share of profits and are normally allowed to vote at company meetings.

■ The main difference between private and public limited companies is one of size. The shares of some public limited companies can be bought and sold on the stock markets.

■ A co-operative is a business run for the benefit of its members and typified by the well-known Co-op retail group of companies. Other co-operatives include workers' co-ops and trading co-ops.

■ A franchise enables someone to set up in business using a well-known name, but at a cost – a share of the profits has to be paid to the franchisor.

■ Public sector businesses are reducing in number – partly through privatisation and partly through the growth in popularity of Public Private Partnerships where private sector money is invested in public services such as transport and hospitals.

Key terms

Limited company
A business that is owned by its shareholders.

Limited liability
Where the business owner – eg a shareholder – is not liable for all the debts of the business.

Co-operative
A business set up and owned by its members and operated for their benefit.

Franchise
A business which pays to use the name of another established and well-known business.

Private sector business
A business owned directly or indirectly by private individuals.

Public sector business
A business directly or indirectly controlled by the Government.

Privatisation
A public sector business sold off to the private sector.

Public Private Partnership
A public sector service financed by the private sector.

7

Functions in business

Tina and Tania – a working day

Tina and Tania share a flat. Tina runs a busy town-centre hair salon. Tania works in the Finance Department of Prism Solutions, a medium-sized company. They are sitting over a cup of coffee having a heart-to-heart about work. Tina is happy in running her sole trader business, but Tania is bored and looking for promotion or a sideways move. She is complaining:

'It gets so boring. All you get is paperwork piled up in your tray: quotations to prepare, invoices to prepare, statements to send out, customers to chase for non-payment, payroll to process, cheques to bank, credit card payments to put on the terminal. I really fancy more responsibility or more variety. I need a change – like now!' Tina looks concerned and replies:

'The grass is always greener on the other side. My work is varied, but I have to work long hours. I don't get the chance to switch off properly. I have to do everything myself. I have to see to the clients, look after my staff and the premises, arrange the advertising, deal with the paperwork, make sure there is money in the bank. It never ends. But it pays. And it is worth it.'

a point to think about . . .

Running a business involves different areas of activity – 'functions'. If you are a sole trader you end up doing most of them yourself. If you work in a larger business these functions are carried out in different departments.

business functions and your Portfolio

As we have seen, you will have to choose two different businesses for your Portfolio investigation. It is likely that these will be medium-sized or large businesses which will, as the Case Study shows, have departments or distinct operating areas.

It is a good idea to choose departments for comparison in areas which interest you. For example you might choose Marketing, Finance and Human Resources, or you might investigate Production in a manufacturing business. Remember always to look at the links between the departments – they all work closely together.

functions in business

A function in business is an area of activity in the business.

It does not matter if the business is a sole trader or a public limited company, the **functions** (areas of activity) remain the same, for example: buying and selling, dealing with suppliers, dealing with customers, paying bills, making sure there is soap in the cloakroom. Someone has got to do these tasks. It is up to the business to organise them in an efficient way.

different functional areas

You will see from the two Activities which follow that business activities can be classified in functional areas, even if the business is a sole trader who does everything himself or herself.
The main functional areas are:

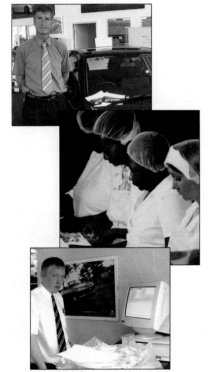

selling, production and using ICT are all business functions

marketing and sales	finding out what products customers need and selling those products to them
customer service	looking after customers' requirements, dealing with their complaints
production/operations	dealing with resources: manufacturing a product or providing a service; researching and developing new products or services
human resources	looking after the employees, for example keeping employee records, training and disciplining
finance	managing the money coming in and out, paying bills, paying wages, keeping the books, raising money for the business
administration & ICT	providing all the backup needed – the day-to-day jobs that have to be done and providing the computer support for the running of the business (Information and Communication Technology)

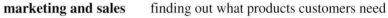

▶ Activity 7.1 – functions in your school or college

Your own school or college is an organisation which in many ways is run along business lines.

You are the customer and your education is the product.

Make a list of the functions which you can identify at work in your school or college.
Provide the names of any departments you can identify or people who have responsibility for a functional area. How do these compare with the business functions listed on this page?

Case Study – a day in the life of Tina Solo

As we have already seen, Tina Solo runs a busy town-centre hair salon as a sole trader business.
She calls it 'Style on Top'.

She employs four stylists and also works in the salon herself.

She works a long day but the business is profitable and she enjoys it.

She is even thinking of opening another branch in a nearby town.

Set out below is a 'log' of what she does during a working day, which, as you will see, does not always end when she leaves the salon in the evening.

08.00	Arrive at salon and open post.
08.15	Sketch out text for new advert to go in the local evening paper.
08.30	Talk to senior stylist Fallon about training of new assistant who started this week.
08.45	Try to pacify customer who rings up and wants an appointment that morning. They are fully booked until the afternoon. Customer not pleased. Manage to arrange a 15.00 appointment. The customer is happy in the end.
09.00	Salon opens. Talk to new assistant about her work and training.
09.30	Deal with bills – write out five cheques.
10.00	Work in salon, styling hair.
12.00	Have sandwiches and make telephone call to book advert in local paper.
12.15	Telephone accountant with a query about tax position of new employee. Is she to be put on an emergency tax code?
12.30	Have to have words with one stylist about the shoes she is wearing. They are not suitable for the job.
13.00	Back to work in salon, styling hair.
15.00	Have a ten minute chat with the new assistant during her coffee break – how is she getting on? Then back to work again in the salon.
17.00	Salon closing time. Door locked.
17.30	Salon alarm set. Go home.
19.00	Tina spends an hour at home writing up the cash book.
20.00	To the fitness centre for a workout. Suggest to a friend that she visits the salon for tinting.

Activity 7.2 – functions at work

1   Go through the list of Tina's activities during the day and decide what function from the following list best describes each activity:

   - human resources

   - finance

   - administration

   - operations

   - marketing and sales

   - customer service

   If you have a computer, draw up a table with six columns on a word-processor or a spreadsheet. Head up each column with the name of a function and list the appropriate activities below each heading.

2   Do all the business activities take place on the business premises?
   What does this tell you about the life of a sole trader?

departments in business organisations

If the business is a large company with many employees, customers and suppliers, each business function is likely to be carried out by an individual **department**. There is no hard and fast rule about what the departments should be. It will all depend on the nature and size of the business: it might be a business manufacturing components, it might be a medium-sized travel company providing holidays.

Business departments are often shown in the form of a **structure chart**, as shown below. On the next two pages this basic structure is developed further (but put on its side) for a manufacturer and a service business. These charts will illustrate the types of activity that take place in the various departments of these businesses.

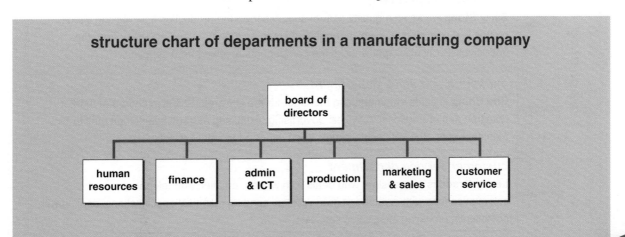

structure chart of departments in a manufacturing company

board of directors

human resources · finance · admin & ICT · production · marketing & sales · customer service

Case Study – departments at a manufacturer

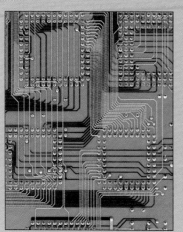

Aztec Electronics makes circuit boards for the electronics industry. It supplies computer and video equipment manufacturers worldwide.

Aztec has a brand-new factory in Sunderland and employs 300 people, mostly on its production lines.

The company sources its components from the Far East.

Aztec is a public limited company and is run by a board of directors, headed by Jo Wynnstay, Chairman.

The internal departments of Aztec are shown in the boxes in the diagram below, together with profiles of some of the employees who work in the departments.

managing board of directors

human resources department
Neeta Patel is a senior manager. She is in charge of 'hiring and firing' – she is on the interviewing panel when the company is recruiting new employees and deals with disciplinary matters. She also helps to plan the training programs in the departments.

finance department
Jim Nesbitt is an accounts assistant. His work is mostly involved with checking financial documents such as invoices and orders and putting them on the computer. He also deals with making up the wages and paying money into the bank.

administration and ICT department
Helen Cosgrove is an assistant who has just joined the department. Her work involves dealing with the incoming and outgoing mail, filing, photocopying and computer operation. She is training on Microsoft Word and also on Access for database input.

production department
Barty Stoop works as a quality control supervisor on the production line. Making circuit boards is a precision task which requires a clean environment and accuracy from the operatives. Barty also 'spot' checks the components received from suppliers.

marketing and sales department
Cho Ching is sales and marketing manager for the UK area. She is in charge of market research and promotional activities: advertising, exhibiting at trade fairs, direct mail to TV manufacturers. She sets sales targets each year and monitors results.

customer service department
Lenny Gradd is an assistant who deals with written, emailed and telephone communications with customers: giving prices, sending technical specifications, dealing with complaints, providing after-sales service.

Case Study – departments in a service business

Skiway Holidays specialises in ski holidays to the French Alps. The company employs twenty staff in the main office in York, but takes on two hundred temporary employees each season (December to April) to look after its chalets in the ski resorts.

Skiway Holidays is a private limited company run by the Moran family, who own all the shares. Ken Moran is Managing Director.

Although the ski season is relatively short, the company keeps busy all year, renovating existing chalets and building new ones. A major task is the annual recruitment of chalet staff and ski guides and the preparation of the new brochure.

Skiway's busy but small departments and some of the staff are described in the chart below.

managing board of directors

human resources department

Katie Crispin works in York as a recruitment assistant. She helps plan adverts for new staff and maintains the large database of existing and prospective employees. Each month she operates the computer payroll to ensure all the staff are paid on time.

finance department

Ron Moran is Finance Director. It is his job to draw up financial plans for each year's trading: to estimate costs, to set prices for holidays and to make sure there is enough money in the bank account, and if there is not, to raise finance.

administration department

Joan Moran works as office manager in York. She organises all the office backup needed for this international operation. The computer system is very important: it holds details of staff, bookings and accounts. All the chalets are linked on-line with York.

operations department

Ken Moran is in overall charge of 'operations' – the equivalent of a manufacturing production department. He co-ordinates staff, flights and chalet management so that his clients receive a quality holiday 'product' and will want to come again next year.

marketing and sales department

Josie Peters is in charge of marketing and sales. She is responsible for the annual brochure, press advertising and public relations – making sure the company appears in the media. She makes the most of customer feedback comments when writing the brochure.

customer service department

Kerry Norden works in the York office dealing with customer enquiries and complaints. A major part of her work is processing the written questionnaires completed by clients at the end of their holiday. She passes valuable feedback to the directors of Skiway.

Activity 7.3 – departments in business

Read the two Case Studies on the previous page and answer the questions below.

1   What are the 'products' of the two businesses?

2   In what sectors of industry do the two businesses operate?
    (You may need to look at Chapter 2 if you need reminding about sectors of industry).

3   What are the similarities between the 'production' department of Aztec and the 'operations' department of Skiway Travel?

4   Why are the following departments particularly important to Aztec and Skiway?
    (a)   marketing and sales
    (b)   customer service

working to a common aim

It is a mistake to imagine that departments in a business are completely separate and carry on regardless of each other. When you carry out your investigations for your Portfolio you should always bear this in mind.

It is important to realise that a decision by one department will affect the workings of other departments. Sometimes there may be a conflict between departments. It is true to say, however, that a well-organised and successful business will have departments which:

■   work to a common **aim**

■   communicate with each other – making the most of computers and networks (see Chapter 14 for more on the use of **ICT**)

what common aims?

The subject of business aims was covered in detail in Chapter 3. Important business aims include:

■   making a profit

■   providing a quality product and quality service to customers

■   corporate social responsibility – eg helping charity, going 'green'

Activity 7.4 – business aims at Skiway Holidays

Discuss in class how the following business suggestions at Skiway affect the 'other' departments. Look at the three points in the text above: profit, quality and social responsibility.

1   Human Resources department wants to increase the wage rates to attract better staff in France.

2   Marketing and Sales wants to offer bigger discounts in order to sell more holidays.

3   Finance department wants to cut back on customer questionnaires because of the high cost.

4   Customer Services department suggests offering special holidays for disabled skiers.

security services and
telephone answering –
business functions which
can be outsourced

outsourcing – a growing trend

We saw at the beginning of this chapter that the sole trader may turn
to specialists to help carry out some of the day-to-day business
functions, eg employing a book-keeper to write up the books.

In the same way larger businesses are now increasingly turning to
specialist companies to provide some of the business functions
formerly carried out by the business departments. This is known as
outsourcing. These providers include businesses that will:

- process the payroll and carry out other finance functions

- provide security services

- answer customer telephone enquiries and complaints

You may well find that the businesses you are investigating are
outsourcing some of their functions. If you are looking at Lloyds
TSB Bank, for example, you will find that they use another
independent company to process and clear their cheques.

 ## Nutshell summary

- Small and large businesses all have to carry out the
same functions.

- In a small business such as a sole trader, the owner
will normally carry out most of the functions himself
or herself, or may employ specialists to help.

- Larger business are structured into departments.
These include:

  - marketing and sales

  - customer service

  - production (manufacturer), operations (service
provider)

  - human resources (dealing with employees)

  - finance

  - administration and ICT (computers & networks)

- It is important that departments work together to
achieve common business aims. Conflicts between
departments do occur, and should be resolved.

- There is a growing trend for larger businesses to
'outsource' some of the business functions, ie use
other companies to do those activities for them.

Key terms

Function
An area of activity in business.

Department
A section of a business which is
organised to carry out a particular
function.

ICT
Information and Communication
Technology (sometimes also
called IT) – the computer and
communication technology which
is nowadays essential in business.

Aim
What a business sets out to
achieve.

Outsourcing
A business using a separate
specialist company to carry out
one of its internal functions.
The word means 'sourcing from
outside'.

8
Marketing and sales

Virgin – a marketing legend

In the first chapter of this book we looked at entrepreneurs – people who have the energy, enthusiasm and flair for promoting a business idea, and are willing to take all the risks involved.

Entrepreneurs are not content to sit back and watch the world pass by – they are constantly thinking of new products which customers need and can be persuaded to want. They expand their businesses and invest in new ventures, involving other entrepreneurial managers who can be trusted to make a success of the new projects.

A prime example of this type of entrepreneur is Richard Branson, founder of the Virgin brand which has given its name to so many successful businesses.

In 1970 Richard Branson started his first venture, Virgin Records, as a mail order business which then became a retail store. The Virgin record label followed and signed up the Sex Pistols and Boy George. In 1984 the airline Virgin Atlantic was launched and in 1991 Virgin Retail Group and W H Smith set up the Virgin Megastore chain as a joint venture. Virgin Vodka and Virgin Cola were introduced in 1994 and in the following year Richard Branson founded the financial services company Virgin Direct. Since then Virgin Bride, Virgin Rail and Virgin Mobile have all become well-known names.

What is the secret of this success? Marketing. Knowing what product the customer wants, providing it at a competitive price, giving it a 'brand' name that is instantly recognisable, and using all types of promotional activity to persuade people to buy it – and then making it available.

Successful marketing also means beating the competition. In the case of Richard Branson and Virgin this has been achieved by creating a recognisable and trusted value-for-money brand.

points to think about . . .

Marketing means persuading people that a product they need is a 'must have'. Something they need becomes something they want.

Marketing is also selling products that don't come back to people who do. A quality product results in a satisfied customer.

marketing and your Portfolio

You will have to choose a number of departments in two different businesses for your Portfolio. Marketing and Sales is a good choice because it is important to the main aims of most businesses:

- putting the customer at the centre of what the business is doing
- making a profit

what is marketing?

some definitions

Marketing has been described as:

Getting the right product to the right people at the right price.

The marketing function is crucial to the success of any business. Products which have been 'flops' can often attribute their failure to poor marketing:

- a product which nobody wants
- a product at the wrong price – too expensive or too cheap
- a product aimed at the wrong type of person – motor bikes for grannies, alcoholic drinks for children

Successful marketing results from concentrating on what is known as the **4 P's.**

Product

Finding out and producing what the customer wants, for example a type of car or a type of holiday. This will require detailed market research to see what people want and what demand there is for the product.

Price

Fixing a price at which the customer will buy the product. This will require research into what the competition are charging and what the customer is prepared to pay.

Promotion

Deciding how you are going to promote the product using advertising, publicity and special offers.

Place

This is where the Sales function comes in – deciding on where and how you are going to sell the product – whether locally, nationally, over the counter, by phone, over the internet.

As you will see above, **Sales** is the last part of the Marketing function. You need a product, price and promotion first. Sales is the process of the customer purchasing the product.

products and consumers

Marketing involves getting the product right in the first place. This requires market research – getting to know the customer and the customer's needs. But who is the customer? Different types of people require different types of product, eg different types of clothing, holidays, music, and so on.

customers and consumers

A **customer** is the person who buys a product.
A **consumer** is the person who uses it.

Normally the consumer **is** the customer, but not always. Think about TV adverts for children's toys. The pressure is put on the child – the **consumer** – to want the Barbie doll or computer game, but it is often the parent – the **customer** – who has to go out and buy it.

Activity 8.1 – different types of consumer

Carry out a brainstorming session in groups in class:

Draw up a list of as many different consumer 'types' as you can, eg students, the over-50s ('wrinklies'), males, females. If you are short of ideas, think of current TV ads for drinks or cars – who are they aimed at?

Appoint someone in the group to write the types down.

Discuss your findings in class.

consumer types

market segments

The buying public is not one single market, it is made up of a number of different market **segments** – different types of consumer.

Businesses need to classify consumers into market segments so that they can direct their marketing effort towards the right people. There would be little point, for example, trying to sell expensive holidays to people who cannot afford them. Consumers can be classified by:

- age
- gender (male or female)
- wealth and income
- geographical area
- lifestyle (fashion and taste)

We will now look at the ways in which businesses approach these market segments.

classification of consumer by age and wealth

Producers of goods carefully distinguish between different age groups when marketing their products, as we saw in the case of the doll and computer game. Commonly accepted age groups include:

age	buying group	typical weekly income (£)
0 – 12	child	2
13 – 17	teenager	10
18 – 35	young working person	400
36 – 59	mature working person	600
60 plus	retired person	400

Of course, people in marketing are always on the lookout for new market segments, as is seen in the Case Study which follows.

Case Study – products for 'Tweenagers'

The new target market for High Street fashion retailers is the 'tweenager'.

What is a 'tweenager'?

It is a sophisticated, fashion-conscious young person aged between 10 and 13 who is now able to influence his or her parents to spend what it needs to provide fashion gear.

Take Sarah, aged 12, who wears designer label clothes and reads magazines such as *Shout* and *Mizz*. Her weekly pocket money is £2 and she receives extra money for doing jobs around the house.

She is able to persuade her parents to buy her the fashion clothes and accessories she needs, because, as she says 'I need to keep up with all my friends.'

She has a mobile phone, internet access and has set up her own website. Sarah is a marketing phenomenon.

Activity 8.2 – products and age groups

1   Read the Case Study above and look at the age groups in the text at the top of the page. Think of another age group <u>within</u> the age ranges given (ie like the tweenage group) and suggest products that could be marketed specifically for that age group. If you can, think of a name for the age group you have identified.

2   What age groups are targeted by the two businesses you are investigating for your Portfolio?

classification of consumer by gender

Although we live in an age where the sexes are supposed to be equal, there will always be differences between what men want and what women want. Businesses will always exploit those differences by marketing products for gender groups – products 'for him' and products 'for her'. These differences can be obvious, as in the clothing and cosmetics industries. They can also be more subtle, as you should be able to find out in the next Student Activity.

Activity 8.3 – products for 'him' and 'her'

Divide into groups of three or four students and find examples of products – for example, cars, drinks, cosmetics – which are more attractive to one sex than to the other. Try not to argue too much!

Compare your findings with those of other groups.

Discuss in class what it is about the products that makes them appeal to one sex rather than the other.

Does advertising have anything to do with it?

classification by where you live

Businesses are able to classify customers according to the type of area in which they live. Country and city areas will clearly have different types of consumer living in them. Classification is also possible by postcode. You will know that in your locality certain areas are different from others. One form of computer database classification by postcode is ACORN:

A Classification **O**f **R**esidential **N**eighbourhoods.

As a postcode covers a relatively small number of households, it is possible to classify each postcode area into a specific neighbourhood 'type'.

classification by lifestyle

This type of classification is less straightforward than the examples of segmentation already given. The basis of this type of classification is to view each consumer as a 'type' which will combine elements of social class, personality and attitude and will require very specific types of product. Lifestyles are often given catchy names:

DINKY   =   dual income, no kids yet

SITCOM   =   single income, two kids, oppressive mortgage

SOPPIE   =   sensible older person with pension and insurance

L-PLATE LAD

The L-plate lad is young, single, lives at home with his parents and has started work. He is into lager, girls, TV and sport and buys CDs and junk food. He frequently gets legless and so is unable to pick up girls. Instead he staggers home to play computer games into the small hours.

Activity 8.4 – products for lifestyles

1   Listed below are two more lifestyle types. Suggest some products (items or services) for each type of consumer which you think would be suitable for that lifestyle.

EWES (Experts With Expensive Style)
Aged 25 to 34, with high income, large mortgage, no children. The high life.

OWLS (Older With Less Stress)
Aged over 55, mortgage paid off, children left home, healthy and wealthy.

2   What lifestyles (if any) are targeted by the marketing function in the two businesses you are investigating for your Portfolio?

market research methods

It is the role of the Marketing function in a business that is making a product or providing a service to be aware of the different classifications of consumer – the segmentation of the market described here.

Different types of consumer will require contrasting types of product, eg different types of cars, clothing, holidays. Businesses are also aware of changing patterns of consumer behaviour: certain products will stop selling well, other products will suddenly 'take off'.

Market research involves the collecting of information about what is happening in the mind of the consumer and in the market segments to which the consumer belongs. Information can be gathered in two ways – **field research** and **desk research**.

street interview – field research

field research

Field research, also known as 'primary research', means communicating directly with consumers – in the street, over the telephone, through the post – by means of interviews and questionnaires. The questionnaire at the bottom of this page is part of an extensive national shopping survey.

Nowadays more sophisticated shopping information can be obtained by retailers who issue 'loyalty cards' to their customers. Each time a shopper uses a 'loyalty' card every single item purchased is recorded, which when linked with the purchaser's address, enables the seller to build up a very accurate picture of who buys what, and where they live.

a consumer questionnaire

desk research

Desk research, also known as 'secondary research', involves looking at published material – reference books, statistics, and marketing reports by specialist companies. This allows the Marketing and Sales Department to find out about trends relating to consumers' income and expenditure.

You might find a Government publication 'Social Trends' in your library. It is a mine of information about income and consumer spending, covering areas such as population changes, household and family income and spending and leisure activities.

pricing – fixing the 'right price'

The second 'P' of marketing is **pricing**. Once the first 'P' of marketing – **product** – has been decided and the market researched, the price will need to be fixed. It is important that the business gets the price right. There are a number of different factors it will need to consider. Many of them relate to the basic aims of the business:

making a profit

The business will want to cover the cost of its product, or it may make a loss. If it is producing a hi-tech product such as a games console or digital TV it will also want to recover the cost of research and development – which is why prices of these products can be high on launch, but then drop down after a period of time.

beating the competition – maximising sales

The business may be able to get people to buy its product rather than a competing product by pricing it below the price of competing products. This is done to achieve the business aim of maximising sales. When it is carried out on a large scale by competing businesses it is known as a 'price war' and can often have the effect of dramatically cutting business profits. This has happened in product areas such as games consoles and sliced bread.

providing a quality product at a quality price

A business should always make sure that it is not undercharging for a product, particularly if it is a quality product. People sometimes buy a product because it is expensive and it is seen by other consumers as being a quality product – eg a BMW car or a designer label jacket.

low pricing and
premium pricing

Activity 8.5 – getting the price right

1 Investigate the cost of 'cut-price' sliced bread in your local supermarket and compare it with the price charged at small independent food stores. Choose a standard type of loaf such as medium-sliced white for your comparison. Write down your findings in a suitable table format.

    (a) Where can you get the cheapest bread?

    (b) Why do supermarkets cut the price of bread?

    (c) What effect do you think this price cutting has on the profits of a supermarket?

2 The Ferrari is a high performance quality car built in limited numbers in Italy. Many models cost over £100,000 each. Why do you think people will spend so much on a car when there is not even room to put the shopping in the boot?

3 How do the prices set by the two businesses you are investigating for your Portfolio compare with the competition?

packaging is promotion

promoting the product

the promotion process

The third 'P' of marketing is **promotion**.

The overall promotion process involves the marketing function of a business in a number of different and distinct processes:

■ advertising – informing the public about the product

■ branding – creating an image of the product at the point of sale

■ packaging – presenting the product in an attractive way

■ publicity in the media, special promotions and sponsorship

advertising

Advertising involves:

■ identifying the right market segment(s) for the product

■ identifying the right media for the advertising – newspapers, magazines, TV, radio, cinema, leaflets

■ creating the right message in the adverts

■ getting the timing right (advertising sunshine holidays in winter!)

■ getting the cost right – making sure that you are getting value for money for your promotion

promotion through branding

Branding means identifying a product in the minds of consumers by creating a name or logo for that product which will persuade the consumer to buy it.

 ## Activity 8.6 – advertising and branding

1   Identify the logos shown above. What products do they sell?

2   To what extent do the two businesses you are investigating 'brand' their products?

combining branding and packaging

promotion through packaging

Packaging means more than just the box or wrapper a product is sold in – it involves all aspects of presentation. The marketing function has to make sure that the packaging gives the consumer the 'right image' of the product. This can involve:

- its shape and size and general appearance
- colour (look at the use of white for hygiene products)
- ease of use (can it be opened easily – sometimes a problem with modern packaging!)
- environmental factors – is the material bio-degradable?

publicity and public relations

Publicity means appearing in the news. Publicity is always the objective of any producer of goods and services, and will help greatly with promotion – for example, the lady climber rescued in the Scottish Highlands, who, when dug out of a snowdrift, said: 'I could just do with a glass of Guinness.'

Public relations, on the other hand, is the area of the Marketing Department which looks after the public image of the business, making public statements when things go well or badly.

'special promotions'

Promotions involve a business marketing a specific product, or range of products, by using special offers and techniques which will attract the interest of the consumer. These methods can include:

- money off this purchase – two for the price of one, coupons, bulk packs
- extra benefits – eg 'air miles', free gifts, money off next purchase

TWO FOR THE PRICE OF ONE

BUY TWO – GET ONE EXTRA FREE

COUPON
5p off your next purchase of Britax furniture polish

5% discount for purchases of 6 or more bottles of wine

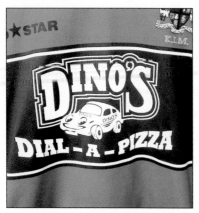

football sponsorship on a local scale

promotion through sponsorship

Sponsorship is a well-known means of promoting the name of an organisation. Many sports and arts organisations rely on support from sponsors: in return for a money payment, the name of the sponsor is mentioned prominently on publicity material and at the sponsored event.

The best form of sponsorship for a business is where there is TV coverage. Many televised sports events carry the sponsor's name prominently.

'place' – the sales function

The fourth 'P' in marketing is **place**. Place involves selling a product – a manufactured item or a service – and getting it to the consumer. This process is often known as 'sales and distribution' and is an important part of marketing. In a larger business this function may be carried out by a separate department.

Sales can be direct or indirect.

Direct sales are made when the provider of the product sells direct to the consumer without any middle person such as an agent or wholesaler being involved. Remember that a product can be a manufactured item or a service.

direct sales

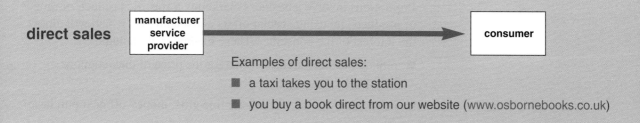

Examples of direct sales:

- a taxi takes you to the station
- you buy a book direct from our website (www.osbornebooks.co.uk)

Indirect sales are made when the provider of the product sells to the consumer through a shop, possibly supplied by a middle person such as an agent or wholesaler. In this process products pass through what is known as the **supply chain**.

indirect sales

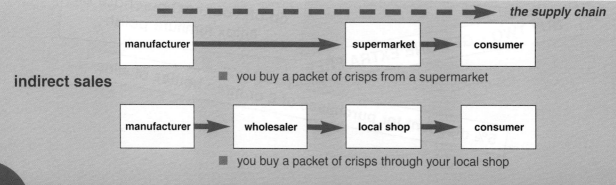

- you buy a packet of crisps from a supermarket

- you buy a packet of crisps through your local shop

other sales methods

Businesses are increasingly selling to their customers using methods which by-pass the traditional shop. Some common sales methods are described below.

E-commerce is described in more detail in the next section.

direct mail

Businesses obtain computer databases of names and addresses and send catalogues to selected market segments so that customers can buy direct by mail order. This method is used both for selling to the public and to other businesses. Much of this sort of sales material can end up in the bin!

telesales

a telesales worker

Selling by telephoning the customer direct – telesales – has become very common, both when selling to the public and to other businesses. It is used extensively by organisations like financial services companies and also by business suppliers.

the growth of e-commerce

Selling through websites is now the fastest growing sales method worldwide. Manufacturers and mail order companies are easily accessed on-line and through net 'searches'. Popular products sold using this method include books, CDs, cars and holidays. If you have access to the internet try the on-line store www.amazon.co.uk or shopping sites available through the web search engines such as Yahoo. This form of selling by 'e-tailers' poses a serious threat to the traditional retailers. Read the newspaper article below.

Internet threat to town centres

By Anita Howarth

Town centres, already hammered by out-of-town developments, face a devastating new attack from home shopping on the internet, according to a top retail boss.

Barry Gibson, chief executive of the mail order and pools firm Littlewoods, says towns will have to reinvent themselves as places for leisure and entertainment rather than shopping centres if they are to survive.

Though the government has closed the planning doors that allowed out-of-town superstores, it is encouraging the growth of internet shopping.

Gibson says this will tear the heart out of many town centres, just as superstore developments have done.

He believes that 'e-tailing' could be the straw that breaks the back of many shopping districts. Some have already suffered up to a 3 per cent fall in turnover because of out-of-town retailing.

He admitted that the drop in custom might not sound much. But with retailers having already driven down costs, any 'further reduction in turnover could have a disproportionate impact on profits'.

'It could become a landslide,' he added.

Source: The Mail on Sunday

Tesco.com – 'you shop, we drop'

Some retailers have now responded positively to this threat by 'if you can't beat them, join them' and have opened their own online shopping and home delivery facilities.

Tesco.com is an example. You can order your weekly shop on-line and have the goods delivered to your door.

Other successful businesses which are using the internet to sell their products are the 'cut-price' airlines such as Ryanair. Not only can you book a flight on line, but once the company has your email address they will continue to send you information about special offers.

Marketing could not be quicker or cheaper.

Activity 8.7 – the growth of e-commerce

Investigate examples of businesses which have set up websites for selling their products on-line. You can do this either by reading articles in the press about IT developments, or by looking at sites on-line. Most search engines such as Yahoo give easy access to on-line shopping.

1   What are the advantages to customers of buying on-line?

2   What are the disadvantages to customers of buying goods on-line?

3   What are the advantages to a business of selling on-line?

4   Do the businesses you are investigating for your Portfolio have a website and an on-line shop? How does e-commerce benefit the business?

organising marketing and sales in business

The way the marketing function operates in a business will depend on the size of the business. If the business is a sole trader, the owner is likely to do all the marketing.

A larger organisation – such as the businesses you may be investigating as part of your coursework – is likely to have a Marketing and Sales Department along the lines of the type we have seen so far in this chapter.

A typical structure showing the marketing and sales functions in a limited company is shown on the next page to help you in your investigations. This business could equally be a manufacturer or a services provider – a biscuit company or a bank.

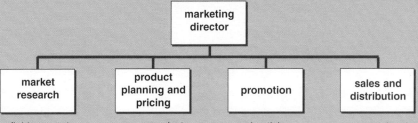

the functions within a marketing and sales department in a limited company

marketing director

| **market research** | **product planning and pricing** | **promotion** | **sales and distribution** |

market research
- field research
- desk research
- analysing feedback from customers
- monitoring the competitors

product planning and pricing
- new product development
- creating brands
- analysing competitors' pricing

promotion
- advertising
- publicity
- public relations

sales and distribution
- organising the sales campaigns
- organising distribution

Nutshell summary

- Marketing is a process which involves the **4 P's**:

  - **P**roduct: finding out who the customers are and what products they need and want

  - **P**rice: setting a price at which the consumer will buy a product

  - **P**romotion: communicating a product to the consumer in a variety of ways

  - **P**lace: ensuring that the product can be bought, and is available – this is the sales process

- Successful marketing is based on identifying groups of consumers – market 'segments' – and then designing products for them. Market segmentation can be by age, gender, wealth, where you live and lifestyle (fashion and taste).

- Market research is essential for identifying market segments and their needs.

- Successful pricing is setting a price that is 'right' for the product: competitive, not too cheap, not too high.

- Promotion is a 'mix' of different communication methods: advertising, packaging, special offers.

- Sales means getting the product to the right people at the right time. Many businesses are now turning to selling on the internet – 'e-commerce'.

Key terms

Marketing
Getting the right product to the right people at the right price.

Sales
The process of the customer buying the product.

Customer
The person who buys the product.

Consumer
The person who uses the product.

Field research
Direct research into consumers.

Desk research
Research involving published resources.

Promotion
Communicating the product to consumers.

Branding
Identifying a product by creating a name or logo for a product.

E-commerce
Selling through websites.

9

Customer service

Putting the customer first

Nikki is studying Business Studies at school. In her coursework she has to observe a variety of businesses at work. Part of her observation involves looking at customer service – the ways businesses deal with customers. She does this on a Saturday just by walking around the town. Nikki is surprised at the different way she is treated by staff in different shops. Here are some of the situations she encounters:

Shop assistant to Nikki in a music store when she asks for a compilation CD :

'I've no idea when that album will be in. We keep getting promised them. I really have no idea.'

Shop assistant in another music store:

'I'm sorry we do not have that album in stock just now. If you can wait for a second I will check on the screen to see when it will be in. Yes, it should be in on Tuesday. Do you want me to reserve one for you?'

Shop assistant in café when Nikki asks for an iced tea and a Mars bar:

'Certainly. Would you like lemon with your tea?'

a point to think about . . .

Customer service is not only about attitude – and attitude problems – it also involves knowing about customer rights and complying with consumer law.

customer service and your Portfolio

For many businesses, putting the customer first is a prime aim.

Customer Service forms part of your Unit 1 coursework as it is a function of a business. You are likely to be comparing the way Customer Service works in the two businesses you are investigating.

Customer service is also covered in Unit 2 'People and Business' when you study a single business in detail. For more on this subject, please read Chapters 25 to 28.

This chapter gives an overview of the way Customer Service works.

what is involved in customer service?

As the Case Study on the opposite page suggests, **Customer Service** is more than just serving customers and being nice to them. It involves a range of 'services' – from providing information to knowing what happens when something goes wrong with a product.

The application of Customer Service is known as **Customer Care**. It involves:

- making sure you know about the available product range
- making sure the product range can be delivered if necessary
- making sure the product is safe and reliable
- providing information about products and giving advice
- providing credit facilities (finance) where appropriate, allowing the customer to pay over a period of time
- providing after-sales service – guarantees, spare parts, help-lines

There are laws which provide protection to consumers buying goods and services. Businesses should know their obligations under these laws; it will help them maintain a high level of customer service. **Consumer Protection** law is dealt with in detail in Chapter 28.

where does customer service happen?

Most businesses stress to all their employees that customer service is important, not only for staff working in a Customer Service section or Department, but for all staff. This idea extends to the concept that customer service should also be **internal** – employees should treat their colleagues as 'customers' and the business will benefit from smooth and efficient internal working.

External Customer Service is commonly seen operating from a desk or counter in a shop – providing information, taking customer orders and giving refunds, treating customers in a friendly way.

Customer Service with a smile at Tesco

why have customer service?

It should be the aim of every business to provide the highest level of customer service.

Businesses need their customers to buy their products or to use their services in order to survive and make a profit. The way that they treat their customers is therefore very important. Many businesses have a laid-down policy of Customer Care which involves putting the customer first in all situations. Read the Case Study about the Royal Bank of Scotland on the next page.

Case Study – Customer Care at the Royal Bank

The Royal Bank of Scotland is one of the UK's leading banks. It operates branches throughout the country.

The bank's policy on Customer Care is set out in its National Service Standards, which are designed to 'deliver the level of service we should achieve to be sure of meeting our customers' needs.'
These standards are classified in terms of:

- efficiency of staff
- customer problem solving
- courtesy to customers
- dealing with customers who are waiting
- knowledge of the bank's products and services
- personal appearance of bank staff
- use of the telephone by bank staff

Set out below are extracts from some of these National Service Standards.

efficiency
- aim to be 100% error free
- answer all letters within 2 days of receipt
- advise customers of delivery timescales

problem solving
- take ownership – don't blame others
- resolve complaints within 2 to 10 working days
- follow up afterwards to ensure that the customer is satisfied

courtesy
- greet customers and smile
- use customer's name
- give customer 100% of your attention

dealing with customers who are waiting
- serve all customers within 4 minutes
- apologise if a customer is kept waiting
- make visible efforts to reduce waiting times

product and service knowledge
- explain products and services clearly
- explain charges and fees clearly
- if unsure, don't guess – refer to someone else

using the telephone
- answer before the third ring, if possible
- speak clearly to customers, use their name and check their understanding of what you say.

Activity 9.1 – customer care at work

Read the National Service Standards on the previous page and answer the following questions:

1 What response times – eg for answering the telephone – are set down for Royal Bank of Scotland staff who deal with customers?

2 How does the Royal Bank of Scotland avoid the situation where someone dealing with a customer problem says, 'I'm sorry but the person who told you that is at lunch – and anyway, he shouldn't have said that – we don't do it like that here'?

3 How does the Royal Bank of Scotland ensure that the customer is given full and accurate information about its products?

4 How does the Royal Bank of Scotland ensure that its employees are polite to customers?

5 Customers who are kept waiting can get very angry and frustrated. How does the Royal Bank of Scotland aim to avoid this situation?

additional activity

Invent a situation where you are working in a job where you deal with the public – for example in a shop, a travel agency, or as a sales telephone operator for a mail order company. If you work part-time, use that situation.

Draw up a list of what you think are the ten most important 'service standards' you will have to achieve in order to provide a good level of Customer Care.

Nutshell summary

- Customer Service is more than just an information desk in a shop. It involves all the areas in which a business meets the needs of its customers.

- The range of activities involved in Customer Service includes:
  - providing information and advice
  - providing finance facilities for the customer where they are needed and are appropriate
  - making sure the product can be delivered
  - providing after-sales service, eg guarantees, repairs, help-lines

- Some businesses require their employees to treat each other as 'internal' customers.

- Customer Care is Customer Service in action.

Key terms

Customer Service
The areas of activity in which a business deals with and meets the needs of its customers.

Customer Care
The ways in which employees put Customer Service into action.

Internal Customer Care
Treating colleagues as one would treat an external customer.

Service Standards
Targets for external Customer Care set down by a business.

note
This chapter provides a brief overview of Customer Service. Read Chapters 25 to 28 for an in-depth study.

10

Human resources

A business is all about people

Laurie is a marketing specialist, and like all marketing specialists he is very much in demand for his services. He has been working as a consultant for fifteen years – in other words he has not been an employee, but has been his own boss. He has worked for many different businesses and has been involved in writing marketing plans and monitoring sales campaigns for his clients.
His income has been good as he has charged as much as £500 a day for his work.

But he wants a change. He is tired of travelling around and wants to join a go-ahead business as a permanent employee. He realises that he has a lot to do:

■ he will have to draw up a detailed CV

■ he will have to look at job adverts in trade magazines and on the internet

■ he will need to research marketing salaries

■ he will need to look at his present skills and training needs

■ he will have to buy a new suit and prepare for interviews

a point to think about . . .

A business is very much the end-product of the people that work for it. The Human Resource Departments that eventually interview Laurie will need to plan carefully how they recruit, interview and select the right people. They will need to train, develop and promote them so that they are motivated. They may also need to get rid of them if they are no good. The success of a business very much depends on its people.

Human Resources and your Portfolio

Human Resources forms part of your Unit 1 coursework as it is a function of a business. You are likely to be comparing the way Human Resources works in the two businesses you are investigating.

Human Resources forms the main part of Unit 2 'People and Business' where you study a single business in detail.
For more on this subject, please read Chapters 16 to 24.

functions of Human Resources

In this chapter we look at the **Human Resource**s function which deals with the hiring, firing and well-being of staff. People are an important resource and businesses need to make sure that employees are treated fairly and are encouraged to work well. This will benefit the effectiveness of the business as a whole in achieving its aims.

The main functions of Human Resources include:

- recruiting and keeping staff
- disciplining and dismissing staff
- training, developing and promoting staff
- maintaining good working conditions and Health and Safety
- looking after employer/employee relations
- dealing with employee organisations and Trade Unions

website recruitment:
www.jobsite.co.uk

Employers and employees have **rights** and **responsibilities** to each other. It is up to the Human Resources function to make sure that people know about them and to see that they are observed.

The interests of employees are protected both by **Trade Unions** (independent organisations which operate nationally) and by **staff associations** (which operate within organisations).

The rights of employees are also protected by **employment law**. The most important of these protect employees against discrimination on the grounds of sex, race and disability.

the Human Resources department

Most organisations, apart from very small ones, have a Human Resources Department or section. Traditionally it is known as a 'Personnel' department although the term 'Human Resources' department is becoming more common, often in its abbreviated form 'HR'. In this chapter you will find references to 'Human Resources' and 'Personnel'. They mean basically the same thing – dealing with employees.

a job interview

Human Resources and the organisation

Even in very small businesses a manager will include human resource management as one of his or her job roles.

As some HR departments are very small we shall look at a department that would be typical of a big company or local authority. How is the Human Resources department structured and what job roles does it cover? Read the extended Case Study – which includes a structure chart – on the next few pages.

Case Study – Human Resources at work

Arial Print plc is a large printing company. It prints mainly books, but it has also diversified into calendars and greetings cards. The company employs over 350 staff in its newly built factory near Nottingham.

Arial Print has a busy Human Resources Department. The structure of this department is shown in the chart below. On the next few pages some of the Human Resources employees explain what they do. Read this Case Study and answer the questions that follow.

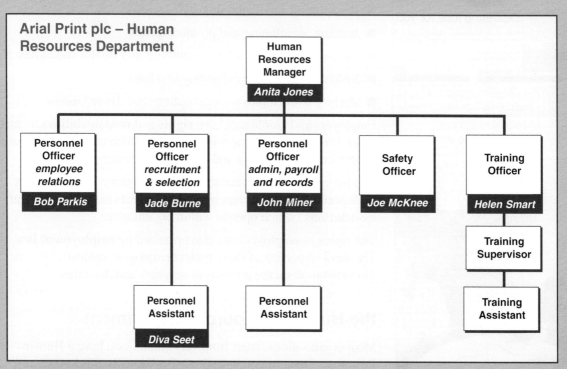

Arial Print plc – Human Resources Department

- Human Resources Manager — *Anita Jones*
  - Personnel Officer *employee relations* — **Bob Parkis**
  - Personnel Officer *recruitment & selection* — **Jade Burne**
    - Personnel Assistant — **Diva Seet**
  - Personnel Officer *admin, payroll and records* — **John Miner**
    - Personnel Assistant
  - Safety Officer — **Joe McKnee**
  - Training Officer — **Helen Smart**
    - Training Supervisor
      - Training Assistant

Anita Jones

Human Resources Manager

'My main roles include:

1   Carrying out the instructions of the company Board of Directors.

2   Ensuring my Department reaches its targets. For example, in this department last year our target (set by the Finance Department), was to reduce the level of sickness absence from 6.5 days lost per employee per year to 4 days. We actually got it down to 3.5!

3   Ensuring staff throughout the business are trained properly, so that they do their jobs well and enjoy what they are doing.

4   Carrying out the administration of the department – this includes the supervision of my five section officers.'

Bob Parkis

Personnel Officer – Employee Relations

'We operate a large factory employing 356 people and 189 of these belong to the Transport and General Workers Union (TGWU). The 189 are represented by the TGWU representatives (known as 'shop stewards'). My job is to make sure that the relationship between our employees and the company works effectively and without too many disputes. We have a series of agreements (sometimes called 'procedures') with our employees which set out how we deal with them from day to day. These include: Disciplinary Procedures, Grievance Procedures, and Redundancy Procedures.'

Jade Burne

Personnel Officer – Recruitment and Selection

'My main job involves the recruitment and selection of the right quality and quantity of staff.

Firstly, I have to talk to departmental managers who want to replace staff or recruit extra staff. They have to tell me exactly what they are looking for. I write out the job adverts and place them in the newspapers and with on-line agencies. Then I have to choose candidates to interview, often from hundreds of applications, and then invite them over for a selection day.'

John Miner

Personnel Officer – Administration, Payroll and Records

'I used to be a factory assembly worker but had to give that up fifteen years ago after I had a bad injury at work. My job includes putting all newcomers onto the computerised payroll system and sorting out the pay arrangements for leavers. I handle all queries and complaints from staff about pay and I deal with the appropriate person in the company accounts department. I look after all the personnel records, including holidays and sickness. I deal with pension enquiries from staff and deal directly with the company pension scheme administrators. I also manage the company car fleet!'

Joe McKnee

Safety Officer

'Being an ex-ambulance man, like me, means you pick up on unsafe workplace situations or dangerous equipment more quickly than other people. I have to ensure that Arial Printers fulfils all of its duties under the Health and Safety at Work Act. This means I have to run a Safety Committee which consists of managers and employee-appointed safety representatives. I also have to run training courses for safety representatives and for supervisors and managers. More recently I had to carry out disability awareness programmes for all staff under the Disability Discrimination Act.'

Helen Smart

Training Officer

'My main role is the development and training of staff. My main concern is employee development. This means making sure that staff are motivated to perform as well as they possibly can and the best use is made of everyone's skills and abilities.

Basic training on the equipment in the factory is administered by my Training Supervisor, Pete Davis. Like most people in his position, he has had years of work experience in the factory.'

Diva Seet

Personnel Assistant

'In Human Resources departments like this one, a personnel officer or a training officer will have an assistant to carry out much of the routine clerical work. I work as Personnel Assistant to Jade Burne, who is in charge of recruitment and selection. Jade gives me loads of opportunities to do a wide range of personnel work. I joined Arial Printers two years ago from the local college and I am using a lot that I learnt there on my Business Studies course – mind you, it never works out exactly like they tell you in the books! For example, Jade gets me to look after all the lower grade vacancies. I have to plough through dozens of candidates, then short-list about ten candidates and fix up all the interviews for them. Sometimes I have to book hotel accommodation for those coming a long way. Then half of them don't even turn up . . .'

Activity 10.1 – Human resources at work

Read the Arial Printers Case Study on the previous pages and answer the following questions:

1 What Trade Union has a substantial membership at Arial Printers? Who represents the employee members and who represents the employer? What are the various agreements that set out the way in which the employer deals with the employees?

2 Who is directly responsible at the company for recruitment of new staff? List the processes that are involved in the recruitment of staff for a company like Arial Printers.

3 What day-to-day activities are involved in administering the work of a Human Resources Department? Why do you think it is important that people involved in this work keep the information they deal with under lock and key, or in a secure part of the computer system?

4 What does the Human Resources Department do to make sure that it maintains a safe workplace for Arial Printers' employees? What do you think might happen to Arial Printers if one of its machinery workers suffered a crushed arm in a printing machine as a result of the company not repairing a broken guard rail around the machine?

5 How does Arial Printers benefit from implementing a thorough training programme for its employees?

6 Anita Jones, as Human Resources Manager, is involved with other parts of the business, as well as being responsible for her own department. Suggest how her work might bring her into contact with other areas of the business.

Nutshell summary

■ Human Resources is an important function within business because it deals with employees.
The manner in which a business obtains and treats its employees is critical to its success.

■ The range of activities involved in Human Resources includes:
  - staff recruitment and staff motivation
  - disciplining and firing staff
  - maintaining good working conditions
  - maintaining Health & Safety
  - looking after employer/employee relations
  - dealing with employee organisations and Trade Unions

■ A business is the people who work in it.

Key terms

Human Resources
The function of a business which deals with employees.

Trade Union
An organisation which upholds the rights of employees.

Staff Association
A committee within a business which upholds employee rights.

Employment law
Laws which protect the rights of employees in areas such as sex, race and disability discrimination.

note
This chapter provides a brief overview of Human Resources. Read Chapters 16 to 24 for an in-depth study.

11

Operations management

What resources will I need?

Ella is starting a new business offering computer and internet training. She is calling her business 'Webwise'. She realises that starting a new business is a challenge which will take up all her time and energy for a long time to come. She doesn't mind this because, as a true 'entrepreneur', she has the necessary dedication and 'sticking power'. Her organisational powers are stretched because she has to deal with so many different **resources** in order to produce her training courses – her product. Ella needs:

- buildings – premises in which to set up her business
- equipment – furniture, computers, fax, telephone, photocopier
- people – staff to help her in computer training, keeping the accounts, marketing, and all the requirements of the day-to-day running of the business
- materials – training materials such as books and computer software, and basic office requirements such as printer cartridges, disks, pens, paper, paperclips

One of the basic functions of business, therefore, is the management of resources. This is essential for the '**operations**' of Ella's service business. If Ella had decided to manufacture a product, the organisation of her resources would be concentrated in the '**production**' of the product.

a point to think about . . .

Ella's business is small. She has to do most things herself. In a large business, such as a travel company or a car manufacturer, the 'operations' or 'production' will be dealt with by a large department.

definitions: 'operations' and 'production'

'Operations' is the process of transforming business resources such as buildings, equipment, materials and people into a product.

The term '**operations**' can be used to describe the production of goods and services, although the traditional term '**production**' is commonly used to describe the management of resources for a manufacturing business.

business resources

As we have seen in the Case Study on the previous page, when a business manufactures a product or provides a service it will need a variety of resources (which include items it owns) and people. These resources will vary with the type of business involved but could include:

land and buildings used by the business

. . . for example, farmland, mines, fisheries, offices, factories, warehouses, shops, hotels, keep-fit centres

machinery and equipment used by the business

. . . for example, production-line machinery, vans, cars, computers, communication equipment

people who work in – and for – the business

. . . for example, managers, supervisors, assistants, specialists, consultants, accountants, solicitors

materials and stock used by the business

. . . for example, goods bought in by a shop to sell to customers, raw materials and components bought in by a manufacturer to produce the finished product

Now look at and compare the diagrams which follow.

business resources needed

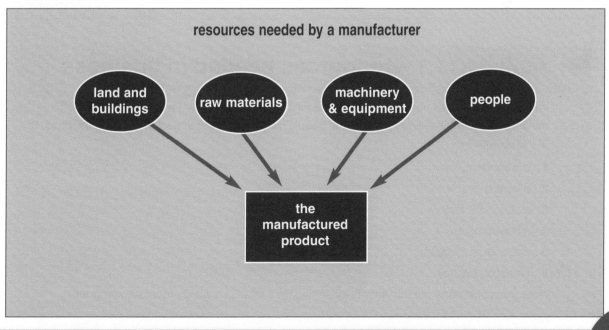

resources needed by a manufacturer

- land and buildings
- raw materials
- machinery & equipment
- people

the manufactured product

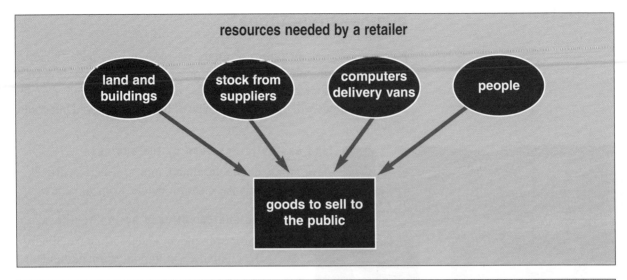

resources needed by a retailer

resources needed by a travel agent

Activity 11.1 – resources needed in business

Identify the resources needed by the businesses listed below and classify them under the four headings: land and buildings, equipment, people, materials. State in each case what the product of the business is:

1 a dairy farm
2 a dentist
3 a chocolate factory
4 a bus company
5 a television company
6 an escort agency

Note: you could carry out this activity by setting up a table in a word-processing program.

the production process

factors of production

'Production' is the process of turning all these resources into a product – a manufactured item or a service – which can be sold by the business. These resources are sometimes known as the **factors of production** – they are combined to produce the product.
The main factors are:

- **land** – the land and buildings used in production
- **labour** – the people who work to produce the product
- **capital** – the money invested to produce the product
- **enterprise** – the input of the entrepreneur (see Chapter 1) without whom the product would not get off the ground

how do you add value to apples?

adding value

When a business manufactures an item or provides a service it uses its resources to '**add value**' to those resources.
This means that the product can be sold at a higher price when it has gone through further production processes.

Take, for example, a fruit farm which grows apples.
The farmer combines the resources of the land, the trees, the labour cost of maintaining them and picking the fruit.

He could sell the apples at 70p a kilo to the passing public.
But he could also add value to them by turning them into juice or cider, and selling the final products for more money.

production costs and profit

The resources used by a business will have to be paid for.
They result in costs for the business which have to be covered – wages, rent, cost of materials, stock, electricity, phone bills and so on. All of these have to be dealt with by the Finance Department. This is covered in more detail in the next chapter.

When a business is planning to produce a product – whether it is a manufactured item or a service – it will need to make sure that the day-to-day costs will be covered by the money received from sales. The greater the added value, the greater the possible profit:

profit = money from sales – running costs

Clearly if the money from sales does not cover running costs, the business will make a loss. It is up to the business owner to make sure this does not happen. See Chapter 29 on business costs.

Activity 11.2 – adding value

How do you think you could add value to the following basic resources by using them in some form of business venture?

State what extra resources you might need to add value and make a profit.

1   a pile of seasoned timber

2   a lake stocked with fish

3   you find you are a genius at writing computer games

methods of production

The way a business manufactures a product will depend on the type of product involved.

There are three main methods of production: job production, batch production and continuous production.

job production

With **job production** one item is completed at a time. This method is suitable for large or 'one-off' projects such as ships, buildings and anything that is built to order.

batch production

A **batch** is a term used in baking. Batch production involves completing a group of items – a 'batch' – at the same time and then moving on to the next group.

A tray of bread rolls or loaves being prepared and then baked in the oven is a common example. Batch production therefore involves a series of operations repeated time and time again.

continuous production

Continuous production is the commonly accepted idea of 'production-line' manufacture. A product is assembled on a continuous moving line and parts and processes added as it moves along.

The processes can be carried out by hand or by robots. The modern car production line is a common example and is highly automated. For many products such as food products the process ends with wrapping and packaging.

The illustrations on the next page show examples of all three methods of production.

job production – a building

continuous production of Toyota cars

batch production at a bakery

methods of improving production

efficiency and productivity

You will know that you need to be efficient to achieve good results. **Efficiency** means that you have to make the most of your resources. If, for example, you are producing a piece of work, you should make the most of your notes, textbooks, websites, your tutor and your time. Businesses also need to make efficient use of their resources.

Efficiency shows how well all the resources are being used. One useful measure of efficiency is **productivity**. This calculates the number of items produced (or services sold) by the employees.

Some employees are paid a bonus if they produce (or sell) more than a given number of items – so it is in their interest to be productive!

One way of calculating productivity is to divide the number of items produced by the number of people employed. If a car factory produces 30,000 cars a month and employs a workforce of 1,000 over the month . . .

$$productivity \ = \ \frac{30,000}{1,000} \ = \ 30 \ cars \ per \ employee \ per \ month$$

Activity 11.3 – productivity

A factory producing TV sets records the following staffing and output levels for three months production:

	employees	output of TV sets
Month 1	1,250	200,000
Month 2	1,100	187,000
Month 3	1,300	195,000

1   Calculate the productivity (the number of TV sets per employee) for each of the three months.

2   Is productivity at its highest when the output is at its highest level? If not, why not?

a quality product

Businesses sell their products in a competitive market. A business producing a quality product can be reasonably confident that the product will sell.

quality control

Quality control on the production line of a manufactured item involves a process of inspection of a set number of items.

Any faulty items will be rejected and the cause of the problem investigated. Quality control of a service product is equally important and involves monitoring of the service and feedback from customers received by the Marketing Department.

Quality Assurance

It is important to appreciate that quality is not only desirable in the finished product, it should also be applicable in every process and system within the business. This is known as **Quality Assurance**. Businesses which show that they can match up to and maintain high standards may apply for one of a range of internationally recognized certificates of Quality Assurance (the BS EN ISO 9000 range). Anyone dealing with a business with this certificate can be confident that it is dealing with a 'quality' organisation.

Activity 11.4 – aiming for quality

This note is packed with every pair of children's shoes which leaves Start-rite Shoes Limited in Norwich. Read it through and answer the questions which follow.

1. What is the specific business aim relating to customers set out in the statement?

2. How will the company meet the requirements of BSEN ISO 9002?

3. What are the four main aims of the company's manufacturing strategy?

4. Which department would be responsible for producing this statement?

QUALITY POLICY STATEMENT

It is the policy of Start-rite Shoes Limited to provide footwear which will give total satisfaction to our customers with their fit, fashion, comfort, service and price. To help achieve this objective the Company has established and will maintain a Quality Management System designed to meet all the requirements of BSEN ISO 9002. This programme complements and co-ordinates the Company's overall manufacturing strategy which includes:
* Providing materials and components of an approved specification.
* Up-to-date fashion interpretation.
* Modern, well maintained machinery and support systems.
* On-going training at all levels.

---

using information technology in production

Computers are now employed extensively in the production process in a number of ways:

CAD

Computer Aided Design (**CAD**) is now commonly used to draw up plans for new products. It is cheap and efficient as it works entirely on-screen and enables concepts to be drafted rapidly and changed as required.

CAD works in 3D (three dimensions) and so is used a great deal by architects and designers of products such as cars.

robots

Some modern production lines use programmed **robots** to assemble products. This is common where the product is complex and needs a very clean environment. Car production is a well-known example. The picture on page 99 shows Toyota Corollas being assembled by welding robots.

CAM

Computer Aided Manufacture (**CAM**) uses computers to ensure that the product process has the required materials, components, stock and labour as and when they are needed.

The Case Study below shows how a car manufacturer uses computers to design cars and also enables the customer to 'build' their own vehicle.

Case Study – computers and car design

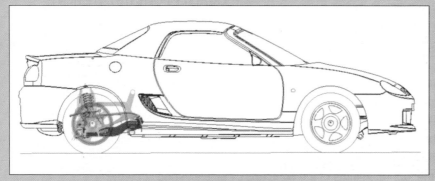

design by the manufacturer

MG Rover Group is a leading UK independent manufacturer of sports cars and sports saloons bearing the famous MG badge.

Computer Aided Design plays a great part in the design process of its cars. Designers are able to draw up plans on the computer and show them to senior management, including Production, and modify them as the project progresses. The car shown above is the company's MGTF sports car in its development stage. Visit www.mg-rover.com for further details of the group and its cars.

design by the customer

Volvo cars have always had a reputation for quality and safety. One feature of Volvo manufacturing is the ability of the customer to order a new car, using an on-line system. The car colour, engine size, interior trim and wheel design can all be specified, either at the dealer or at the website www.volvocars.co.uk and passed with the order to the production line.

Activity 11.5 – using ICT in car design

Read the Case Study on the previous page and answer the following questions:

1   How does the MG Rover Group use computers in the car design process, and what are the advantages of this method of design?

2   How does Volvo Cars UK Limited use computers to help customers design cars?

3   What method of production has traditionally been used to manufacture cars? Does your answer to **2** (above) change this situation at all?

Nutshell summary

- 'Operations' is a word used in business to describe the transforming of business resources into a product – a manufactured product or a service.

- The main types of business resources are:
  - land and buildings
  - machinery and equipment
  - people who work for the business
  - materials and stock used in the business

- Other business resources include:
  - capital – the money investment in the business
  - enterprise – the energy and ideas of the entrepreneur who runs the business

- Businesses need to cover their running costs from sales income, or they will make a loss. Many businesses achieve a profit by adding value in their production process – making a product which will sell for a higher price.

- There are three main types of production: job production, batch production and continuous production.

- Businesses also make a profit when they are efficient and make the most of their resources. Efficiency is often measured by productivity.

- A quality product sells well. Quality of production is maintained by quality control inspection. A quality organisation is achieved through Quality Assurance.

- Computer technology is used to make production more efficient in the areas of design, management of resources and robotics in assembly lines.

Key terms

Operations
The process of transforming business resources into a product (goods or services).

Production
The process of transforming business resources into a manufactured product.

Factors of production
Resources such as land, buildings, machinery, materials and people which are used in production.

Job production
Production where one item is completed at a time.

Batch production
Production where a group of items is completed at the same time.

Continuous production
Production where the product is assembled on a production line.

Productivity
The number of items produced (or services sold) by an employee.

Quality control
Inspection of products produced to monitor and ensure quality.

Quality assurance
The maintenance of quality in every process and system within the business.

12

Finance

Where has the money gone?

Six months ago, Homer Samson started a business importing speciality chocolates from Europe and selling them into shops and supermarkets. He employed a staff of twenty – including a Finance Manager – and rented a storage warehouse on the edge of town. The business seemed to be doing very well but suddenly Homer ran out of money. He did not have enough cash to:

- pay the wages
- pay his overseas suppliers
- pay the rent on the warehouse
- repay his bank overdraft

He could not understand what had happened because he was owed a lot of money by his customers – but they seemed so slow in paying. Then his Finance Manager resigned and he was left to sort out the wages, write up the books and pacify the bank.

Eventually, at a meeting with his accountant and the bank, Homer was offered a 'rescue' loan by the bank – on the understanding that he exercised stricter control over his finance and chased up his customers for the money owing.

a point to think about . . .

It is all very well having the business resources to provide a product (as in the last chapter), but if a business cannot manage its finances it will run into trouble – even if it is owed money by its customers.

Finance, your Portfolio and Unit 3

Finance forms part of your Unit 1 coursework as it is a function of a business. You are likely to be comparing the way Finance is managed in the two businesses you are investigating.

Finance is dealt with in much greater detail in Unit 3 'Business Finance' which is externally assessed and covered in Chapters 29 to 42 – the final section of this book.

In this chapter we give an overview of business finance.

the finance function

The finance function in a business is closely involved with the production of goods and services and so links up with other function areas in the business, including the senior management.
Look at the table of activities below.

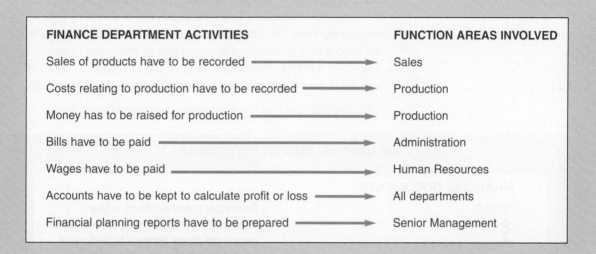

FINANCE DEPARTMENT ACTIVITIES	FUNCTION AREAS INVOLVED
Sales of products have to be recorded	Sales
Costs relating to production have to be recorded	Production
Money has to be raised for production	Production
Bills have to be paid	Administration
Wages have to be paid	Human Resources
Accounts have to be kept to calculate profit or loss	All departments
Financial planning reports have to be prepared	Senior Management

finance department structure

Set out below is a structure chart of a typical finance department showing the main functions that it carries out.

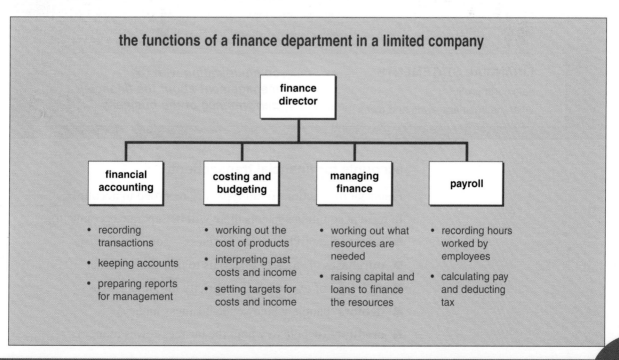

the functions of a finance department in a limited company

finance director

financial accounting	costing and budgeting	managing finance	payroll
• recording transactions	• working out the cost of products	• working out what resources are needed	• recording hours worked by employees
• keeping accounts	• interpreting past costs and income	• raising capital and loans to finance the resources	• calculating pay and deducting tax
• preparing reports for management	• setting targets for costs and income		

financial accounting

The box on the left-hand side of the structure chart on the previous page shows the **financial accounting** function.

the financial accounting system

Later in this book (Chapter 39) we will be looking in detail at the financial documents involved in buying and selling. These documents form the first part of a process which ends up with the production of financial reports such as profit statements. These are used by the management of the business in seeing how well the business is performing and meeting its objectives.

The stages in the process are shown in the diagram below.

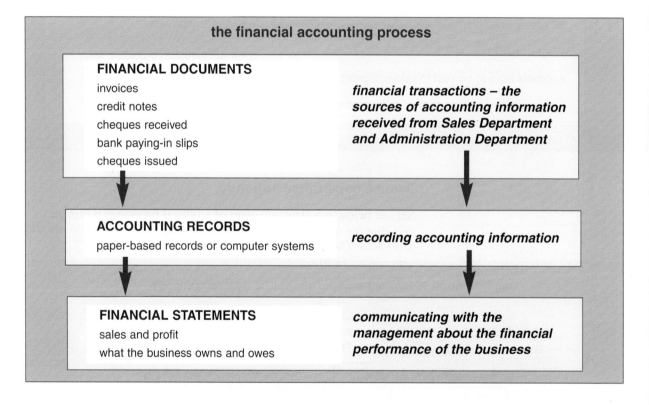

accounts for financial transactions

Financial transactions of all types are recorded in **accounts**.

In most accounting systems there will be separate accounts for:

- **sales** of the product of the business – goods or services
- **purchases** of stock or materials to make the product
- each type of **expense**, eg electricity bill, rent, wages
- **debtors** (people who owe the business money)
- **creditors** (people to whom the business owes money)

double-entry accounting

The basis of many accounting systems is the **double-entry** book-keeping system. You do not have to study double-entry for your course, but it is useful to know what the system involves.

Double-entry book-keeping means making two entries in separate accounts for each transaction. For instance, if you are paying for wages by cheque you will make an entry in Bank Account (because you are paying out money) and an entry in Wages Account (because you are recording the amount you are paying for wages). If you are using a manual accounting system you will make the two entries in separate accounts by hand (the accounts are set out below).

If you are operating a computer accounting system you will make one entry on the keyboard, but indicate the other entry with a code number (see the example at the bottom of the page).

Bank Account			Wages Account		
	30 Nov Wages	£1553.46	30 Nov Bank	£ 1553.46	

computer accounts

As noted earlier, many small businesses and almost all large businesses use computers to handle their business transactions.

If you use an accounting program, you input the transactions into the computer where they are stored on disk. The principles of double-entry book-keeping remain the same – when you input the data you use input codes to identify the two accounts involved in each transaction, eg 1200 = Bank Account, 7500 = stationery account, as in the example shown below from a computer program screen.

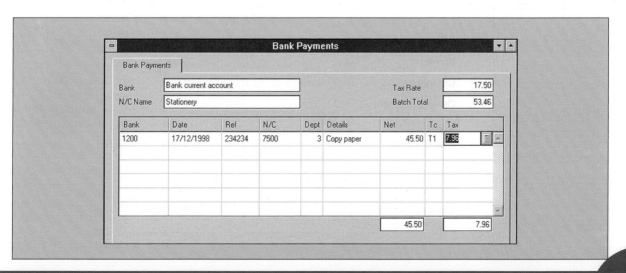

financial statements

The Finance Department regularly draws up financial statements for management. These report on areas such as sales and profit and help management monitor the main objectives of the business.

These statements are prepared from the information held in the accounting records. Some computer accounting programs will print out these statements automatically.

The two main statements are the profit and loss statement and the balance sheet:

■ the **profit and loss statement** shows the sales figure, the expenses and profit

■ the **balance sheet** shows how much a business owns and owes

Read the Case Study below and answer the questions in the Activity which follows.

Case Study – financial statements

Bentom Music is a business which sells mail order CDs.

The figures shown on this and the next page have been taken from the accounting records of the business at the end of the year.

The Balance Sheet below shows items owned by the business and also where the finance has come from: money borrowed from the bank and money invested by the owners.

BENTOM MUSIC	
Balance sheet figures (extracts)	
	£
Office and storage premises	80,000
Furniture	25,000
Computers	20,000
Other equipment	15,000
Stocks of CDs	40,000
Bank account	2,000
Bank loan	22,000
Owner's Capital	160,000

The Profit and Loss statement below shows the sales income of the business at the top. It then deducts all the running costs, including the CDs purchased, and shows the profit at the bottom.

BENTOM MUSIC
Profit and Loss Statement

	£	£
Sales of CDs		260,000
less purchases of CDs		100,000
equals		160,000
less expenses		
rent and rates	5,000	
postage	2,500	
insurance	1,500	
telephone	2,500	
wages and salaries	80,500	
electricity	3,000	
advertising	25,000	
Total expenses		120,000
PROFIT		40,000

Activity 12.1 – financial statements

Read the Case Study above and answer the questions that follow.

1   The balance sheet shows you what the business owns. What is the total value of what the business owns?

2   Where has the money come from to finance the business?

3   The profit and loss statement lists the money from sales and expenses of the business. What is the sales figure?

4   Where has the sales figure come from?

5   Apart from the CD purchases figure, what is the largest item of expense for the business? Where has this figure come from?

6   What is the profit of the business over the period of the profit and loss statement? Which groups of people and functions in the business would be interested in this figure?

costing and budgeting

costing

It is the job of the Finance Department to find out information about the cost of producing a product – whether the product is a manufactured item or a service. **Costing** can involve a wide variety of resources:

- the raw materials purchased (for a manufactured item)
- the cost of stock (if the business is a shop)
- the cost of paying the wages for the employees producing the product
- other expenses known as 'overheads' which have to be paid anyway, for example electricity bills, advertising, rates, stationery for the office

It is up to the Finance Department to liaise with the various function areas and calculate the cost of producing the product to ensure that:

- there is sufficient finance to cover the cost
- the business is making the most efficient use of its resources

budgeting

It is the responsibility of the Finance Department to set **budgets** (targets) for future periods. For example:

- a **sales budget** to forecast the income that will be received by the business from sales
- a **production budget** to plan the number of items produced and to work out what they will cost

As time goes on, the Finance Department will monitor actual figures against the budgeted figures. If there is a problem – for example, if sales are not as high as budgeted – they will have to liaise with the other Departments and adjust their forecasts.

raising finance

Money is the lifeblood of any business. Money is needed for:

- **long-term needs** such as investing in premises, machinery, computers
- **short-term needs** such as buying stock and raw materials, paying bills, paying wages

It is the job of the Finance Department to co-ordinate the raising of money for the different function areas of the business, eg Production, Marketing.

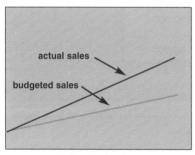

INVOICES

£?

the costs of running a business

actual sales

budgeted sales

sales budgeting

The finance raised is normally either short-term or long-term:

■ **long-term** in the form of investment from the owner (known as **capital**) and bank loans repayable over a period of time

■ **short-term** in the form of:

– money received from sales of the product

– credit from suppliers (the money is available because the suppliers have not yet been paid by the business)

– short-term borrowing from the bank on an overdraft

Look at the diagram below.

the flow of money in a business

SOURCES OF FINANCE

long-term finance

owner's investment

bank loans

short-term finance

money from sales

credit from suppliers

bank overdraft

USES OF FINANCE

long-term investments

premises

machinery, computers

short-term needs

paying for stock and materials

paying bills and wages
bank overdraft

Activity 12.2 – raising finance to meet costs

1 What sorts of cost are taken into account when the Finance Department of a manufacturing business calculates the cost of making a product?

2 Why would a business need to examine the costs of making a product or providing a service?

3 What is a sales budget?

4 Why would the Production Department need to know about the sales budget?

5 What sources of finance might a business use if it wanted to buy some new premises?

6 What sources of finance could a business use if it needed extra stock?

payroll

Payroll is the function in the business which works out the pay and deductions (income tax and National Insurance) of its employees.

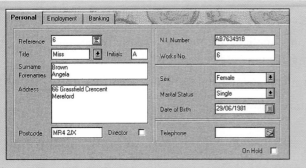

employee record screen from a Sage Payroll program

Some businesses 'farm out' payroll and pay specialist bureaux to do the job for them. Most businesses process payroll within the Finance Department, which gets its information from the Human Resources Department.

Payroll can either be done manually using the forms and instructions provided by the Inland Revenue, or it can be done by computer using programs such as Sage Payroll. More and more businesses are now using computer payroll programs as they are faster and very accurate.

Case Study – jobs in a Finance Department

JOHN CARDWELL – SALES LEDGER CLERK
'My main job is issuing invoices to customers who order goods from us. I have to check their purchase order forms carefully and also make sure they are good accounts and not bad payers. We used to type out the invoices ourselves but we now have a computer system which prints them out in batches. The computer does all the calculations, which is great, but we still have to check our work carefully.'

JACK POUND – COST ACCOUNTANT
'I get involved in most aspects of costing work. Just now I have been calculating the cost of materials that we use in manufacture. My next task is to analyse the costs of our overheads – our rent, our wage bill and all the other running costs. It is important work because you need to know what things cost in order to plan ahead and draw up budgets. In the end it is all about making a profit – which, of course, benefits everyone.'

TANYA REYNOLDS – PAYROLL ASSISTANT
'Although we occasionally have to work out wages manually, most jobs are computerised now – all we have to do is to enter the hours worked by each employee onto the computer, and it automatically works out the pay and prints out a payslip. Some employees still get paid in cash – and I have to work out a cash analysis and get the right notes and coins from the bank. I find the work interesting because I like working with figures.'

Nutshell summary

- The Finance function in a business is closely linked with the other functions because it deals with the basic business resource of money.

- The Finance function can be subdivided into a number of different areas:
  - keeping accounts (financial accounting)
  - costing and budgeting
  - raising and managing finance
  - payroll

- Financial accounting involves three main processes:
  - recording financial transactions from documents
  - entering the transactions in accounts – which can be manual or computerised
  - presenting the information in financial statements such as profit and loss statements and balance sheets

- Financial statements are important because they tell the management of the business – and other stakeholders – how much profit (or loss) has been made and how financially strong the business is.

- Costing is another vital financial function as it tells the business what it will cost to produce any level of production. This in turn enables the business to work out how profitable it will be.

- Budgeting looks forward and projects financial and other targets for the business. It provides a 'yardstick' for monitoring and assessing actual performance.

- All businesses need finance to operate and to expand. Generally short-term financial needs (eg stock) are met by short-term loans and long-term needs (eg a factory) are met by long-term loans and capital from the owners.

- Payroll – paying employees – is an essential financial function. It can be carried out by the business Finance Department, or it can be contracted out to independent payroll bureaux.

 # Key terms

Financial accounting
The recording of financial transactions in accounts and the presentation of financial reports.

Account
A record – manual or computerised – of financial transactions.

Double-entry
An accounting system in which two entries are made in the accounts for each financial transaction.

Profit and loss statement
A financial statement which shows the sales, purchases, expenses and profit (or loss) of a business.

Balance sheet
A financial statement which shows what a business owns and owes and the way in which it is financed.

Costing
The process of finding out how much the various expenses of a business actually cost. This helps with the budgeting process.

Budget
A forecast of the likely future performance of a business, eg in sales and in production.

Capital
The money invested by the owner(s) in a business.

Payroll
The part of the business which works out the pay and deductions of its employees.

---

note
This chapter provides an overview of Finance. Read Chapters 29 to 42 for an in-depth study of this subject.

13

Administration and ICT

Keeping the business together

Rachel has just got a job as an administrative assistant at Presto Limited, a company that makes sauces to accompany pasta and stir-fries. Rachel has recently completed a course in Business Administration at the local college and has also done work experience at the local Trading Standards Department.

Her supervisor has asked her to carry out a wide variety of tasks:

■ computer operation – working with databases, spreadsheets and word-processed documents

■ dealing with the incoming mail and the outgoing post

■ processing emails

■ filing

■ photocopying

■ checking the First Aid supplies

She has just finished her first week and is having a drink with a friend.

'It's all go,' she says, 'I feel as if I have been hit by a tornado. It's "Rachel do this" and "Rachel do that" from people from all departments of the business. I have to organise myself to get everything done, otherwise the paper piles up on my desk. But the people are really nice.'

a point to think about . . .

Administration is sometimes seen as a routine area to work in, but it is a vital function of business – it keeps everything going. If the administration is well-organised, the business can go places.

administration and ICT

Whatever the size of a business, it will need a great deal of back-up administration work to be done. Much of this will require the use of ICT (Information and Communication Technology) support.

ICT support involves a wide range of computer applications: databases, spreadsheets, word-processing, in-house publishing (eg training material), accounts packages, computerised payroll, internal email and external email.

what is administration?

Administration is making sure that the right resources are in the right place at the right time.

Administration means that a business runs smoothly – that there is paper in the photocopier and paper in the loos, that the premises are clean and safe, that customers are sent the right documents and that telephone messages do not get lost or emails go unanswered.

administration and communication

Many administration tasks involve communication.

Information and messages – enquiries, orders, complaints – will come into the business from **external** sources by post, by fax, by phone and email. Callers with and without appointments will arrive. All have to be dealt with efficiently.

The different functions within the business (eg sales, finance, production) need to communicate **internally** with each other in the day-to-day running of the organisation. The methods used can include paper documents, telephone, fax, intranet (internal email) and meetings. These are dealt with in detail in the next chapter.

dealing with the telephone

who does the administration?

If you are a sole trader, administration is likely to be something that you have to do yourself.

If the business is larger, many of the administration activities will be organised within the departments concerned. For example, a Sales Department will keep records of customers, and the Finance Department is likely to process the accounts and the payroll. Many of these activities are likely to be carried out on computers.

Although many administration tasks are done in the departments, there will be activities which are needed by the whole organisation, for example:

- opening and distributing the post when it arrives
- collecting and stamping the post going out at the end of the day
- operating the telephone switchboard
- dealing with callers to the premises
- designing and printing forms
- filing and database maintenance
- making sure the premises are clean and secure

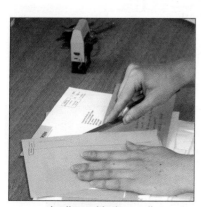
dealing with the mail

Activity 13.1 – administration at school or college

Find out what department or section is responsible for the following activities in your school or college. Identify the activities which are carried out by people who are not employees of the school or college.

1   dealing with the post – incoming and outgoing

2   processing all the photocopying and teaching aids needed by teachers /lecturers

3   dealing with visitors during the day

4   operating the telephone switchboard

5   cleaning the premises

6   making sure all the computers are working correctly

7   catering

organising the administration function

There are a number of options available to a business with separate departments when it is organising its administration:

■ each department can be made responsible for its own administration

■ the business can set up its own administration department

■ the business can use other businesses to carry out some of its administration work; this is known as **outsourcing** – examples of this include cleaning and security services and the use of outside telephone **call centres** which will take telephone enquiries and orders on behalf of the business (see next page)

Study the three diagrams and read the Case Study that follows.

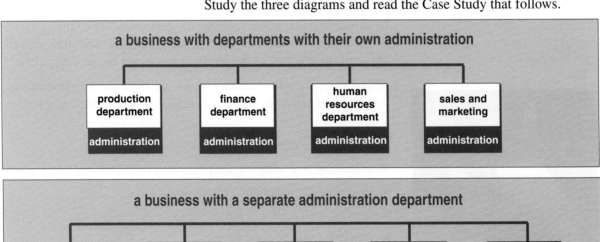

a business with departments with their own administration

production department — administration
finance department — administration
human resources department — administration
sales and marketing — administration

a business with a separate administration department

production department | finance department | human resources department | sales and marketing department | administration department

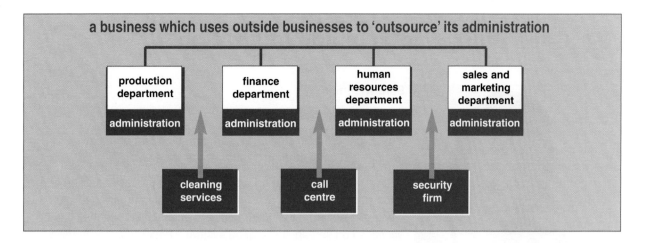

a business which uses outside businesses to 'outsource' its administration

production department	finance department	human resources department	sales and marketing department
administration	administration	administration	administration

cleaning services	call centre	security firm

Case Study – using call centres

Source: Call Centre Focus

A business that wishes to outsource its telephone contact with the public – providing information and taking orders – can use a call centre. A call centre is a business employing a large number of trained telephonists who will answer calls for other businesses.

It is an industry which has been growing rapidly. In 1997 there were 1,800 call centres with 144,000 call centre telephonists in the UK. In 2001 there were 3,300 sites employing 540,000 telephonists.

Developments in ICT have made it possible for call centres to be set up overseas. The falling cost of transmitting calls and low wage rates have made it possible for British Airways and BUPA, for example, to set up call centres in India to answer calls from the UK.

But call centres are not ideal for all businesses. A case was reported of a man, whose bank was in London, being connected to a call centre in Scotland. 'I was wondering,' he asked the telephonist, 'if I might have left my glasses on the counter when I came into the branch this morning?'

Activity 13.2 – the growth of call centres

Read the Case Study above and answer the questions that follow.

1   What is a call centre?
2   How have call centres grown over the last few years? Calculate the percentage increase in centres and employees.
3   Why would a business want to set up a call centre in a different country?
4   What are the advantages to a business of using a call centre?
5   What are the possible disadvantages to a business of using a call centre?

Case Study – jobs in administration

Sara Wiseman

Administrative Assistant

'I work in the Administration Department on a part-time basis. I work with fifteen other assistants and a supervisor.

The work is certainly varied. I do mostly word-processing, filing and photocopying. We have recently been converting the filing to an electronic system – the documents are scanned so that they can be accessed on screen. It is a good system – better than rummaging around in a filing drawer to find that someone else has taken the file out!

We deal with all the paperwork involved with the running of the company, so we get to see what all the other departments are up to. I like working here, the atmosphere is good – the supervisor is strict, but has a broad sense of humour!'

Gerry Freidman

Mail Room Assistant

'I have worked in the mail room for three years now. We open the incoming mail, date-stamp it and sort it into the various departments: anything to do with stock goes to Production, cheques go to Finance, job applications to Human Resources and so on. We have to make sure that the mail gets to the right person as quickly as possible.

We also deal with outgoing parcels. The carrier we use has a tracking system where you can look at their website and see where each parcel has got to. Each parcel has a barcode which identifies it. It is a great system because you can tell customers where their goods have got to at any one time.'

Mina Morris

Health & Safety Representative

'I work in the Administration Department and a Health & Safety Representative for the company. I am in charge of assessing safety risks on the premises and organising staff training in Health & Safety. I have also written a Health & Safety Policy document for the company. I rely a lot on my computer for updating the Policy document, designing notices and producing training material.

Nobody has been injured here yet, but we need to be prepared!'

Activity 13.3 – investigating administration jobs

Read the Case Study on the opposite page and answer the questions that follow.

1 In what ways do computer applications support the work that Sarah does?
What are the main advantages of organising a filing system on a computer?

2 In what ways has the work of a mail room such as Aftab's been improved by Information Technology? Who benefits from these improvements?

3 Maintenance of Health & Safety is a legal requirement in all but the smallest businesses. What are Mina's responsibilities in this area and how is she supported by ICT?

4 What evidence can you see, from reading about the three employees, that the work of an Administration Department affects the running of the other departments? How would the aims of a business be affected if the Administration Department became inefficient?

Nutshell summary

■ The Administration function in a business makes sure that the business has the essential back-up resources it needs to function efficiently.

■ The Administration function relies heavily on Information and Communication Technology (ICT) to function efficiently. Computer applications widely used in business include:
- word-processing and in-house publishing
- spreadsheets and databases
- accounts and payroll packages
- internal and external email

■ Administration inevitably involves communication – both inside and outside the business.

■ Administration may be carried out within individual departments, or by a separate Administration Department.

■ Many Administrative tasks, such as cleaning and security, are now carried out by 'outsourcing' – by using external businesses to provide the necessary service.

■ The greatest growth area in outsourcing is in telephone call centres which employ over half a million people in the UK.

Key terms

Information and Communication Technology
The use of computer and communication technology to support the running of a business.

Administration
Making sure that the right business resources are in the right place at the right time.

Outsourcing
Using another business to provide an essential business function, such as cleaning and security.

Call centre
A business which provides telephone answering and calling services for other businesses.

Health & Safety
The legal responsibility of a business to maintain a safe and secure workplace for its employees.

14

Communication and ICT

The communication revolution

Jack was talking to his grandad, who used to work in a company office in the middle of the last century.

'I can't believe,' his grandad was saying 'how offices these days need so few people. In my day we had scores of typists typing away in a typing 'pool' as it was called. All documents had to be typed by hand – there was none of this word-processing stuff. We had about thirty accounts clerks writing up the books by hand, and anything we wanted printing, like forms and invoices, had to be sent to a proper printing firm where the printing plates were set up by hand.

We did have telephones, but they were not mobile – and there was none of this email nonsense, where it seems to me that you are bombarded with messages all day long and have to reply so quickly.

In my day, you had time to think about things and to take decisions properly. It seems that these days everything has to be done straightaway. It tires me out to think about it!'

'Yes,' said Jack, 'but you have to keep up with technology or you will get left behind and lose out to other businesses.'

'I think I'd rather be left behind,' muttered his grandad.

a point to think about . . .

The ways in which businesses communicate have been revolutionised by information technology. But it may not all be to the good.

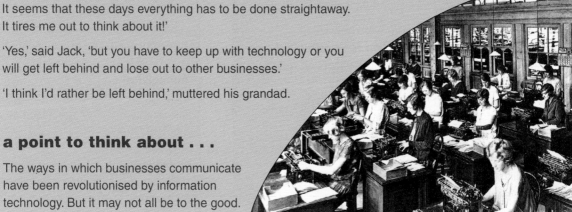

a mid-twentieth century typing 'pool'

communicating in business

communication flow

Communication means getting a message across.

Businesses need to communicate on a very regular basis with people outside the business – with customers and suppliers, for example. They also need to communicate internally: departments need to pass information to each other, managers need to talk to supervisors, assistants need to complain to supervisors, and so on. As you will see from the arrows on the diagram below, the communications flow in many directions:

■ in and out of the business

■ vertically – between the different levels of authority

■ horizontally – between departments or functions

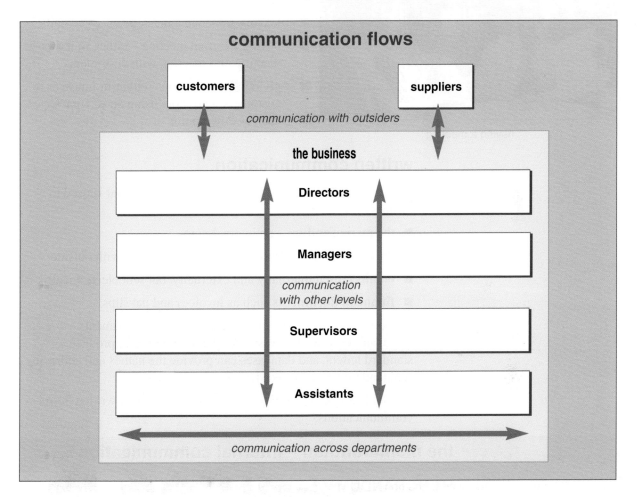

forms of communication

Communication in business can take a variety of forms:

■ **oral** (word of mouth) communication – eg telephones, meetings

■ **written** communication – eg memos, letters, financial documents, adverts, emails, email attachments

■ **graphical** communication – eg using images sent by fax

■ **video** communication – eg webcams, videoconferencing

We will give examples of these and explain how ICT is generating more and more electronic communications.

oral communication

Oral (word of mouth) communications include:

having a meeting

- meeting someone face to face and talking to them, eg serving a customer in a shop
- talking to someone on the telephone, eg answering a customer enquiry
- leaving someone a message on voicemail
- having a formal meeting – either an in-house meeting or a meeting with customers
- giving a presentation – either in-house or to customers – possibly using an ICT package such as Powerpoint

written communication

There is a wide variety of written communication that is used in business:

- the **memorandum** – an internal note
- the **letter** – a more formal communication used with outsiders
- **emails** – used internally and externally, but sent electronically
- **financial documents** such as invoices and payslips

ICT is used widely in the production of written documents. For example, word-processing packages are used to produce standard letters, and databases can provide the names and addresses for standard 'mailmerged' letters.

Set out below and on the next page are examples of written business communications.

the memorandum – internal communication

details of the sender, recipient, subject, and who is being sent a copy →

the text →

<u>no</u> signature →
items enclosed →

MEMORANDUM

To	K Roach, Finance Manager		
From	Tim Blake, Sales Manager	**Ref**	KR/AC/1098
Copies to	Departmental Managers	**Date**	26 June 2002
Subject	Product A163 Launch SuperSucker cleaner		

Please attend a presentation of our new A163 SuperSucker cleaner on 24 July in the Ground Floor Conference Room. Details of the new product are attached and a fully working example will be demonstrated on the 24th.

enc

the business letter – external communication

Wyvern Double Glazing Contractors
107 High Street
Mereford
MR1 9SZ
Tel 01605 675365 Fax 01605 765576

reference → Ref DH/SB/69

date → 14 December 2002

name and
address of → Mr J D Sutton
recipient   23 Windermere Close
Crofters Green
Mereford MR6 7ER

salutation → Dear Mr Sutton

heading → Double Glazing of 23 Windermere Close

Thank you for your letter of enquiry dated 11 December.

body of
the letter →
We are pleased to enclose a brochure with details of our double glazing units, all of which comply with the most up-to-date building regulations.

We will be happy to give you a quotation for glazing your new extension. In order to do this we will need to send our surveyor to measure up your property. We shall be grateful if you will kindly telephone us to arrange a visit at a convenient time.

We look forward to hearing from you.

complimentary
close →
Yours sincerely

signature → *D M Hunt*

name and job
title →
Derek Hunt
Sales Manager

enclosures → enc

123

electronic communication

The growth of information technology (ICT) has resulted in a revolution in the way communication takes place between businesses and also inside businesses.

intranets and email

Many businesses are now linked internally by an **intranet**. This is a network system whereby people working in a business are supplied with computer workstations which are linked together electronically. This means that they can all have access to information held on computer by the business, eg customer details, product details, diary systems.

In addition to accessing all this data, they can send each other **emails**. It can be very informal. You may find that your school or college has an intranet installed. An intranet will normally be linked up on-line to the internet (see below and next page), usually referred to as 'the net'. Note that an intranet and the internet are far from being the same thing!

the internet and email

emails routed by satellite

The **internet**, or 'net', is a rapidly expanding network of private, public, commercial and non-commercial computers linked via telephone lines by internet service providers (ISPs) who operate servers connecting their subscribers together. ISPs communicate with each other by telephone links, largely by satellite. Any person or business who is 'on the net' just has to dial up through the computer to be able to contact other internet users, anywhere in the world, using email or 'messenger' services.

an email – a response to a customer enquiry

```
  rpnelson@goblin.com, quotation                                          1

          To: rpnelson@goblin.com
        From: books@ritabooks.co.uk
     Subject: quotation

Dear Mr Nelson
Thanks for your e-mail enquiry of 1 December.
The title 'Bonsai for Beginners' ISBN 0 9510650 72 is available at £17.95. You can obtain it from most
bookshops and also from our website on mail order www.ritabooks.co.uk

Regards
H Bach
Customer Services
```

a business intranet linking up with the internet

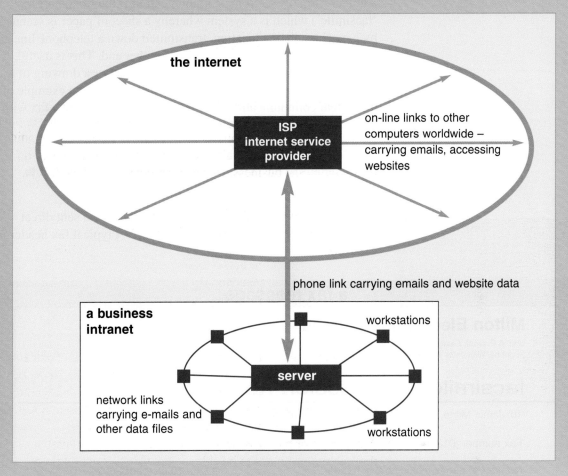

the internet

ISP
internet service
provider

on-line links to other
computers worldwide –
carrying emails, accessing
websites

phone link carrying emails and website data

a business
intranet

workstations

server

network links
carrying e-mails and
other data files

workstations

websites

More and more businesses are coming on-line and setting up
websites, not only for promoting their products but also for selling
their products 24 hours a day, worldwide.

A **website** is a series of interlinking pages set up on a computer
server provided by an internet service provider (ISP). It is a 'shop
window' for the business, and so successful have websites become
that some businesses, for example the on-line bookshop
www.amazon.co.uk, trade only from their website.

A website normally has a 'contact' page which enables any visitor to
the site to email the business. A business with a website therefore
has to deal with incoming electronic messages from the site in
addition to the normal sources of email.

A Case Study of online trading follows on page 129.

fax

Another form of electronic communication is the **fax** (short for 'facsimile') which is a system whereby a sheet of paper is scanned by a machine in one location, transmitted down a telephone line and printed out by a similar machine at the other end. This is useful, for example, if you want to send a map, a price list or a drawing of a product to someone who wants it in a hurry. This is an example of **graphical** communication. It is normal practice to send a fax with a 'fax header', which is a piece of paper which sets out:

- the name and address of the organisation sending the fax
- the details of the person and organisation it is being sent to
- the date and the number of pages being sent

Faxes may also be generated on a computer file and sent direct down the telephone line from the computer. A typical fax header is shown below.

a fax message

Milton Electronics Limited

Unit 4 Everoak Estate, Bromyard Road
St Johns, Worcester WR2 5HN

facsimile transmission header

To: Jamie Milne, Buying Office, Zippo Computers

Fax number: 01350 525504

Number of pages including this header: 1   Date: 10 October 2002

message
Jamie
Just to let you know that the consignment you called about this morning was despatched last Thursday (5 October) and should be with you soon.
Regards
Jon Smart
Despatch Dept

videoconferencing

Videoconferencing involves an image generated by a camera on top of a computer being sent down the telephone line and displayed on a computer screen at the other end. This is useful for meetings where one or more of the people cannot be present. It is now possible for images generated by a small camera (**webcam**) to be sent over the internet, which is a cheap and cheerful form of videoconferencing. These are both examples of **video** communication.

a BT impression of a teleworker's workplace

teleworking

Some employees are required to work at home or in custom-built 'telecottages' in the country.

'Tele' means 'at a distance'. Teleworkers are generally linked on-line and communicate by telephone, fax and email with their employer and clients.

Teleworkers enjoy the advantages of a pleasant working environment (as seen in the picture on the left) and avoid the stresses and expense of travel.

On the downside, teleworkers miss out on the social life of an office and interaction with colleagues. Some employers have countered this by introducing company 'chatrooms' and 'bulletin boards' which can be accessed online by the teleworkers.

Activity 14.1 – choosing communication methods

written communications

What methods of communication would you use in the situations set out below? In each case, say why you would use that method of communication.

1   Derek Hunt, who has written the letter on page 123, now has the estimator's quotation for glazing the new extension. He wants to send the quotation to Mr Sutton, together with the drawings for the job.

2   You are the Manager of the Administration Department and want to tell the other Departmental Managers the dates next year when the business will be closed for public holidays.

electronic communications

You are working in business. What form of electronic communication would you use in the following situations, and why? Assume that your business is equipped with fax, is on-line and has a website with details of all its products.

3   You receive a telephone call from a customer who is coming to visit your business tomorrow. He does not know where your premises are. It is too late to send him a letter and the road systems around you are so complicated that it will take you a long time to give him directions.

4   One of your directors has to go to Paris for the day from London. The meeting is tomorrow. She wants to know very quickly if it is quicker and cheaper to get there by rail rather than by air. How could you find out from your office without having to contact a travel agent?

Read the two Case Studies that illustrate how communication is supported by IT. Then answer the questions in the Activities.

Case Study – communication: the sales rep

Rob – the travelling sales rep

Rob Williams works for Compsupplies Limited, a company based in Warwick, Central England, that sells computers and computer equipment to other businesses throughout the UK.

Ron is a senior sales representative. He spends most of his time on the road, travelling throughout the UK, visiting existing customers and prospecting for new ones.

Despite being away from the office for four working days or more each week, he needs to be in touch with the main Warwick office for information including:

- customer details such as names, addresses, contact numbers, dates visited, any orders placed
- product details such as computer specifications, prices, availability, special offers
- financial information such as the value of goods sold, transaction dates, discounts given and whether or not the customer pays up on time

All this information is held on an intranet database at Warwick, which employees on site can access through their workstations.

Rob also has access to this intranet when he is travelling. He uses a laptop computer which has on-line access through his mobile phone to the database information held in the Compsupplies Warwick main office intranet.

Rob gives a quotation and gets an order

Rob has been asked by Turner Associates, an existing customer, for a quotation for a Comcell desktop PC with a flat screen display. Turner Associates are based in York.

Rob dials up the Warwick office, giving his password to the company intranet, to find out the specifications, price and availability of the equipment. He is then able to print out a quotation for the customer, who decides to place an order there and then. The order is sent on-line through the laptop so that the customer will get the equipment and invoice three working days later.

Rob will, of course, have first checked from the intranet that Turner Associates have paid up on time before and are seen by the Finance Department as good customers.

The deal is done, hundreds of miles from base.

York, Northern England

Rob Williams + customer
- **laptop**
- **printer**
- **mobile phone**

online ↕ *communication*

Compsupplies intranet:
- **customer details**
- **product details**
- **financial status of customer**

Warwick, Central England

Activity 14.2 – the sales rep

Read through the 'sales rep' Case Study and answer the questions that follow.

1 What information is held on the Compsupplies intranet?

2 What ICT equipment does Rob have which enables him to log into this intranet from anywhere in the UK?

3 How does Rob log into the Compsupplies intranet?

4 What are the advantages to Rob of using this communication system?

5 What are the advantages to Rob's customers of placing orders this way?

Case Study – using e-commerce

If you wanted to buy a copy of this book, how would you go about it?

You could go down to the local bookshop, but as it is a very specialised type of book, it is unlikely they will have it in stock. They would probably look it up on their computer database of published books and see that it cost £14.95 and was available from a wholesaler or Osborne Books.

If you ordered the book from the bookshop it might take a few days to come in. You would have to trek down to the bookshop again to pick it up and pay for it. They would probably scan the barcode on the back of the book to adjust their stock records and locate the price on their database.

Because of this inconvenience, many businesses are now turning to selling on the internet – this is known as **e-commerce**. This works especially well when you know what the goods are and what they look like. It may not be suitable, for example, for clothes and trainers when you want to see them, feel the quality and try them on first.

But for a book, the internet is an ideal marketplace as a book does not come in different styles and sizes. Successful businesses like amazon.co.uk do not have bookshops in the High Street, but trade entirely on-line.

Book publishers also use e-commerce. This Case Study shows how you can order and pay for this book on-line using up-to-date developments in ICT.

The first step is to select the shop on the Osborne Books home page (see right).

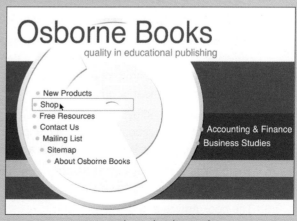

The next screen will show the on-line bookshop 'doorway' with the various categories of books which are available to look at.

You should click on the 'Business Studies' category which will show you all the Business Studies books to browse through.

The books are set out as on a bookshop shelf and you can add the items you want to buy to your 'basket' by clicking on the relevant button.

In this case you would click on 'GCSE Applied Business.'

You now proceed to the 'checkout' where you will be asked to complete your name, postal address for despatch, email address and debit or credit card details (not shown here for security reasons!).

You will then be asked to confirm the order and will receive an email confirmation

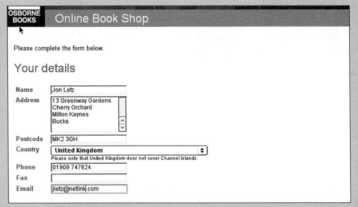

how ICT is used in on-line shopping – from 'mouse to house'

1 You place the order on-line through your computer.

2 You receive an automatic email confirmation of the order from the seller's website.

3 The credit or debit card details will be processed by on-line link from the seller to the card company and the seller's bank. The money transfer will be sent electronically. This transfer is made using very secure processes. The risk of anyone 'hacking' into the system and obtaining the credit card number is very low.

4 The seller is advised by email of the order and processes the order at the warehouse – using a computer accounting package which prints out an invoice and a mailing label.

5 The book is despatched using a carrier which tracks the parcel electronically by means of a barcode on the package.

6 The book arrives and is signed for.

Activity 14.3 – buying on the internet

Read the Case Study on the previous two pages and answer the questions below.

1 What is e-commerce?

2 Choose an item you would like to buy on the internet and make a list of the ways in which ICT (ie information and communication technology) is used when

    (a)   the item is bought at a High Street shop

    (b)   the item is bought on the internet

3 Describe the advantages to the customer of buying goods (or services – eg a holiday) on-line.

4 Describe the advantages to the business of selling goods (or services) on-line.

5 What might put customers off buying goods on-line in terms of the goods themselves, making payment for them, or any age limits which might apply?

Nutshell summary

■ Good communication is essential to the efficient functioning of a business.

■ Communication can be internal within a business – between function areas (departments) and between different levels of authority.

■ Communication can also be external – for example, dealing with customers.

■ Communication can take a number of different forms:
   - oral (word of mouth), eg telephones, meetings
   - written, eg memos, letters, documents, emails
   - graphical, eg drawings, maps, sent by fax
   - video, eg webcams, videoconferencing

■ Communication is increasingly taking place by email, both within internal intranets and on the internet.

■ ICT is also making working away from the office more common, eg teleworking

■ One of the biggest revolutions in communication is the growth of e-commerce which enables goods and services to be sold from websites. E-commerce is largely made possible by advances in ICT which links the customer to the seller electronically and enables payment to be made over the internet.

Key terms

Communication
Getting a message across.

Email
An electronic message sent from one computer to another.

Intranet
An internal computer network set up within a business.

Internet
A worldwide network of computers linked by telephone line.

Fax
A visual image of a page sent by telephone line to another location.

Videoconferencing
An image from a camera sent by telephone and displayed on a computer at another location.

Teleworking
Employees who work away from the office, often at home.

E-commerce
Selling through the internet.

15

External influences on business

A business of survival

Matt Pope and his wife run a small shop – a 'convenience store' on a main road.

They sell a wide variety of goods and services which people need on a day-to-day basis: newspapers, magazines, snacks, drinks, groceries, cards and stationery. They also rent out videos and operate a small Post Office counter. The business is hard work. The hours are long and Matt cannot remember the last time they went on holiday.

'Why do you do it?' people ask. The reply is normally, 'We are here for our local customers. We know them and they know us. We get a buzz out of doing our own thing.'

But recently things have not been very easy. 'The supermarkets are the main threat,' says Matt, 'they are cheaper, some are open 24 hours a day, and parking is easier there.

Then there is the cost of wages – the Government's Minimum Wage has been a real pain, and they have just put up interest rates again, making borrowing more expensive. Then there are all the regulations for food labelling. It really is a problem keeping up with all the red tape . . .'

a point to think about . . .

Running a business is very often a case of survival in a world of fierce competition, government regulations and restrictions. It is often only the fittest that survive.

external influences

Businesses experience **external influences** on the way they operate from three main areas:

- business competitors – eg the supermarket up the road

- government measures and economic conditions – eg the Minimum Wage and interest rates for bank borrowing

- the need to sustain the environment, eg restrictions on air pollution and river pollution

threats to the business

All these three external influences can pose threats to the business. They can affect the ability of the business to sell its products and to make a profit, and eventually to survive. In this chapter we will look at these three areas in turn.

threats from competitors

The business world is not always polite and good mannered. Businesses are out there to beat their competitors and, in some cases, put them out of business. Winning means getting and keeping customers, often at the expense of other businesses. This is known as increasing **market share.**

Market share is the percentage of sales made within a market by a single product or business.

Some businesses survive by being small, some by being large. How do they do it?

pricing

It is no secret that customers like low prices and value for money. Some businesses aim to provide products at the lowest possible prices and in so doing attract customers. Here are some examples:

low-cost airlines have increased market share by offering very low fares

supermarkets attract customers by selling essential products at low prices which do not make much profit

quality

Customers are also attracted by **quality**:

- quality of the **product** itself
- quality of **customer service**

Competing businesses must provide both of these types of quality. The airline Virgin Atlantic, for example, achieved much of its initial market share at the expense of British Airways, not through charging low fares but by providing a higher level of customer service.

availability

Customers like a product which is **available**.
This means a number of things:

■ customers must ideally be able to obtain the product at any time of the day

■ they must be able to buy the product easily – they do not want to have to travel a hundred miles to get it

■ the product itself must be in stock (for goods) or providable (for a service)

A business that wishes to gain customers at the expense of its competitors must achieve this **availability**. The Case Study below shows how this and the other factors of **price** and **quality** can be achieved by using e-commerce – selling on the internet.

 # Case Study – Amazon.co.uk success story

www.amazon.co.uk

Amazon.co.uk, owned by Amazon.com of the USA, is an online store which sells books, music, DVDs, videos, electronics, software, PC and video games and products for 'kids'. It also hosts online auctions. The site is open 24 hours a day, offers rapid postal delivery and substantial discounting of its products. Amazon.co.uk is a 'dot.com' business success story and has become one of the UK's major book retailers.

Amazon.co.uk has been described by one of its customers as 'an extraordinary company, doing business on the Web in a real customer-oriented way.'

PRESS REPORT 20 MARCH 2002 (extracts)

'Amazon.co.uk today announced it has passed the five-million cumulative customers landmark.

Customers continue to respond to Amazon's mission to be a retailer that consistently serves customers by driving down prices.

Amazon.co.uk was responsible in February 2002 for 16.6% of all UK e-commerce. The site in February 2002 had 2.7 million visitors. Over the preceding Christmas Amazon.co.uk shipped over 4.7 million items.'

Activity 15.1 – beating the competition

Read through the Case Study on the previous page. Answer the following questions:

1   What evidence is there in the Case Study that Amazon.co.uk has been successful in attracting customers since it first started in business?

2   Are the customers of Amazon.co.uk likely to be local, national or international? Give reasons for your answer.

3   How has Amazon.co.uk attracted customers by using pricing?

4   How does Amazon.co.uk use quality to attract and, importantly, to keep customers?

5   How has Amazon.co.uk achieved its success by using the factor of availability?

6   What are the disadvantages to the customer of purchasing books online? Do they matter?

7   What type of customer may not have heard of Amazon.co.uk, and why may this be the case?

competing through market segmentation

We saw in Chapter 8 ' Marketing and Sales' (pages 72 to 75) that the buying public is not one single market, but is made up of a number of different market **segments**. Consumers can be classified, for example, by:

■   age

■   gender (male or female)

■   wealth and income

■   where they live

■   lifestyle (fashion and taste)

Businesses can turn this to advantage by concentrating on marketing their products to specific market **segments**. This can be a threat to larger businesses if they do not rely on segmentation.

Take holidays, for example. Smaller holiday companies can win market share by offering very specific types of holiday – to different age groups, or social groups, for instance.

Larger holiday companies also increase market share by appealing to different age group **segments**. The brochures shown on the left include '2wentys' holidays from First Choice and 'Golden Times' from Cosmos.

The age distinction is very clear from the cover images.

holiday products for different age groups

the influence of the economy

the economy – a delicate balance

The state of the economy of the UK will be reflected in:

- the level of **inflation** – ie the level of price rises each year
- the level of **interest rates** – how much it costs to borrow money
- the strength of the £ – which affects the **exchange rate** – the cost of trading with overseas countries

These are factors which affect **businesses** that need to plan ahead and **consumers** whose spending keeps businesses going.

The UK Government is responsible for managing the economy – setting targets for inflation, interest rates and the stability of the pound. Important players in this operation are the Chancellor of the Exchequer and the Bank of England (the state-owned UK Central Bank which supervises all the other banks).

The Government aims to help businesses through:

- control of inflation (keeping price rises low)
- low interest rates
- low taxation

keeping businesses and consumers happy

The main objective of the UK Government is to provide a stable economic environment for businesses and consumers. This will win them votes as well as benefiting the economy as a whole.

Businesses need to be able to:

- make reliable plans for expansion
- know how much it is going to cost to borrow over the long term

Consumers need to be able to:

- save for the future
- borrow for the present
- spend on things that they need

So, what do we mean by a 'stable economic environment?'
At the time of writing this means keeping inflation at a target level of 2.5%. Look at the chart below and see how inflation has fluctuated.

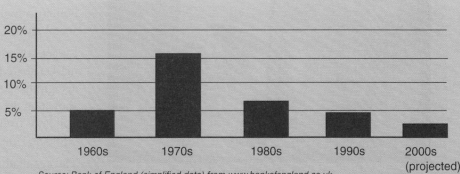

inflation rates over the decades (1960s – 2000s)

Source: Bank of England (simplified data) from www.bankofengland.co.uk

inflation and interest rates

inflation

Inflation has been defined by the Bank of England as

'a widespread rise in the level of prices across the economy.'

Inflation is measured as a percentage rate which indicates the amount by which prices increase over a year. Rates of inflation have varied widely over the last thirty years or so. In the 1970s, for example, inflation averaged at least 13% per year and reached 27% in 1975 – a very unstable situation. Since then inflation rates have dropped every decade – an encouraging sign.

What happens to businesses when inflation is high?

- future money values become very uncertain
- planning decisions become very short term
- price lists keep changing
- interest rates are high and so borrowing is expensive

High inflation damages business confidence:

- **financial planning is made difficult**
- **prices keep changing**
- **borrowing is expensive**

interest rates

The **interest rate** is measured as a percentage and is

the cost of borrowing money.

Interest is normally charged to borrowers by lenders such as banks. So if a business borrows £1,000 for a year and the interest rate is 5%, the interest charge will be £1,000 x 5% = £50.

The higher the interest rate, the more expensive it becomes to borrow money. The result of this is:

- the higher the interest rate, the less businesses will want to borrow and invest and expand
- the lower the interest rate, the more businesses will be encouraged to borrow and invest and expand

Look at the graph below and see how the basic interest rates in the economy fell from nearly 14% in 1990 to 4% in 2001.

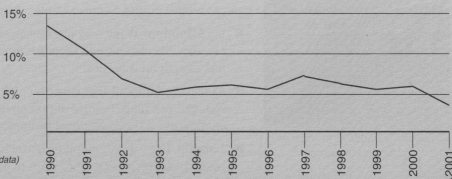

interest rates 1990 – 2001

Source: Bank of England (simplified data) from www.bankofengland.co.uk

price rises

We have seen on the last two pages that **inflation** measures price rises and that interest rates can add to price rises by increasing the cost of borrowing.

There are two further external influences which can add to the costs of a business and reduce its profit:

- exchange rate fluctuations
- legislation introduced by the Government

exchange rate fluctuations

The exchange rate is the conversion rate from one currency to another.

If you travel to the USA you may be told that the £ to US$ exchange rate is 1.49. This means that for every £1 you will get US$1.49. This rate may fluctuate from time to time as economic conditions change in the two countries.

How does this fluctuation affect businesses dealing with the USA?

- for the UK exporter of goods, a rise in the £ means that the goods will be more expensive in the USA, which is bad news
- for the UK importer of US goods, such as computers, a rise in the £ means that the foreign goods will be cheaper in the UK, which is good news

a rise in the £ means fewer tourists coming to the UK

Exchange rate fluctuations can also have a serious affect on tourism:

- if the £ rises in value, overseas tourists will find it more expensive in the UK, which will put them off coming, which is bad news for the UK tourist trade
- if the £ falls in value, the UK will be cheaper for overseas tourists, which is good news for the UK tourist trade

price rises from Government legislation

The Government can sometimes make things difficult for businesses by introducing laws and regulations which increase business costs and so reduce profits. Some examples include:

- the **Minimum Wage** – by law businesses cannot pay any wage rate they like, but have to keep to a minimum hourly rate – this can put up wage costs
- increasing **National Insurance** – employers have to pay National Insurance (a form of tax) on the earnings of their employees - a rise in National Insurance can put up wage costs
- **Landfill Tax** – a tax on tipping waste has added to the costs of businesses which use a lot of skips to get rid of rubbish

Landfill Tax adds to the cost of getting rid of rubbish

Case Study – running a hotel

The Towers is a hotel in a seaside resort on the south coast of England. It is run by Ben Fortey who has been in the hotel business for over twenty years.

He has been having a hard time recently, and he has struggled over the last year to cover his costs and to break-even.

'The hotel trade used to be a safe bet,' says Ben to a friend. 'We used to be fully booked over the holiday season and we'd be turning away foreign tourists – particularly Americans – every day. We don't seem to be getting them now. They can't afford holidays in the UK, so they say.

Also, our wage costs seem to be going through the roof now that the Minimum Wage has come in. Gone are the days of cheap casual labour. National Insurance has also gone up. I don't know what this country is coming to! I suppose the only good thing is that food prices have been fairly stable and interest rates have been low, which has helped with the loan we got from the bank for renovating the hotel. Anyway, "roll on retirement" is what I say!'

Activity 15.2 – coping with external influences

Read the Case Study above and answer the questions that follow.

1   What, apart from the weather, is the factor that is most likely to deter foreign tourists from visiting the UK and keeping hotels like The Towers in business?

2   What rises in costs are adding to the expenses that The Towers has to pay?
    Who is responsible for them? What effect will they have on the profits of The Towers?

3   What positive factors in the economy are helping to keep The Towers afloat financially?

4   What would be the effect on the profitability of The Towers if there was a sudden rise in the rate of inflation and the Government raised interest rates?

5   If Bas was good at marketing and there was a continued decline in overseas visitors, what could he do to increase his occupancy rate (the number of people staying at the hotel)?

businesses and environmental constraints

Another area in which businesses are restricted in what they can do is the problem of **pollution** and the **wastage of natural resources**, which can directly affect people and the environment. Pollution by business can take a number of forms:

■   air pollution
■   noise pollution
■   water pollution

In addition, the wastage of materials and energy which originate from natural resources ultimately damages the environment.

air pollution

Businesses are prevented by law from undue pollution of the environment. Businesses also often publicise a 'green' (ie protecting the environment) policy, not only because they need to obey the law, but also because they want to be seen to be 'green' by their customers. Businesses that are seen to have a responsible attitude to the environment will gain customers. Being 'green' is therefore also an important aspect of marketing.

dealing with pollution

The main types of pollution – air, water and noise – are covered by a number of laws including the Environmental Protection Act, the Clean Air Act, the Water Resources Act, and the Noise Act. Visit the site www.environment-agency.gov.uk and its excellent NetRegs section for further details and local Case Studies.

Any reported cases of suspected pollution will be dealt with by the Local Authority – for example excessive smoke and gases, toxins poured into a river or a very loud club disturbing residents at night!

corporate social responsibility (CSR)

Many businesses, especially the PLCs which are well-known to the public have adopted a policy of **Corporate Social Responsibility** (see also page 30). This normally includes an environmental section. These are often available on the company website, as in the Tesco Case Study which follows.

Case Study – Tesco's Environment Policy

Tesco's environmental policy is to be found at www.tesco.com in the Corporate Information section in the 'CSR Review'. Some screen extracts are illustrated below. The Environmental Policy also states:

'Tesco is committed to reducing its energy consumption and emissions of greenhouse gases responsible for climate change.

Tesco's Nature's Choice Code of Practice covers 'the rational use of pesticides, fertilisers and manures, pollution prevention, protection of human health, efficient use of energy, water and other natural resources, recycling and re-use of materials, wildlife and landscape conservation and enhancement.

We are always looking for new and innovative ways to minimise packaging, such as biodegradable packaging for organic fruit.

Tesco has removed GM ingredients from all own brand products.'

Tesco is committed to protecting the environment, using its commercial strength to put principles into practice. Our standards apply to every aspect of our business and Tesco also asks its suppliers to adhere to many of these environmental practices.

Waste and Recycling

Tesco is committed to minimising the amount of waste produced and to recycle it wherever possible.

In November 2001, Tesco launched the scheme to encourage customers to recycle old and unwanted mobile phones and help raise money for charity at the same time.

Our target is to recycle 1 million mobile phones.

Activity 15.3 – Tesco's Environmental Policy

Read the Case Study on the previous page and, if you are able, read the Tesco Environmental Policy on www.tesco.com. Then answer the questions that follow.

1 How is Tesco's Environmental Policy committed to improving the atmosphere?

2 What evidence is there in the Policy of minimising waste and recycling materials?

3 In what ways does Tesco's Environmental Policy protect 'Nature' and natural methods of food production?

4 How would the Marketing function and the Finance function within Tesco view the Policy?

Nutshell summary

- Businesses experience external influences on the way they operate. These influences come from three main directions:
  - business competitors
  - economic conditions and Government measures
  - the need to sustain the environment

- These external influences can pose threats to the business and its ability to make a profit, and ultimately its survival.

- Threats from business competitors can be responded to by policies involving pricing, quality of product and service, and availability.

- Businesses, particularly smaller businesses, can often compete by identifying and concentrating on a specific market segment, and also by using ICT.

- The success of a business also depends on the economic conditions in which it operates. Businesses can be affected by:
  - changes in the level of prices (inflation) in the economy; high inflation leads to instability
  - changes in the level of interest rates; a high interest rate means borrowing becomes expensive
  - changes in exchange rates; a high £ means exports cost more abroad but imports are cheaper

- Businesses are also affected by environmental constraints: the need to contain pollution and cut down on wastage of natural resources.

Key terms

Market share
The percentage of sales within a market which is made by a single product or business.

Market segment
An identifiable consumer group which needs and wants specific types of product.

Inflation
A widespread rise in the level of prices across the economy.

Interest rate
The cost of borrowing money, expressed as a percentage of the amount borrowed.

Exchange rate
The conversion rate from one currency to another.

Minimum wage
The legal minimum hourly wage rate an employer can pay.

Pollution
Contamination of the air, ground or water by a business.

Corporate Social Responsibility
The responsibility of a company to Society at large.

People and Business

A business is its people – its employees and its customers.
This unit will involve you in investigating these people and studying
one business in detail. The unit will enable you to find out about:

■ the relationship between employers and employees, and what
happens if there are disagreements

■ the legal protection given to employees

■ the way in which people are organised and trained in a business

■ the processes of recruiting employees and applying for a job

■ the need for a business to keep its customers satisfied

■ the protection given in law to consumers

Chapters in this Unit...

16

Business stakeholders

A stake in Whittakers

'My name is Jack Patel and I own the convenience store opposite Whittakers PLC. My shop is open from 6.30 in the morning to 12.00 midnight and Whittakers' employees rely on us for all sorts of things – snacks, cans of drink, cigarettes, sandwiches and newspapers.

Over the last five years the company has expanded and they have taken on 60 extra staff, including my own son. He works in their Accounts Department – he says shopkeeping is not for him. He would hate the hours!

I've just added new lines like burgers, baked potatoes and video rentals. My son reckons that the food in the canteen is awful, so the potatoes should sell well.

There are only a few houses around here so we get most of our money from Whittakers. If it ever closed, we'd be finished.'

Whittakers PLC is a manufacturer of labels for a wide variety of business customers. Employing 420 men and women on a two shift working system (7 - 3 and 3 - 11, Monday to Friday) the company sells its products throughout the UK.

Whittakers has one factory – where the offices are also based – in Wakefield, West Yorkshire.

a point to think about . . .

Jack is not the only person who would be affected if Whittakers closed. There would be all the employees, customers, suppliers and anyone who is connected with the factory and its products.

stakeholders

In this chapter we will be looking at business **stakeholders**.

A stakeholder is anybody who has an interest in a business.

This does not mean that a stakeholder has to own part of the business – they just have to **be affected by it** in some way.

Whittakers has a number of stakeholders. One of these is Jack Patel because most of his income comes from Whittakers' employees who buy goods such as newspapers or food as they walk or drive past his shop.

If the factory closed, he would be forced to close down the shop.

owners and shareholders

Whittakers PLC is a **public limited company**. The directors and employees can buy its shares, and so can the general public on the Stock Market. In this way they are also stakeholders as owners and shareholders.

People buy shares in companies like Whittakers PLC for two main reasons:

- they get an income from the shares, known as a dividend
- they can make money if the shares go up in value

Because the public can own shares in a PLC like Whittakers, they will expect the business to act responsibly and in a politically correct way. If the business, for example, was polluting the rivers or exploiting cheap labour overseas, the shareholders – and probably the newspapers – would make their opinions known.

Owners of smaller businesses – partnerships and private limited companies – also look to the business to make a profit and provide them with a return on their 'stake' in the business.

employees and their managers

There are plenty of other jobs locally but Whittakers **employees** are paid well above average rates and there is a good pension scheme. Employees feel part of a family.

Another interest of an employee is in a safe job. Whittakers' staff work hard to achieve success and profit for the business.

Managers get well paid – often with bonuses – to produce products in the most efficient and profitable way.

Some managers in Whittakers come with university degrees and others, like Vic Tillman, have worked their way up from the bottom. 'From apprentice to Manufacturing Manager in fourteen years' is Vic's proud boast.

Vic – a hard-working manager

Activity 16.1 – what's in it for an employee?

Tom works in the design studio at Whittakers. He creates designs for labels for customers and also produces designs for brochures – all on the computer. The company is paying for him to go to College, one day a week, to get a design qualification. He hopes eventually to become a Design Manager.

Tom started working there two years ago. He started, straight from school, as a computer operator but the company soon saw he was very hardworking and they wanted to give him a chance to get on in his career. Tom is now in the company pension scheme and he has just bought some shares under the employee share scheme. As he says, 'You have to have some faith in your own employer – after all they are paying your wages!'

1   What are the main attractions of Whittakers to Tom?

2   Why are Whittakers so interested in helping Tom?

3   Why do companies sell shares to their employees like Tom?

4   Why are people like Tom interested in buying them?

financiers as stakeholders

Organisations that lend to business and provide money capital – the **financiers** – are important stakeholders. Their main interest in the business, of course, is making sure that their money is repaid or that their investment is safe.

Most businesses deal with **banks**, and many borrow, either long-term, eg to buy premises and equipment, or short-term, on overdraft. Whittakers have a long relationship with their bank – the founder of the business, John Whittaker, borrowed money from the same branch eighty years ago to set the business up. Whenever Whittakers invests in new equipment or buildings they borrow from the bank at a favourable rate of interest.

a bank is a financial stakeholder

customers as stakeholders

Most of Whittakers' output is the supply of 'brand labels' used by food and drink manufacturers. Millions of their labels are used every year, for example, on milk cartons. The company also supplies boxes of computer labels sold under the 'Whittaker Wise' brand name to stationery chains, post offices and mail order stationery catalogue companies.

Customers can buy labels from many other manufacturers, many of them based overseas, but Ben Whittaker, the Managing Director,

customers have an interest in the product itself

is pleased to see that many customers stay with them: 'they like the quality of our designs and artwork. We are also very competitive.'

As we have already seen in this book, customers have three main interests in a product: quality, price and availability. As a producer, Whittakers can fulfil all these expectations.

suppliers as stakeholders

Whittakers buys raw materials from dozens of different **suppliers**. Their biggest purchases are paper, of various qualities, and card. They get these from two companies, one British and one French.

Suppliers value large contracts with companies like this one because they are steady, secure, business. In return the supplier will offer Whittakers a good discount for steady orders. If they do not do this, they know that Whittakers can always go elsewhere.

the Government as stakeholder

Whittakers is important to the **Government** because it provides local jobs. Without these jobs the Government would have to pay out money in jobseekers allowances to more unemployed people.

Whittakers also pays taxes to the Government.

The Government uses a variety of laws to protect employees working at firms such as Whittakers. These are dealt with in Chapter 18.

As a stakeholder in organisations such as Whittakers, the Government must ensure that employees get all the rights they are entitled to. They will also want employees to know what they can do, and whom they can go to, if they are not given their legal rights.

pressure groups

These are independent organisations which fight for particular causes, eg www.greenpeace.org.uk. All businesses are bound to be affected by pressure groups to some extent. Let us look at two examples . . .

Suppose Whittakers dumped chemicals from its production processes into a nearby river? A local **environmental group** would almost certainly complain to the National Rivers Authority – this would lead to the criminal prosecution of Whittakers, meaning they would have to pay a large fine.

Suppose Whittakers began to deliver raw materials to the factory late in the evening. Local residents might set up an **action group** to stop this because the noise upsets householders and makes it more difficult to get to sleep. Their action might include writing to the local MP and the city councillors, leafletting local houses and blocking the road with street protests.

water pollution – a case for an environmental group?

the local community

The local community has a substantial interest in many large businesses such as Whittakers. The company is the main workplace in that part of Wakefield, so if it closed, or even just cut back, the impact would be serious.

Apart from this, the community benefits because:

- other local firms supply Whittakers – local caterers supply the factory canteen, a local firm cleans the windows, local buses deliver staff to the factory gates, Jack's shop (see page 144) supplies the workforce with a variety of goods
- Whittakers pays thousands of pounds in **business rates** to the local council

Activity 16.2 – dealing with pollution

You live in an estate near a large chemical factory owned by Petra Chemicals PLC.

When the wind blows from the east the fumes from the factory are very unpleasant, and people on the estate often complain of sore eyes and headaches. Employees of the company often have the same problem.

Many people are concerned and they want to set up an action group to try to do something about it. Greta Sykes, a local doctor, says 'if we don't take action about this, nothing will happen and someone could become seriously ill.'

questions

1   What stakeholders of Petra Chemicals are potentially being harmed by this pollution – in terms of the people who work in the factory and the people who live nearby?

2   What stakeholder sets down the regulations for this type of pollution? Refer to the previous chapter and find out what the regulations are.

3   What stakeholders are actually prepared to do something about the problem?

4   If you were faced with this problem, whom would you approach with your complaint?

financial stakeholders

We will again deal with stakeholders in Chapter 37 'Who needs financial statements?' when we examine the financial aspects of being a stakeholder.

Now study the diagram at the top of the next page, which shows how a business is affected by stakeholders.

akeholders of a business

shareholders	local community	customers
interested in the profit made and the dividend paid	interested in jobs, environmental and social issues	interested in the success and stability of the business

pressure groups		employees
interested in social and environmental issues	**the business**	interested in whether the business will keep their jobs going

suppliers	banks	managers
interested in stable trading and income received	interested in the business being able to repay its loans	interested in the bonuses for helping to make a profit

---

 ## Nutshell summary

- A stakeholder is anybody who has an interest in an organisation, and who is affected by what it does and the way it operates.

- All organisations have a number of stakeholders, although larger organisations tend to have more than small ones.

- A stakeholder may have a direct financial interest in an organisation. Shareholders/owners and employees are the best examples.

- Other stakeholders may not be financially involved, but the organisation will affect their lives in important ways.

- Stakeholders can behave in a way that forces an organisation to change its plans and the way it operates.

 ## Key terms

Stakeholder

A person with an interest in an organisation.

Shareholder

A person who has bought a financial interest (shares) in a limited company.

Customer

A person who buys goods or a service from an organisation.

Supplier

A person who supplies goods and services to an organisation.

17

Employers and employees

The dismissal

Sara is a packer in the Despatch Department at Whittakers. She packs computer labels which are sent to the major retail 'High Street' stationery stores. Sara joined the company about seven months ago, after two years waitressing in a café. She is 20.

Sara had been off work with a bad cold for three days. It was a genuine cold, not a 'sicky', so, on returning to work, she was amazed to be told by her Manager that she was being dismissed with one month's notice. Admittedly, she had been verbally warned, three weeks ago, about the quality of her work. She was fast enough – not surprisingly, since she was on a bonus scheme, so the more she packed, the more money she was paid. The trouble was she was clumsy and she rushed the job – then Quality Control complained about the standard of her work a number of times.

Sara went home to tell her mother about this. 'Surely I've some rights, haven't I?'

Her mother promised she would ring the Citizens Advice Bureau the next morning . . .

a point to think about . . .

The success of any organisation depends on a good working relationship between an employer and the employee. For the employer and the employee to work together well, both need to be clear about what their rights are and what their responsibilities are.

employee rights

contracts of employment

A contract is a legally binding agreement between two people.

A **contract of employment** means that a person offers to work for an organisation. In return the employer must pay that person to do the work.

Employees are generally given a written statement of the 'terms and conditions of employment' setting out the terms of their contract of employment. Look at Sara's contract shown on the next page.

CONTRACT OF EMPLOYMENT

employer	Whittakers PLC, Albany Estate, Halifax Road, Wakefield, WS2 5HN.
employee	Sara Cassidy.
start date	6 January 2003, fixed term contract for 12 months.
job title	Despatch Assistant.
place of work	Whittakers PLC, Albany Estate, Halifax Road, Wakefield, WS2 5HN.
hours of work	09.00 to 17.00, Monday to Friday, or as otherwise mutually agreed.
remuneration	£13,000 p.a., overtime at £10 per hour, overtime hours worked as mutually agreed. Productivity bonus as agreed.
annual holidays	22 working days paid holiday plus statutory holidays and other days at employer's discretion. Holiday dates as mutually agreed.
sickness pay	A employee sick pay scheme is in operation which provides payment during periods of certified sickness for 3 months in any 12 month period.
grievance and disciplinary procedures	Grievance and disciplinary procedures will be dealt with by the Manager, Despatch Department. A copy of the procedures will be supplied.
notice of termination to be given by employer	1 month.
notice of termination to be given by employee	1 month.

Any amendment to this statement will be agreed with you and confirmed in writing within one month.

G T Wanderbee
....

For and on behalf of the employer,

I acknowledge receipt and agree to the terms of this statement.

Sara Cassidy
....

Employee

6 January 2003
....

Date

6 January 2003
....

Date

Apart from basic details such as the names of the employer and employee, job title and place of work, this **statement** includes the main rights of the employee. We will now look at these.

hours of work

The employer must tell you the number of hours you are required to work and the times of starting and finishing work each day. Employees may be expected to vary their starting and finishing times and to work overtime.

pay rate

The **pay rate** is the amount due to the employee under the contract. Note that the employer must pay at least the Minimum Wage set by the Government.

Pay can be in the form of

■ a weekly or monthly **salary**

■ **piecework** – payment for the number of items produced on a production line

■ **commission** – payment based on the number of products sold

■ **bonus** – an additional payment which may be made when the business is doing well and working efficiently

At Whittakers, office staff and managers get monthly salaries. Production staff get paid piecework and the sales staff get salary plus commission. Sara gets a salary plus a productivity bonus.

holidays and sick pay entitlement

At least four weeks paid holiday per year is a legal requirement. Sara will get 22 days holiday entitlement plus bank holidays.

The contract must say if the employee is entitled to employer sick pay or whether the employee will only get Statutory Sick Pay (SSP) (a far lower payment). Sara will be paid in full for up to three months certified (ie by the doctor) sickness.

at least four weeks holiday a year

notice periods

If the employee decides to leave or if the employer decides to dismiss the employee it is important to know how much paid notice is required. Here it is the legal minimum of four weeks but in many high level professional jobs it is three or six months, or even a full year.

grievance and disciplinary procedures

The statement needs to state to whom, in the first instance, the employee can refer if he or she has a grievance. It will also state who is responsible for disciplinary procedures. Sara will have been given a copy of the 'procedures' which set down what to do in these cases.

period of contract

It should be noted that Sara's contract starts on 6 January 2003, but lasts for one year only, after which Whittakers PLC can renew it if the company wants to. Short term contracts are becoming more and more common nowadays.

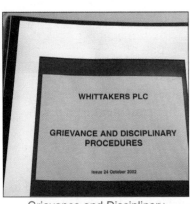

WHITTAKERS PLC

GRIEVANCE AND DISCIPLINARY PROCEDURES

Issue 24 October 2002

Grievance and Disciplinary Procedures are given to employees

Activity 17.1 – what are Sara's rights?

Read through the Case Study and the Statement of Main Terms and Conditions of Employment. Then answer the questions.

1 What is the reason for the disciplinary action being taken against Sara?

2 How is this covered in the Statement of Main Terms and Conditions of Employment?

3 What other document should she look at for information about her situation?

4 Where could she get advice about her situation?

5 From the facts that have been given to you, give your own assessment of Sara's case.

further rights of employees

Health & Safety

'**Health and Safety**' means that employees should be given a healthy and safe place in which to work. This topic is covered in the next chapter under the Health and Safety at Work Act.

proper training

Employees must be properly trained to do the job they are given.

Good employers will also give employees the chance to acquire wider work experience or to get extra qualifications in order to help them to get better jobs later on. This is called **staff development**.

Unison is a Trade Union that represents workers in the public sector: www.unison.org.uk

Trade Union membership

A Trade Union is an independent organisation which represents the interests of employees.

All employees are legally entitled to join any trade union, if they wish to. In fact, only about 8 million out of 25 million employees in the UK are trade union members.

Employers often see trade unions as trouble makers that will harm their business. However, recent legal changes mean that an employer can be forced to bargain with a trade union if enough employees in the workplace vote in favour of it.

access to confidential records

Employees now have the right to see their employment records, in return for a small fee. This means that employees can see their disciplinary records and any job references that have been written. Employers now have to be very careful about what information they keep about their employees.

employee duties

Employers are entitled to expect certain things from their employees in return . . .

employees must be available, willing and capable to work

This is fairly self-explanatory! 'Capable to work' means that the employee must be physically and mentally able to do the job.
If physical or mental problems make it difficult for the employee to do a job properly then the employee may be forced to give it up.

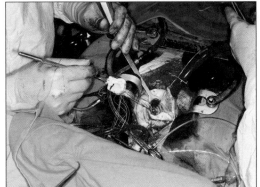

the importance of taking care and using skill – a surgeon

employees must take reasonable care and use skill when doing the job

The rule about **care** is that employees are expected to be as careful as any reasonable person would be.
Experienced trained staff should know what they are doing, how to do it and what the dangers are, but should avoid timewasting through excessive checking.

Employees must ensure they work safely and they must not put their workmates in any danger. They must not ignore safety requirements when doing a job.

As far as **skill** is concerned, all jobs require some basic skills and an employer can expect the employee to be skilled enough to carry out the job they are paid to do. Once they are fully skilled it is assumed that they can be expected to work safely and competently without close supervision, as in the case of a surgeon!

employees must take proper care of their employer's premises and equipment

If an employee loses equipment owned by the employer or if they intentionally damage or destroy it they can lose their job.

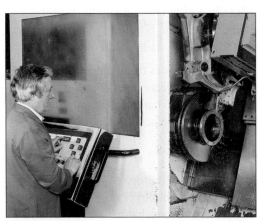

The rule is that an employee should take the same care of their employer's premises and equipment as they would do if the equipment was their own.

employees must obey reasonable orders

Employees must do any work which is covered by their contract of employment.

employees must always play fair with the employer

An employee should not, for example, work for a competitor at the same time, work directly in competition with an employer, or give away 'trade' secrets.

taking care of equipment – a machine operator

Activity 17.2 – Sara's problems as an employee

Sara Cassidy tells you a bit more about what has been happening at work over the last few weeks. Read the comments and answer the questions below.

'It's all very well them criticising me at work, but the Despatch Room is an awful place to work in – the light is terrible and I keep damaging my hands on the equipment.

I know I keep making mistakes, but the Supervisor is rubbish – he didn't really tell me what to do properly – no wonder things go wrong!

I wanted to see what had been written about me after my last verbal warning, but the Supervisor said I couldn't because they were confidential to Management and couldn't be released to employees.'

1   What **rights** as an employee has Sara got in each of the three situations she describes above?

2   If you were the Supervisor, what **duties** of the employee would you quote in your defence?

 # Nutshell summary

- If employers and employees are to work well together they both need to know what they are expected to do and what their rights are.

- An employee is normally issued with a Contract of Employment, often set out as a written Statement of Main Terms and Conditions of Employment. This covers subjects such as pay, hours, holiday and sick pay entitlement, notice periods and disciplinary and grievance procedures.

- In addition employees have the rights to a safe and healthy workplace, proper training, Trade Union membership and access to employee records.

- But the employer can also expect from the employee a willingness to work, the use of care and skill, reasonable obedience and loyalty.

- The laws relating to employer and employee rights are covered in the next chapter.

 # Key terms

Contract of employment
Legally binding agreement between employer and employee, setting out the terms and conditions of employment.

Health and Safety
The provision of a safe, risk-free and healthy working environment.

Staff development
Training staff and giving them the opportunity to acquire qualifications.

Trade Union
An independent organisation which represents the interests of employees.

18

Employees and the law

Sophie visits the doctor

Sophie works in Whittakers' Accounts Department. She uses a VDU (computer screen) for most of the day. She has a properly designed workstation. The VDU has a protective screen over it – at least it did have but Sophie took it off because she didn't like it. Nor does she like the computer chair, so she sits in an ordinary office chair.

Her Supervisor is constantly telling her all about using proper chairs and the use of VDU filter screens but Sophie says that they do not suit her. She had an appointment for the free yearly eye tests that staff are entitled to under the 1992 VDU Regulations, but she forgot to go.

Recently Sophie went to the doctor's with pains in her lower arms and wrists. She has also been suffering from headaches. She was worried about RSI (Repetitive Strain Injury). She said to the doctor 'All this is Whittakers' fault . . . I'm thinking of talking to my solicitor or my union rep about it. I should get some compensation for this . . .'

'I wouldn't be so hasty,' the doctor replied, 'you really should use the proper equipment at work. It will not make your aches and pains vanish overnight but at least they will not get any worse. You certainly cannot blame Whittakers.'

a point to think about . . .

There are laws to protect employees' rights in a number of different situations, but it is important that the employees know what those legal rights are, or they may lose the protection given.

legal protection for employees

In this chapter we examine the main laws which affect the employer/employee relationship.

One of these relates to the situation that Sophie has got into – although, as we will see, it is not all plain sailing for her.

All employees are protected by a variety of laws that have been introduced over the last few years. They cover areas such as discrimination, Health and Safety and the rights of part-time and temporary workers.

no grounds for discrimination here

www.eoc.org.uk – a site set up by the Equal Opportunities Commission to provide information about discrimination issues.

www.disability.gov.uk – a site set up by the Department for Work and Pensions to provide information about the rights of disabled people.

websites to visit

Sex Discrimination Act 1975

This Act states that employers should not discriminate on the grounds of gender. It makes it illegal to discriminate against men or women when:

- advertising to fill jobs
- appointing people to jobs
- promoting employees into better jobs
- deciding what the terms and conditions of the job will be
- offering employees the chance to get more training and career development

There are a number of examples where the Act does not apply. These include private clubs (eg 'men only'), some areas of the armed forces and acting jobs (eg no females playing James Bond).

Equal Pay Act 1970

This states that men and women should be given the same pay and working conditions for the same type of job.

Race Relations Act 1976

This Act makes discrimination on grounds of race illegal under the same circumstances covered by the Sex Discrimination Act 1975, ie when advertising and filling jobs, promoting and training staff.

Again, there are a few exceptions to the Act, including ethnic restaurants (Chinese waiters for Chinese restaurants), social worker jobs dealing with specific ethnic groups, and acting roles which require a specific nationality actor..

Disability Discrimination Act 1995

This Act – which applies to organisations employing over 20 people – improved the protection given to disabled people, and made discrimination against them illegal in many circumstances, eg when:

- advertising jobs and inviting applications for job interviews
- offering jobs after interviews have taken place
- when deciding on the terms and conditions of the job

The Act requires that the employer must take **reasonable steps** to ensure that a disabled person can work there, unless, of course, the job is unsuitable. These are examples of reasonable steps:

- modifying the buildings (entrances, ramps, lifts etc)
- allowing extra training so that the disabled person can do the job
- putting a disabled person in a more convenient work location (eg the ground floor rather than three floors up)

Activity 18.1 – discrimination?

Here are a few extracts from adverts for job vacancies. Study each of them and state which law they involve, and whether or not they break that law.

1 'Barman required at the Fox and Grapes Inn, Ludlow.'

2 'Local man required to play the role of Santa Claus from 15th November onwards. Write to Russell and Smith Ltd, Department Stores, Milton Keynes.'

3 'Social worker required to deal with local Indian community. Indian nationals preferred.'

4 'Temporary labourers needed for City Centre building site. Able-bodied applicants only, please.'

maintaining safety in the workplace

HEALTH AND SAFETY LAW

What you should know

Your health, safety and welfare are protected by law. Your employer has a duty to protect and keep you informed about health and safety. You have a responsibility to look after others. If there is a problem, discuss it with your employer or safety representative, if there is one. Below is a brief guide to health and safety law. It does not describe the law in detail, but it does list the key points.

Visit the Health & Safety Executive: www.hse.gov.uk

Health and Safety Laws

We have already introduced the idea of the employer providing a safe and healthy workplace. The principal law covering this area is the **Health and Safety at Work Act 1974.**

This says that an employer must provide:

■ safe entrances and exits

■ safe equipment and machinery and systems of work

■ training to ensure that staff work safely

■ a system of recording accidents in an 'accident book'

■ a 'written statement' of a Health and Safety policy

This 'written statement' must be made available to all staff – a good employer will give copies of it to all new staff. Employers are also required to carry out a **risk assessment** in the workplace.

other Health & Safety measures

As well as the 1974 Act, other legislation has brought in further protection for employees:

The **C.O.S.H.H.** ('control of substances hazardous to health') Regulations (1994) lay down very strict rules on how dangerous chemicals are to be handled, stored and recorded.

The **Health and Safety (Display Screen Equipment) Regulations (1992)** introduced tight controls over the use of visual display units on word processors and computers, to help prevent headaches, eye strain and related symptoms.

Activity 18.2 – Health and Safety at work

Read the Sophie Case Study at the beginning of this chapter. Answer these three questions:

1   What are Sophie's rights against her employer in this case?

2   What law covers the use of VDUs (computer screens) in the workplace?

3   Would it make any difference to her position if Sophie had developed her pains and her headaches after using the correct chair and screen filter?

Sophies' case relates to the general subject of Health & Safety. Write down what you would do in the following circumstances, and what aspect of the Health and Safety at Work Act 1974 is involved in each case.

4   You find a huge pile of cardboard boxes stacked against a fire exit door.

5   You slip on a wet floor and sprain your thumb.

6   A colleague is injured in a road accident just outside the factory gates.

protection of employees

There are also a number of other Acts of Parliament which protect the rights of the individual employee. A number of them originated in the European Union (EU) as **directives**. A directive is a set of regulations issued by the the EU which are then to be incorporated into the laws of the member states, including the UK.

The Employment Rights Act 1996

This covers a wide range of employment issues, including:

- the employer must give an itemised pay statement, listing all deductions (tax, National Insurance, pension contributions)

- where an Employment Tribunal decides that an employee has been unfairly dismissed the employer must pay them compensation, or give the employee their job back, or give them a different job at a similar pay and status level to their old job

- employees must get compensation payments if they are made redundant

National Minimum Wage Act 1998

This Act started off as an EU directive and has now been passed as an Act of Parliament.

It is now a legal requirement to pay all employees a minimum hourly rate of pay. This normally goes up every year in line with the rise in the cost of living.

Visit www.dti.gov.uk/lowpay for up-to-date details.

a legal right to time off for parents
of young children

Working Time Directive

This is a directive from the European Union which has the force of law. It is now forbidden to make employees work more than an average 48 hours per week, unless the employee 'opts out'.

Parental Leave Directive

All employees with young children are now entitled to have unpaid time off work to look after them. The directive was incorporated into the Employment Relations Act 1999.

Part Time Workers Directive

This states that part-time workers now have similar rights to people working in full-time jobs. If they work for, say, 50% of a standard working week, they will be entitled to 50% of the holiday pay that a full-timer would get.

Temporary Workers Directive

This states that even if a person is only employed for a few weeks – as is often the case with 'temps' – they will be entitled to holiday pay and other benefits.

Data Protection Act 1998

The aim of this Act is to regulate the use of data about individuals – eg consumers – held on computer and written records. It prevents this data being passed to other people and organisations without permission; it also allows the subject of the data to have access to the information.

The Act relates to employees because employers must keep written and computer-based records of employees confidential. Under the provisions of the Act, employees have the right of access to their personal records.

| The Register of Data Controllers | Education & Training | News & Events | Freedom of Information |

Principles of Data Protection

The rules

Anyone processing personal data must comply with the eight enforceable principles of good practice. They say that data must be:

- fairly and lawfully processed;
- processed for limited purposes;
- adequate, relevant and not excessive;
- accurate;
- not kept longer than necessary;
- processed in accordance with the data subject's rights;
- secure;
- not transferred to countries without adequate protection.

visit: www.dataprotection.gov.uk

---

laws to protect the employee – a summary

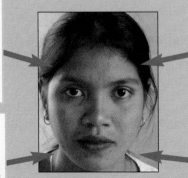

protection against discrimination:
Sex Discrimination Act
Race Relations Act
Disability Discrimination Act
Equal Pay Act

Health & Safety
Health & Safety at Work Act
C.O.S.H.H.
Screen Equipment Regulations

pay and hours:
Equal Pay Act
National Minimum Wage Act
Working Time Directive
Parental Leave Directive
Part Time Workers Directive
Temporary Workers

confidentiality of employee records:
Data Protection Act

Activity 18.3 – discrimination?

What is legal position of the employees in the following situations? What laws have been passed to protect them?

1   An employer wants his staff to work extra time over July and August because the company is very busy. The average weekly hours will be 52. 'It should work,' he says, 'they want the extra cash, and we did it last year too.'

2   A part-time shop assistant complains because she never seems to get any holiday. She complains: 'The full-timers seem to get all the perks here. I just work my hours, get my pay, and that's it!'

3   The manager of a fruit farm is planning the wages budget for the summer season. 'It's OK,' he says to the owner, 'we can get cheap labour in the summer – foreign students and local casuals won't expect more than £4.00 an hour.'

Nutshell summary

■ Employees are well protected in law and it is the duty of an employer to ensure that the rights of employees are respected.

■ The Sex Discrimination Act protects people from being discriminated against on grounds of gender when they apply for a job or when they are applying for a promotion.

■ The Race Relations Act protects people from being discriminated against because of their race when they apply for a job or when they apply for a promotion.

■ The Disability Discrimination Act protects disabled people from being discriminated against when they apply for jobs or when they apply for a promotion.

■ There are several important laws which require employers to operate safe and healthy systems of work. The most important of these is the Health and Safety at Work Act.

■ Recent legislation includes measures to protect the rights of part-time and temporary workers and to guarantee a Minimum Wage for employees.

Key terms

Discrimination
When an employer treats an employee or a job applicant unfairly because of their gender, race or disability.

Health and Safety
The provision of a safe, risk-free and healthy working environment.

Minimum Wage
The legal minimum hourly rate which employers can pay their employees.

Directive
Regulations created by the European Union which are adopted into the law of all countries belonging to it, including the UK.

19
Job roles in organisations

Bob Parkis

Bob is a line manager in the Despatch Department at Whittakers. He has twelve people working for him.

He joined Whittakers from a printing company six months ago. He is a very straightforward guy who expects his staff to work hard. In return he feels he is fair to them – every few weeks he treats them to cakes and drinks. Staff like him and rarely leave his team. He is well thought of by Ben Whittaker who sees him as a future factory manager. He is very clear about what his job is all about

'Look. I have to meet the targets given me by the factory manager. If the labels are not packed on time they get delivered late to our customers. If they are not packed right, customers will complain about the damage to the product. So my job is to train staff so they are quick but also careful. Poorly packed boxes of labels are very easily damaged if they are not packed properly.

Recently I had to speak to a new girl, Sara, because she was rushing the job and we had endless complaints from customers. Our bonus system is to blame because employees rush the job to make more money. Still, we are stuck with it, I suppose. Anyway, I can't afford to keep staff who are no good, so I recommended to the Manager that she be sacked.'

points to think about . . .
Do you feel Bob has been hard on Sara?

What do you think the Manager could do instead of sacking Sara?

job roles in organisations

In this chapter we will study the main roles held by people in a typical business organisation – a limited company such as Whittakers – and examine their responsibilities and powers. Other organisations, such as public sector bodies and charities, provide similar job roles.

The main job roles we will examine are:

- the director
- the manager
- the supervisor (line manager)

- the operative
- support staff

The diagram below shows how these jobs all fit into a typical business. Note the four function areas in the red boxes.

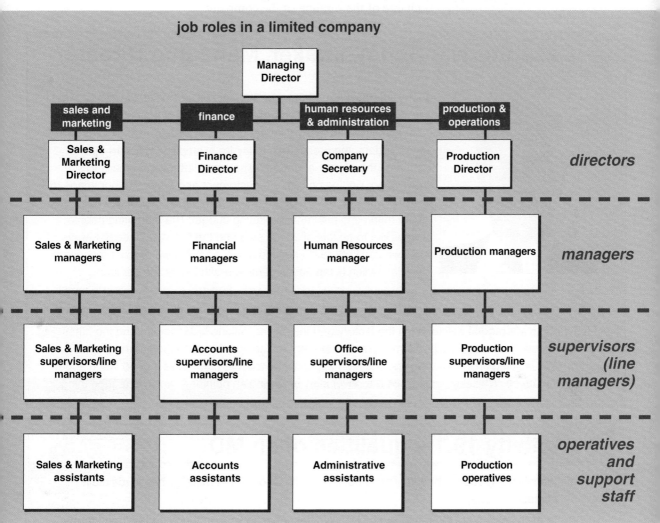

job roles in a limited company

We can now examine these roles, one by one . . .

directors

The Companies Act 1985 requires that all **limited companies** must have at least two **directors** to:

- make long term plans for the organisation
- appoint the right managers to ensure that these plans work properly
- keep control over company finances

- look after the shareholders' interests
- ensure that the company is able to achieve its main aims

Directors are very well paid and receive many 'perks'. At the top of the structure chart is the **Managing Director** who is in overall charge of the running of the company.

Case Study – Ben Whittaker, Managing Director

I am Ben Whittaker, Managing Director (MD) of Whittakers PLC. My job is to be in overall charge of the running of the company. I have to deal with many different groups of people – employees, shareholders, the press. Take today for example. I will start off with scanning the papers and reading selected letters and emails to see how we are getting on with our customers and projecting our image to the public. I then have a board meeting with the other directors to look at the marketing plan and marketing budget. The marketing people always like to do lots of advertising and the Finance Director always says we can't afford it. I have to make sure that we reach a reasonable decision which is the best and most profitable for the company.

Then I am due for lunch with one of our prime customers, the MD of a dairy company for whom we print labels. I have to keep them sweet because they are always trying to screw lower prices from us.

Some of the afternoon I will spend in the factory and the offices, talking to Managers and the other staff and getting scent of any problems. It is so important to keep one's 'ear to the ground' and to know what is going on in the business. The staff appreciate it too. We often have a good laugh about things that go on. Whittaker employees are never slow in voicing an opinion – which is a good thing.

Activity 19.1 – qualities of an MD

1   Identify the groups of people – stakeholders – with whom Ben Whittaker has to maintain contact.

2   In each case, state the reasons why Ben Whittaker has to keep in touch and on good terms with these people.

3   Discuss and list the qualities and skills which you think will contribute to making a good Managing Director.

managers

Each department will be run by a **manager**. The main roles of a departmental manager are to:

- motivate all their employees to work hard for the company
- ensure everyone reaches their targets

- carry out the administration of the department – this will include taking on new staff and sometimes sacking staff who are no good at their job

- share out work between the members of their department so that everyone is as happy as possible

- make sure all the people in their department know what is going on

- encourage everyone to contribute their own ideas on how to run their department

Nowadays managers are very well paid and they usually get the chance to buy company shares at special prices.

We will now look at a Case Study example of a manager at Whittakers. Sarah Phillips is the HR Manager. She runs the Human Resources Department.

 ## Case Study – Sarah Phillips, HR Manager

I am Sarah Phillips, Human Resources Manager. I run a department with three supervisors and twelve staff. I report directly to the Company Secretary (the director who looks after the company administration). One of my main responsibilities is the recruitment and selection of the right kind and quantity of staff. I have to talk to departmental managers who want to replace staff or recruit extra staff.

I have to write the job adverts and place them in the newspapers, at job centres and on websites. Then I have to choose candidates to interview, often from hundreds of applications, and invite them over for a 'selection day'. I ask all the candidates to do a series of job-related tests.

Another aspect of my job is interviewing staff on a regular basis and monitoring all employees' training and progression. Monitoring progression is important because it means we can find out who is doing well and therefore deserves to be promoted.

In short, my life is very busy. I find I am constantly having to solve problems and make decisions. There is no time for dithering! If there is one word I keep in mind all the time it is 'prioritise.'

 ## Activity 19.2 – the work of an HR manager

1 Who works directly for Sarah and to whom does she report?

2 What links does Sarah have with other departments in the business?

3 What are Sarah's main areas of responsibility?

4 Why is it important to monitor employees' progression?

5 Discuss and list the qualities and skills which you think will contribute to making a good manager.

other employees – the 'team'

Under each manager there will be a team of staff. The size of this team can vary considerably. In a factory, the team working for a Human Resources Manager will be very much smaller than the team working for the Production Manager. The members of a team will include:

supervisors/line managers

Nowadays the word 'supervisor' is a bit old-fashioned. Employees do not like the idea that they are being 'supervised' – it sounds as if they are being watched all the time. Nowadays, supervisors are more likely to be called **line managers**.

operatives

A line manager or supervisor in a manufacturing company such as Whittakers has a number of employees called '**operatives**' working under them. The job of the supervisor/line manager is to ensure that:

- the operatives reach their **production targets**
- the operatives produce work of the right **quality** all the time
- those operatives who are not doing a good job are dealt with so that they can be helped to reach their targets – for example, the operative may be given extra **training**
- operatives are made to feel **part of a team** – they are encouraged to work hard because their job is interesting and worthwhile
- operatives are asked for their ideas and opinions . . .

  Nowadays there is increasing emphasis on 'employee involvement' activities in which all employees are encouraged to take part – this includes suggestion schemes and **quality circles** (where all employees meet regularly to think up better ways of doing their job).

assistants and support staff

These employees are at a similar job level to operatives but they are in clerical or administrative workplaces – or in service businesses.

Like operatives they have targets to achieve, in quantity and quality terms.

In recent years they have been badly affected by changes in working conditions. New technology has made redundant many of the lower grade clerical jobs. The growth of the internet and e-commerce has resulted in substantial job losses. Travel agencies, recruitment consultancies and insurance offices are typical areas.

We will now look at a Case Study of Hannah Fairclough, who works as an assistant in the Human Resources Department at Whittakers.

a point to think about . . .

At Toyota Cars in Japan employees give their bosses 660,000 suggestions per year (12 per employee). Some of the suggestions will save Toyota a lot of money.

Case Study – Hannah Fairclough, assistant

I work as an assistant to Sarah Phillips in the Human Resources Department at Whittakers. She has given me a lot of of opportunity to do a wide range of personnel work since I came here two years ago from Liverpool John Moores University.

For example, Sarah gets me to look after all the lower grade job vacancies and she has also asked me to organise the induction courses we hold for new staff coming to Whittakers.

I also help look after the staff records – they are all on computer now – and provide details to the Finance Department when the payroll is run. The work is very varied and Sarah is good to work for – she lets me use my initiative and get on with things, which of course helps her too.

 ## Activity 19.3 – being an assistant

1 To whom does Hannah report, and what are her main areas of activity?

2 In what ways does Hannah work independently?

3 How does this benefit Hannah and her Manager?

4 What skills and abilities do you think an office assistant should ideally have?

 ## Nutshell summary

- Within any business there are a number of key job roles that have to be carried out efficiently. All are important and all are dependent upon one another.

- Directors are in overall control, and in return for the reward of high pay they have much responsibility in directing the business so that it can achieve its main aims.

- The Manager's job involves problem solving and decision making. The Manager needs to be able to communicate with directors and motivate staff.

- The supervisors/line managers carry out a managerial role but at a lower level, which is why they need managerial skills and look for managerial promotion.

- The operatives and support staff are the 'backbone' of a business. If they are well motivated and well paid, they can help the business achieve its aims.

 ## Key terms

Director
Person in overall control of a function of a business.

Managing director
Director in overall charge of managing a company.

Manager
Person responsible for the running of a function area of a business.

Supervisor/line manager
Person who looks after a team of staff in a department.

Operative/support staff
Administrative and clerical employees who provide support in the departments.

20

Recruitment

Using the net

The Whittakers PLC directors decided that they would have to have somebody to look after their website on a full-time basis. The company had already paid for a web design consultant to produce a website for the company and it had become a very successful way of attracting new business. 'It has been worth its weight in gold,' said Ben.

To keep the site up to date, and to add extra pages from time to time, there was a need for a Website Manager. George made some enquiries and found that about £22,000 would be a fair starting salary.

Peter Stoulton applied for this job, having seen it advertised on www.jobsite.co.uk, an online agency. He then found out more about the company and discovered it had grown considerably in size since the mid-1990s. Therefore, it could offer him good long-term career prospects. Having done a web design course at the local college, and an ICT-based degree at Leeds Metropolitan University, he thought he must have a fair chance of getting an interview.

Peter researched the Whittakers website for background information on the company and got an interview. There were two others for interview as well.

a point to think about . . .

The internet is very useful in the recruitment process – not only for placing online adverts, but also to the applicants for finding out information from the websites of the employers.

recruitment and selection

A major job in a Human Resources Department is the recruitment and selection of new employees.

It is very important to define what is **recruitment** and what is **selection**.

Recruitment is from the point when the organisation decides it needs to employ somebody up to the point where a pile of completed application forms has arrived in the post.

Selection begins when the Human Resources Department sorts through that pile of applications, and it ends when the newly appointed employee turns up on their first day at work.

We will look at recruitment first, and then selection.

recruitment – is there a job to fill?

In the Case Study on the previous page, the job is a new one, because the organisation is developing its website. There is a need for recruitment because there is need for a skilled specialist.

filling the vacancy – finding the applicants

The next stage will be to look for candidates. There are two types of candidate – **internal** and **external**.

internal candidates

There will usually be internal candidates who are interested in a vacancy because it is a promotion. If an employer gives an internal candidate a job the benefits are:

- other staff will be pleased to see that they may have a chance of promotion in future

- the organisation will attract better applicants if they see they have a chance of promotion

- internal candidates know the organisation, so they can learn the new job very quickly

external candidates

Here the benefits are:

- there will be a much wider range of people from which to choose, showing everybody that the organisation is an 'Equal Opportunities' employer

- newcomers to the organisation bring in new ideas and skills

In our Case Study there really is no other choice than an external candidate since nobody inside the organisation has the right skills and knowledge.

sources of external candidates

Where would an organisation go to find external applicants? It will depend on the type of job it is trying to fill. There is a wide variety of sources of job applicants, including recruitment websites.

SALES & MARKETING DEPARTMENT

INTERNAL VACANCY

A vacancy has arisen for a market research assistant.

Please apply to Sarah Phillips for details and application form.

GOJobsite

United Kingdom
mygoJobsite

clienthome
aboutus
Find relevant jobs from the p
webdesign
or for more refined resul
Powersear

Monda

Recruiters
Post a job by
Credit Card
Click here for
more information!

Delivering jobs for you

Search jobs UK & Europe-wide. Register for Jobs by Email and award-winning careers, employment and recruitment services from GoJobsite. With over **73498** jobs advertised from 35 industries in the last month alone, you could find your ideal job in seconds.

Job **Hunters**
Job search

Clients
Client Services

www.jobsite.co.uk

Activity 20.1 – sources of job applicants

The main sources are listed below. Think about them in turn and then identify the kinds of job applicant and job vacancies that are appropriate to each.

1 The School Careers Services.

2 Job Centres.

3 University Career Services.

4 Recruitment Agencies – including online agencies such as www.jobsite.co.uk

5 Executive Consultants (sometimes referred to as 'headhunters').

what is the job to be filled?

When Whittakers – or any organisation – is advertising a job it is vital that the company has first decided **what exactly the job is** – the level of responsibility, the range of activities, the skills needed, the type of person needed and the amount the company is prepared to pay in salary.

The two documents used to help in this process are:

■ the **job description** – which describes what the job involves

■ the **person specification** – which describes the type of person needed for the job

For effective recruitment and selection of new employees most organisations now use both of these documents. We will explain these two documents and show how they are used in the case of Whittakers' recruitment of a Website Manager.

job descriptions

A job description describes what the job involves.

More and more organisations have job descriptions for every job – from the caretaker to the managing director.

The main parts of a job description (see page 172 for an example) are:

1 the job title

2 the location of the job

3 a brief outline of what the employer does

4 the main purpose of the job

5 a detailed list of the main tasks required in the job

6   the standards that the job holder will be required to achieve

7   pay and other benefits

8   promotion prospects

9   the person to whom the job holder reports

10 the person(s) who report(s) to the job holder

Points **1** and **2** above are basic details. In **3** the organisation is selling itself to the job applicants – if it looks like a go-ahead, successful sort of place, it will attract better job applicants.

4, 5 and **6** are the essentials of the job description, that all job applicants will need to know about.

7 and **8** are needed as attractions to draw in good quality applicants.

9 and **10** give the applicant a clear idea of how this job fits into the organisation.

To sum up, the job description exists to turn enquiries from capable people into real job applications.

person specifications

A person specification describes the kind of person who is needed to carry out a particular job.

A person specification will be drawn up after the job description has been prepared. Usually a 'seven-point plan' is used to write a person specification. The seven points are:

1   **Physique, health and appearance** – this includes personal smartness, dress sense, voice, hearing, eyesight as well as general health.

2   **Attainments** – what educational qualifications, such as GCSEs, NVQs, A levels, does the job require?

3   **General intelligenc**e – how 'bright' do you need to be to do this job?

4   **Special aptitudes** – what special skills does a person need to do this job? It could be skills with words or numbers for example.

5   **Interests** – organisations will often look for people with lots of interests and hobbies.

6   **Disposition** – what kind of personality is needed to do this job?

7   **Circumstances** – for example, sometimes a job will require the person to live nearby.

The job description and person specification drawn up by Whittakers for the Website Manager are on the next two pages.

JOB DESCRIPTION

Job title	Website Manager.
Organisation	Whittakers PLC, Albany Estate, Halifax Road, Wakefield, WF2 5HN.
Responsible to	Sales and Marketing Manager.
Purpose of job	The Website Manager will develop and maintain the company World Wide Web pages on the internet. The Website is now an important marketing tool for the company both for advertising its products and for promoting the company name and its quality image.
	It is also used for advertising job vacancies and for placing orders for our products.
Duties	To maintain the web pages, ensuring that the site is kept up to date.
	To improve the web pages so that people who look at our site can easily find the information they want.
	To develop our company Intranet server so that it becomes the main method of communication within the company.
	To work with departmental managers to create web pages for their own departments.
	To keep in touch with new developments in web technology so that our system does not become out of date.
	To make sure that the system meets all legal and security requirements.
	To make sure that the system complies with the Health and Safety at Work regulations.
	To take reasonable care of his/her own health and safety and for any other people affected by his/her work.
	To take part in the company management appraisal scheme (on which pay increases will be based).
	To carry out any other duties which might be required from time to time.
Job location	Purpose-built office block next to the factory.
Physical conditions	The Website Manager will have his/her own fully equipped office. Secretarial assistance is also available as and when required.
Appraisals	All managers are appraised each year. Satisfactory appraisal is required in order to qualify for pay increments.
Salary/benefits	£22,000 rising by three yearly increments to £25,000. Subject to satisfactory appraisal.
	Contributory pension scheme. Company sick pay scheme. Share option scheme, subsidised factory restaurant.
Enquiries	Write to Whittakers PLC at the above address or ring Sarah Phillips, Human Resources Manager (01776) 654219 for an informal chat.

PERSON SPECIFICATION

Appearance	*Essential:*	Smart, well presented.
Attainments	*Essential:*	HND in Computing or Graphic Design (or equivalent).
	Desirable:	Some experience of working in a manufacturing environment.
Intelligence	*Essential:*	High level.
Aptitude	*Essential:*	Skilled with words and with figures. Good graphic design skills.
	Desirable:	Artistic skills.
Personality	*Essential:*	Able to work alone or as part of a small team (with the Marketing manager).
		A good communicator who is approachable and able to work successfully with people at all levels in the organisation.
		Must be able to adapt to the changing demands of a fast-growing business.
	Desirable:	A good sense of humour.
		A flexible, positive attitude.
		Patience and tolerance.
Interests	*Essential:*	Sociable – a good mixer with other staff.
	Desirable:	A keen practical interest in new developments in information technology.
Experience	*Essential:*	Experience of web page design using at least HTML.
		Good knowledge of HTML standards and of Javascript.
		Use of graphic tools to produce animated and static images.
		Basic understanding of IIS(NT) or Apache (Linux)
	Desirable:	Experience of using CGI/Perl, Flash 5, ASP.
		Good knowledge of macromedia tools such as Flash, Dreamweaver and Fireworks.
		Experience of setting up and running webservers with IIS or Apache.
		Knowledge of Internet Security systems.
Circumstances	*Essential:*	A successful medical examination.
		Full driving licence.
	Desirable:	Lives within a half-hour drive of Wakefield.

advertising the job

Once the job description and person specification have been written, the job must be advertised. Most job adverts are placed in newspapers, specialist magazines or with an online recruitment site.

writing the advertisement

Before writing the advertisement the employer must determine exactly what is required. The employer must look at the Person Specification (the type of person required) and the Job Specification (the type of job required) before writing the advert.

The advertisement should contain

- the name of the employer and what the employer does (eg label manufacturer)
- the job title – the advert should say what the job requires the person to do
- the type of person required – qualities, qualifications and experience
- pay, hours and perks
- place of work and indication of any travelling required
- how to apply – the advertisement should say whether applicants should write in, telephone or email for an application form

There should not be too much detail about the organisation, but just enough to make it interesting and attractive.

The Whittakers advert for a Website Manager might look like this:

WEBSITE MANAGER

www.whittakersplc.com

Whittakers PLC, a leading label manufacturer, based in Wakefield, requires an experienced website designer/manager to develop and take responsibility for a busy internet site.

The candidate will be responsible to the Sales and Marketing Manager and will be a suitably qualified good communicator, with at least three years' experience of website management.

Salary from £22,000, company pension scheme and other benefits.

Application form available from Sarah Phillips, Human Resources Manager, Whittakers PLC, Albany Estate, Halifax Road, Wakefield, WF2 5HN, telephone 01776 654219, email sphillips@whittakersplc.com

---

Activity 20.2 – assessing and writing adverts

1   Obtain a local newspaper with job adverts. Discuss and assess the adverts in groups, bearing in mind all the features that a good advert should have. Choose in your groups an example of what you think is a good advert and one which you think is less successful. Write down the reasons for your decision.

2   Design an advert for the Whittakers Website Manager vacancy, using the information in the job description and the person specification. Use a computer package if you can.

selection

After the job has been advertised applicants will write in or email Whittakers and will be sent a job application form, a job specification and a person specification.

The large pile of application letters and application forms which arrives at Whittakers must be reduced to a much smaller pile, to decide who can be invited to take part in the **selection process.**

shortlisting

This involves sorting through the letters, putting aside any which are definitely not suitable and then producing a **shortlist** of applicants to call for selection. To get onto the shortlist applicants must:

■   have **all** the 'Essentials' listed in the Person Specification

■   have **some** of the 'Desirables' listed in the Person Specification

■   complete the application form accurately and neatly

By now the company will have produced their final shortlist of people whom they will want to see. Usually this shortlist may consist of perhaps four or five people. In the Case Study at the start of this chapter we saw that there were just three shortlisted people.

selecting the 'right' person

The actual selection process will consist of some or all of the following methods of assessment.

a practical test

Job applicants often have to carry out tests to give a fuller picture of their ability to do the job applied for. In the Whittakers Website Manager example, the applicants could be seated in front of a computer and asked to design a simple web page or asked to change an existing one.

interviews

Job applicants will have one or more interviews. These could be 'one to one' interviews or 'panel' interviews. We will look at the

practical testing

practical aspects of interviewing in the next chapter. For the Website Manager job there were two interviews, one with the Human Resources Manager on her own and one with a panel which also involved the Marketing Manager and the Managing Director.

psychometric testing

Psychometric testing – which often takes the form of a series of multiple choice questions – is designed to provide evidence of the applicant's personality. A common test is a DISC test. This stands for **D**ominance **I**nfluence **S**teadiness **C**ompliance. An example of a psychometric question is shown below. Here the candidate has to state which statement is most like him/her and which is least like him/her. How would you answer?

A	I am very persuasive	Most	☐	Least	☐
B	I see myself as a gentle person	Most	☐	Least	☐
C	I am a very modest type	Most	☐	Least	☐
D	I often come up with original ideas	Most	☐	Least	☐

a psychometric question

Assessment Centre

For some more important job vacancies, job applicants can be required to take part in a group of assessments over a whole day or sometimes two days. They would be required to take part in group exercises (with all the other applicants), aptitude tests and traditional interviews.Using a mixture of assessments like this produces a more accurate result.

references

It is common practice for employers to ask job applicants to provide a couple of references from previous employers and reputable personal acquaintances. An employer can sometimes get a better impression of the candidate by telephoning the referee rather than relying on a written statement which might miss out vital information – eg that the applicant is an alcoholic, for example.

legal and ethical issues when recruiting

Employers should act fairly by never discriminating on **sexual**, **racial** or **disability** grounds. The laws relating to discrimination were explained in the last chapter. The organisation's recruitment advertising must not discriminate against anyone. The way in which people are selected for the shortlist for interview, and the manner of the interview itself, must be carried out **ethically**. This means that the interviewers must be fair and not choose a candidate for personal reasons. For example a girl should not be chosen simply because she looks like Kyle Minogue or a young man because his father happens to play golf with the Managing Director.

It is equally important that the **applicant** is also ethical and does not tell lies or mislead on the letter of application, application form or CV (see next chapter). To do so and be found out could lead to dismissal.

Nutshell summary

- Organisations must have effective recruitment and selection policies to make sure that they recruit the right people to fill their job vacancies.

- Organisations appoint internal candidates to jobs because it is good for employee morale and because the employee already knows the organisation.

- Organisations recruit externally because they want people with a fresh approach and new ideas which might benefit the organisation in the future.

- Job adverts should give an honest picture of the job. They should stress the good points but they should also make very clear what the job requires of the successful applicant.

- Many organisations now use the internet to recruit employees. This can be more effective and cheaper than traditional recruitment methods.

- When shortlisting from a pile of job applications, organisations will have a list of essential features (from the job description) but they will also look at factors such as the overall presentation of the application form and the letter of application.

- When selecting a successful applicant from the shortlist, organisations rely on a mixture of individual and panel interviews. They may also use assessment centres and testing to provide a fuller picture.

- Organisations should act legally and ethically when recruiting and selecting. Applicants should also behave ethically and honestly when they complete application forms and attend interviews.

Key terms

Recruitment
The process from the decision to fill a job vacancy to the point where completed job applications are received.

Selection
The process in which job applicants are selected for interview, to the point where the successful applicant arrives for the first day at work.

Job descriptions
These give an accurate picture of what the job involves.

Person specifications
These give an accurate picture of the kind of person needed to carry out a job.

Shortlisting
The list of applicants who will be invited to come for the selection process.

Psychometric testing
Tests to provide evidence of the applicant's personality.

Ethical
Being ethical is being fair and not being swayed by personal considerations.

21

Looking for a job

opportunities for Sharon

Sharon James, who is 22, lives in Wakefield. When she left school, she found a clerical post at a lighting equipment wholesaler. The company has been good to her, giving her time off work (day-release) to study an NVQ Business Administration course. This certainly helped her to get a promotion into the Human Resources department. Since then she has acquired a lot of experience in a wide range of Human Resources work. Only recently, she had to arrange all the interviews for a major appointment for a Distribution Manager and was praised for her organisational ability.

Although her manager thinks the world of her, she now feels that it is time to move on. There is a vacancy with the local recruitment agency for an Administrative Officer in the Human Resources Department at Whittakers PLC. The work is still personnel-related and Sharon thinks it will be a good career move. On a practical level, it is only a short walk to Whittakers, so she will save both petrol and time.

a point to think about . . .

Nowadays you are not expected to stay with the same employer for your entire working life. More and more people are switching jobs to advance their careers. There is all the more need for the skills developed by Sharon in completing application forms, writing letters and drawing up a CV.

documents needed for job applications

Sharon needs to provide several 'documents' when she applies to Whittakers PLC, or for any job. These are:

- her **Curriculum Vitae** (usually called a CV)

  or

- an **application form** for the job advertised

  plus

- a **letter of application** for the job advertised

We will look at these documents in turn.

the curriculum vitae

A curriculum vitae (CV) is a written presentation of a job applicant's personal details, education and employment so far.

Sharon's CV, which she now needs to update, is her career to date. There are two points to bear in mind about a CV:

- a CV is often used as an alternative to an application form – if the employer sends an application form, it will not always be necessary to send a CV because most of the CV details will go on the application form

- a CV is often sent to support a letter of application

designing a CV

It is important that CVs look good and will impress an employer. There are specialist agencies who prepare CVs for people in a professional manner, but this is not cheap. Sharon cannot afford to pay for this but she does have her own PC at home with a word-processing program, so that she can produce a tidy, well presented CV.

The next question is what to put into a CV. The simplest rule is to include anything which would normally be asked for in an application form. The basic list of contents is:

Curriculum Vitae

1   name and address

2   telephone number(s)

3   date of birth

4   marital status

5   education and qualifications

6   training (where appropriate)

7   employment history (school and college leavers should include part-time employment) – if you have had several jobs, put them in order with the most recent job first

8   hobbies and interests (avoiding 'reading' or 'going to the cinema' or 'music' which sound feeble – they must be activities which are interesting)

9   references (normally two)

Sharon's CV is shown on the next page.

CURRICULUM VITAE – SHARON JAMES

Name   Sharon James

Address   14 Goodwood Drive, Pinders Heath, Wakefield, WF1 8TG

Telephone   01776 452281 (home) 0778 554590 (mobile)

Date of birth   13.8.1981

Marital status Single

Employment history

Organisation   Chapman Lights Limited, Dewsbury Road, Wakefield

Job role   Clerical Assistant (Human Resources Department)

Dates   1998 to present

Duties in role A wide variety of clerical jobs including keeping HR records and organising job interviews

Dealing with personal callers in absence of my manager

Setting up several new office systems to improve office efficiency and installing new software packages

Education   Wakefield High School (1993-1998)
Five GCSEs: Maths, English Language, German, History and Biology

Wakefield College (1998-2000)
NVQ Business Administration (Part-time study)

Other training courses undertaken:
Word-processing course 2001

Interests   Amateur dramatics, fitness training, helping at local hospice.

References   Miss Hilda Spreckley, Headmistress, Wakefield High School, Sutton Road, Wakefield, WF2 1RS.
Ms. Philippa Wyatt, Personnel Manager, Chapman Lights Limited, Dewsbury Road, Wakefield, WF4 9TZ.

Activity 21.1 – assessing Sharon's CV

1 Compare Sharon's CV with the list of contents for a CV on the previous page.
How good do you think her CV is? Write down any criticisms.

2 Write down four questions an interviewer might ask Sharon about what she has written in
her CV.

letter of application

Sharon is also required to write a **letter of application**.

In this letter she should politely ask for the job and state why she would be good at it.

She needs to remember that a letter that is badly structured, poorly expressed and full of spelling mistakes will not help her at all.

Human Resource Department staff may have to read dozens of application letters so it is in Sharon's best interests to pay attention to doing it properly. Key points to bear in mind include:

■ keep the letter brief and to the point

■ the letter should be handwritten, unless the handwriting is hard to read!

■ check the grammar, punctuation and spelling – get someone else to read it and check it for you

letter structure

Sharon's letter should be structured as follows:

■ an **opening paragraph** which explains how she found out about the job and why she is applying for it

■ a **second paragraph** should give basic details about her (the detailed description will be in the application form or CV attached)

■ a **third paragraph** will give the particular reasons why she wants the job and why she wants to work for the organisation

■ a **fourth paragraph** which says when she is available for interview

In the letter, Sharon must show that she is keen to get the job, tell them why she thinks she is suitable and why it will be a good idea for their organisation to employ her.

---

applicant's address and telephone number

name of person in advert
business address

date of letter

Dear ....

body of the letter:
• Paragraph 1 – where the job was advertised
• Paragraph 2 – basic details of the applicant
• Paragraph 3 – why the applicant wants the job
• Paragraph 4 – when the applicant is available for interview

Yours sincerely   (if the applicant is writing to a named person)

Yours faithfully   (if the applicant is writing to Dear Sir or Dear Madam)

signature
name printed beneath

format and elements of an application letter

Activity 21.2 – Sharon's letter of application

Sharon has written down some notes (see below) about what she is going to write in her letter of application, but she has not yet completed the letter itself.

You are to write the letter in full in your own handwriting, but using a word-processing program to produce the draft – so that you can add bits and take bits out as you compile the text.

I wish to apply for the job of training administrator at Whittakers PLC.

I am very interested in training and Human Resources work. Much of the time in my present job is spent on personnel-related work, including course administration for our day-release employees, the organisation of job interviews and keeping employee records up to date.

I consider that it is now time for me to move to a new position in a growing company where I can develop my career further.

I have completed the NVQ Business Administration course. I would be very interested in continuing my studies, in my own time if necessary, to get a professional qualification in personnel management.

Available for an interview at any time.

Sharon's address is 14 Goodwood Drive, Pinders Heath, Wakefield WF1 8TG. She saw the advert in the Wakefield Telegraph last night. It said to write to Sarah Phillips, Human Resources Manager at Whittakers PLC, enclosing a CV. Use today's date for your letter.

the application form

A typical application form will require addresses, next of kin, education, training, qualifications, work experience, non-work interests and, finally, names of referees from whom the organisation can receive a report on personality and performance.

benefits of using an application form

The main benefits to the employer of using application forms are:

- it is easy to match what is written in an application form with what the job description and person specification ask for
- the forms can act as a framework for an interview

  For example the interviewer can ask:

  'Why are there gaps in your employment record?'

  'Why are your school examination results not so good?'

  'Do you have any non-work interests apart from reading?'

- the form from the successful job applicant will become a very useful part of his/her initial employee records

BASSETT CONSTRUCTION LIMITED

applicati

personal de

surname	
Mr/Mrs/Miss	
permanent	
postcode	
nationality	

employment history

employer	job held, duties and responsibilities	dates

education

school/colle

additional information

Describe your present state of health.
Please give details of any serious illnesses or operations over the last 10 years.

Do you have a criminal record or criminal charges pending?   Yes/No

Do you hold a clean driving licence?   Yes/No

Where did you hear of this vacancy?

When are you *not* available for interview?

references

Please give the names and addresses of two referees

name	name
address	address

interests

Please give details of your interests and hobbies, any positions of responsibility held, and any other information which you would like to support this application.

DECLARATION

I declare the information supplied by me in this form is, to the best of my knowledge, correct.
signature of applicant   *date*

extracts from a typical application form

interviews

The final stage in the selection process will be an interview – either with one interviewer or with an **interview panel** of two or three.

preparing for the interview

Sharon in the Case Study was pleased to get an invitation for an interview at Whittakers. As always, she made sure that she was properly prepared:

- as soon as she got her invitation she acknowledged it by letter (telephone or email would also have been acceptable)
- she found out about Whittakers PLC from friends and also from the Whittakers website.
- she wore appropriate, smart, clothes.
- she arrived for the interview a few minutes early.

interview technique

the interview

Sharon's interview was with a panel of two people.

- When she was called into the interview room she introduced herself with her full name and shook hands with both the interviewers.
- Sharon did everything she possibly could to create a good impression. She had read somewhere that most interviewers make their minds up about a candidate within a minute or two of meeting them. This might be very unfair but it is a fact of life.
- She sat upright in the chair and tried not to appear too casual.
- She made good eye-contact with both the interviewers.
- When asked questions she always thought for a few seconds before answering. This gave a good impression that she had considered the questions carefully.
- She always answered the questions as briefly as possible. Interviewers are working to a timetable and often only have half an hour per applicant. If Sharon had talked too much, she would have annoyed them!
- She had prepared two questions to ask at the end of the interview. This showed them that Sharon was really interested in the job. Asking no questions gives a very poor impression.

Activity 21.3 – Sharon's success

Sharon was offered and accepted the job at Whittakers PLC.

1 What areas of Sharon's CV might have impressed the interviewing panel?

2 What aspects of Sharon's interview technique might also have impressed the interviewing panel?

Present your answers in the form of numbered points.

Nutshell summary

- When you are applying for a job you will normally send

  - a letter of application

  plus

  - a CV

  or

  - an application form

- A CV should cover all the key aspects of your life and work so far. It needs to be presented in a professional manner to impress the prospective employer.

- A letter of application must outline why you want the job and what you can offer the organisation in terms of your work experience, qualifications and enthusiasm.

- Application forms are better than CVs in providing information when shortlisting applicants because they are properly structured and easier to follow.

- If you are applying for a job, you must normally provide at least two references to support your job application, including one from your most recent employer.

- There are two types of job interview – the 'one to one' and the panel. Although 'one to one' interviews have certain advantages, panel interviews allow the employer a fuller picture of the job applicant.

- It is vitally important to remember that success in job interviews is all about preparing properly so that you can impress the interviewer(s). It is very easy to create the wrong impression if you are not adequately prepared.

Key terms

Curriculum Vitae (CV)
A written presentation of a job applicant's personal details, education and employment.

Letter of application
A letter accompanying an application form or CV. It outlines the applicant's interest in the vacancy and gives a brief account of the applicant's background.

Application form
A form issued by the employer to the job applicant. It asks for all the information normally submitted on a CV.

References
Statements which are intended to confirm the information put into the application form or the CV. They give opinions about the applicant's ability to do the job being applied for and about the applicant's honesty and reliability.

Interview panels
A group of two or three managers who will each ask a number of questions related to their area of work.

22
Methods of working

Josie and Pat share a job

Josie Sharp is secretary to the Finance Director at Whittakers. She has a young son, Sam, and she wants to work part-time so that she can pick him up from nursery school each day and have some 'quality time' with him. She does not want to give up working because she likes her boss and needs the money.

The Finance Director said that he must have a full-time secretary so this caused a problem for Josie. She would certainly have to give up her job.

At least she thought so until her neighbour, 41 year-old Pat Simkins, asked her if there were any part-time office jobs going at the factory. She had worked there ten years before, as a secretary to Ben Whittaker. Josie said she would see if the Human Resources Manager would agree to them 'sharing' the job.

Sarah Phillips, the Human Resources Manager, was very sympathetic and positive. It would be the first proper 'job share' in the company and it would be a good example for the future. Subject to the Finance Director's agreement she would fix it so that Josie would work mornings and Pat would do afternoons. Both women agreed that this would suit them very well.

a point to think about . . .

Organisations have to be more flexible with their employees today.
If they are not flexible they will not attract good people to work for them.

flexible working

This chapter is all about the different ways in which people work. Nowadays more and more employers use their employees in a **flexible** way – in other words requiring them to vary their hours to suit the pattern of work. This is for two main reasons:

■ so that they can get more value from them – employers argue that without this flexible approach their businesses would close down because they would be too costly to run.

- to attract people to apply for available jobs – as the Case Study shows, if Whittakers had been inflexible they would have lost a very good secretary and there would also have been no vacancy for Pat, another very good secretary

Today organisations try to become as efficient as possible by being flexible in a number of different ways . . .

numerical flexibility

This means that employers alter the **working hours** of their staff from week to week or even from day to day. They may also change the total **number** of staff from day to day or from week to week.

This means they are only paying for staff when they really need them. Not surprisingly, many employees do not like this kind of arrangement because their weekly pay may vary a lot from week to week.

functional flexibility – multi-skilling

a call centre – outsourcing telephone answering

Employees are moved from one job to another as required by the needs of the organisation. This is not popular with some employees because they have to do different jobs – perhaps in the same week and even on the same day sometimes. Some employees, on the other hand, like a change. It also gives them a wider variety of experience which might help them later when they look for a new job.
This ability to carry out a variety of jobs is known as **multi-skilling**.

financial flexibility – outsourcing

This means that the organisation can save money by using other companies to do some of their work. These other companies do this work more cheaply and this saves the organisation a lot of money.

The best known examples are where organisations get other companies to run their staff restaurants, their cleaning, their security services and telephone answering. This is called **outsourcing**.

Activity 22.1 – outsourcing

Some very large companies provide services to businesses, enabling them to outsource some of their activities. Investigate the following – using the internet if you can (try the search engine www.google.co.uk) and describe the services they offer:

Rentokil Initial

Compass Group

Office Response

Group 4

methods of flexible working

We will now look at some of the ways in which organisations work flexibly.

annualised hours

Annualised hours means that an employee has a contract to work a set number of hours per year but the number of hours they work each week varies according to the needs of the business.

In effect it means that when people work overtime their reward is time off later in the year instead of overtime pay – this is not popular with some employees for obvious reasons.

This method of working is only of use to an organisation if the demand for its products or services changes from month to month.

The employee gets the same weekly or monthly pay throughout the year.

annualised hours – a worked example

Let us suppose that the standard working week is 35 hours.

Then assume the employees get 5 weeks holiday. This leaves 47 weeks at work (ie 52 – 5 = 47).

The total number of hours they have to work in the year is 47 x 35 = 1645 hours

When it is busy they might work a 40 hour week for say 10 weeks rather than the normal 35 hours a week. This gives them a credit of 50 hours more than they should have worked (10 x 5 = 50).

To get these hours back from the organisation they might then work 10 weeks of just 30 hours, ie 5 hours less per week than normal.

zero hours contracts

This is where the employee is 'on call' to come into work whenever they are needed.

If they are not needed they earn no money. This is not unusual in retailing where levels of business activity go up and down sharply during a week or even within one day.

Some employees like it because it gives them flexibility as well – after all, if they do not want to come in on a particular day they need not do so. However, for people wanting a secure job with reliable weekly pay it is not very attractive.

job sharing

This means that two employees share a job, as in our Case Study at the beginning of this chapter.

Job sharing could involve a divided day (as in our Case Study) or a divided week (usually the split occurs around Wednesday lunch-time).

The advantage of job sharing is that the employer keeps an employee who can no longer work full time, as in Josie's case.

Job sharing has become quite popular, especially with young women staff who have small children. Even quite senior management jobs are now 'shared' in some organisations.

Problems can happen, however, if the sharers do not work very well together or if one sharer leaves and it is hard to find a replacement.

teleworking

Increasing numbers of people work at least part of their time from home or 'on the road' – they are the 'teleworkers'.

teleworking on the move

'Teleworking' means literally 'working from a distance'.

The introduction of the laptop computer and, more importantly, the advent of email and the internet, have made this far easier to do than it used to be.

For example, salespeople can email sales deals they have done direct to the main sales office and receive emailed instructions directly from there. Reports can be written in Aberdeen and emailed directly to an office in London or New York. The internet provides a wide range of material to teleworkers which would only previously have been available in a library.

Working at home for part of the week has big advantages in terms of the reduction in travel time and travel costs. This cuts down stress, so people feel more relaxed and work more efficiently.

But there can be problems with teleworking:

■ employees can feel cut off from their normal workplace and they can feel that they have been forgotten by their boss and colleagues

■ telework can interfere with the employee's private life, with computers and paperwork cluttering up a spare bedroom

■ the employee's private life can interfere with the telework – particularly if there are young children in the house who want the parents' attention

telecottages and telecentres

One of the problems of teleworking is that teleworkers never really get away from their job. **Telecottages** or **telecentres** are seen as a better bet for some people.

A 'telecottage' or a 'telecentre' is a building designed as a workplace for teleworkers. It has computer links and office facilities and is often only a few miles from home.

Telecottaging is a better alternative than teleworking because it separates 'work' from 'home' and the inevitable conflicts that arise from that situation.

The illustration on the left shows a custom-built 'drop-in' telecottage facility for teleworkers at a motorway services.

a 'Workspace' telecentre at Heston Services
(courtesy the Telecottage Association) www.tca.org.uk

Activity 22.2 – being a teleworker

A friend of yours is a part-time market research assistant who works for a local company. She spends a lot of her time telephoning customers and asking for feedback on products and the customer service provided. She also looks at the websites of competitors. She has been asked by her employer if she is interested in leaving her office-based job at the company headquarters and becoming a teleworker, based at home. She is married, with two children at school.

Prepare for her a list of the advantages and disadvantages of teleworking from home.

Case Study – flexible working at Whittakers

Ben Whittaker, the Managing Director of Whittakers PLC, says that the company operates flexible working wherever it can do so. 'It saves money,' he says, 'which benefits everyone.'

'When our Despatch Department is very busy we get a local job agency to send us some of their people as 'temps'.
We also use van drivers from an agency to help deliver orders when we are busy in the run-up to Christmas.
We would like to put our own delivery drivers onto annualised hours contracts but our trade union would go up the wall about it.

Most of our office staff are now multi-skilled so that they can do a range of tasks and this means we can easily cover people who are ill or on holidays. Staff do not always like doing different jobs but I always tell them it is good experience. Of course, they make more mistakes and they are slower, but they get better with experience and enjoy it in the end.

We save money by using a catering firm to run our staff restaurant. This was because they agreed to do the job for a lower cost than we could ever achieve. When we gave this firm the contract they agreed to keep some of the existing staff but sadly we had to make most of them redundant.'

Activity 22.3 – flexible working

Read through the Case Study on the previous page and answer the questions that follow.

1   In what ways does Whittakers operate flexible working?

2   How do they benefit from it?

3   How do their employees benefit from it?

4   What problems does it cause?

5   Why would the trade union go 'up the wall' about annualised hours contracts?

6   Why do you think a catering firm can run the staff restaurant more cheaply than Whittakers could?

Nutshell summary

■ A flexible workforce enables a business to remain competitive.

■ Flexible working is chiefly for the employer's benefit. However, it suits many employees who could not work under traditional 'inflexible' arrangements.

■ Organisations use numerical flexibility, functional flexiblity and financial flexibility to make them more efficient and to help them to produce their products and services as cheaply as possible.

■ There is a wide range of flexible working options available to suit different organisations in different situations.

■ The introduction of some types of flexible working can be unpopular. They may result in employees being made redundant or being asked to work under less attractive conditions of service.

■ The growth of ICT has made working away from the main office – teleworking – an efficient and value-for-money option. It is not always popular with employees, who miss the office and can be easily distracted.

Key terms

Flexible working
Requiring the workforce to vary their hours to suit the pattern of work.

Annualised hours
Hours worked are averaged out over a year and may vary from week to week.

Zero hours working
Where the employee is only called into work when the business needs them.

Job sharing
A single job shared by two or more employees.

Teleworking
Working away from the main office, often making use of ICT.

Telecottage/telecentre
A building designed as a workplace for teleworkers.

23

Training and development

Being given a chance

Sharon James was appointed as an administrative officer in the Human Resources Department at Whittakers. She worked just as hard as she had done at Chapman Lights – as a result she soon got an excellent reputation and after one year she has her first appraisal with Sarah Phillips, the Human Resources Manager.

Sarah is impressed with Sharon and wants her to start studying for her personnel management professional qualifications. She has some leaflets from the local college about the Certificate in Personnel Practice (CPP) and feels this would be a good starting point for Sharon.

'The CPP course takes one year and it will give you a really thorough grounding in basic Human Resources work. I will help you as far as I can and, of course, we will pay all your course fees and travel expenses. I am afraid that the course is in the evening so you will have to commit your free time to it.'

Sharon knew that going to college one night a week would show her boss how keen she was. If she was successful in the CPP, Sarah would almost certainly let her study for the higher qualifications and this would make it easier to get a really good job somewhere else in a few years time.

If she turned this offer down she would not get a second chance.

a point to think about . . .

When you are interviewed for a job it is always a good idea to ask the interviewer if the organisation helps employees who want to study for professional qualifications. Many organisations will support employees financially because it should mean they will become better at doing their jobs.

employee training

This chapter explains why the training and development of employees is vital to an organisation. It also looks at the main types of training and development and it looks at how organisations appraise their employees.

Employee training means:

Learning knowledge and skills which can be used in employment.

training may mean night classes
for the employee

Most people will have to change their jobs several times in their lives, often switching to completely different types of work. This means good training is very important.

training programmes

Training can be divided into two main categories:

- **'on the job' training**

This means that the employee is trained in the workplace. Many people enjoy this direct link with their job and they can see how important the training is to enable them to do the job properly.

- **'off the job' training**

This means attending courses which may be in a college or a training centre away from the workplace.

skills training

Training is all about getting more skills. Skills can be **non-transferable** or **transferable**.

non-transferable skills

These are skills that are very specific to the job held. They may be of little use in another job. Training to work on a particular machine in a factory provides the employee with a non-transferable skill. It is fine whilst the employee has that job but what happens if they look for a new job or if their skills become out of date later?

transferable skills

These are skills that can be used in a wide variety of other jobs, both now and later on. In the economy nowadays, where people are changing jobs far more frequently than they used to, they must have a selection of 'transferable skills'.

People with transferable skills are:

- more useful to **employers** because they can use them in different jobs (as we saw in the last chapter, organisations want their employees to be able to do a variety of jobs – to be multi-skilled)

- more useful to the **employees** themselves because they can find other, and possibly better, jobs if they have transferable skills

Key skills such as communicating verbally and in writing, numeracy (working with numbers) and ICT (working with computers) are transferable to most jobs.

ICT (computer competency) is a transferable skill

Activity 23.1 – types of skills training

Choose a part-time job that you do or one that a friend does.

Identify the skills required in the job that are non-transferable and those that could be transferable to other jobs.

types of training

induction training for new employees

Induction is the process of introducing new employees to the organisation and showing the employee how the organisation works.

A successful job applicant should be provided with an induction training of some kind.

initial training for new employees

This is to ensure that the job is done competently and safely.

All new employees must, by law, be given training immediately after the induction procedures have been carried out.

updating training

Increasingly, employees are required to learn new skills in place of skills that are becoming redundant, eg in the printing industry the traditional printing processes are gradually being replaced by digital printing which requires completely different ICT-based skills.

In most jobs employees are expected to update their knowledge and skills regularly.

a digital printing press – new skills required, old skills made redundant

multi-skilling training

Multi-skilling means that employees are trained to do several jobs rather than just one.

Employers benefit because:

- an employee can cover the work of somebody who is ill or on holiday
- employees are more motivated because doing several jobs is usually more interesting than doing just one
- the flexibility gained means the total number of employees can be reduced, which will save the employer money

a college-based open learning centre

open learning centres

Many organisations help to encourage 'off the job' training by having 'open learning' centres where their employees can study in their free time. The aim is to get employees to realise the importance of keeping up to date with new developments in industry and in their own particular areas of work.

These can be work-linked topics such as time management or business communications or general interest topics such as 'foreign languages for holidays'.

employee development

Employee development can be described as:

helping the employee by setting targets for improving performance and arranging the necessary training.

If an organisation does not help employees to be more successful they will go to an organisation that will help them. As a result the organisation will lose some of its best people.

To help employees to be more successful, organisations need to examine how well employees are working at the moment. To do this,employees have to be given an **appraisal** by their own manager.

what is an appraisal ?

An appraisal is an examination of an employee's performance over a period of time.

Appraisals are usually carried out every year although better organisations will do it every six months.

Performance appraisal is normally carried out by the job holder's immediate boss. The person who appraises is called the **appraisor** and the person being appraised is the **appraisee**.

It usually works like this . . .

The appraisor will first write an **appraisal report** of the appraisee. It will be structured like this:

APPRAISAL REPORT

- the strengths of the employee
- the weaknesses of the employee
- advice to the employee about the quality of their work in the previous year, and . . .
- an action plan for the next year – this will list the key things that the employee will be expected to do in the next year, for example to go on a training course

the appraisal

the report is drawn up

the interview

performance assessed

new performance targets set

skills assessed

training for new skills arranged

the employee trains and works to meet the new targets set

The appraisor discusses the appraisal report with the appraisee in an appraisal interview. In this interview the appraisee can raise issues that cause trouble – maybe their work is being badly affected because they are being bullied by workmates or because they have problems at home. If these things are not mentioned, the appraisor may think that the poor quality work is just a result of the appraisee being lazy or useless.

When they have both agreed what the appraisee should do in the following year, both of them sign the appraisal form. This is then sent to the Human Resources Department.

the benefits of performance appraisal

- it helps to identify training and development needs

- it may reveal other problems – for example, there may be workplace difficulties with other staff

- it may reveal useful new skills in the appraisee

- it improves communications between employees and managers – a few words of encouragement and praise for doing a good job will really please many employees

- it helps in fixing pay rises – more and more employees now get performance-linked pay rises which may be based upon their appraisal report

methods of developing employees

Organisations provide a variety of different ways to train employees in skills and work situations. This benefits both the employer and the employee.

- **job rotation**

  Giving people a range of jobs in rotation widens their experience and helps to increase their range of skills.

- **job enlargement**

  Allocating people extra tasks in their jobs gives management a better idea of an employee's true ability and determination.

- **job enrichment**

  This is adding more interesting and more difficult tasks to the job. This is done with an employee with promising potential to see just how capable that person really is.

- **understudying**

  An employee is attached to a very senior manager to act as an assistant.

■ **shadowing**

This means that an employee spends some time each week with a manager to learn what they do and to get a better idea of what problems they have to deal with. It is often used to help very able employees to move rapidly into a top job.

■ **mentoring**

An experienced senior manager passes on the benefits of his or her experience and wisdom to a younger employee.

■ **project work**

Giving a promising employee a specific investigative project enables them to get to appreciate many aspects of the organisation and it enables them to get to know senior managers.

■ **internal and external courses**

As we have already seen, employees are often sent on courses, usually at a local college, to learn further skills and to develop abilities.

Some courses will give them the detailed knowledge they will need to be able to take on more responsible jobs (eg courses in law, HR or accountancy). Such courses usually lead to qualifications which can make an employee more valuable to the organisation. It also means that they can find it easier to leave and get better-paid jobs elsewhere.

Other courses will give employees a wider range of general management skills. The most popular ones are those which help employees to manage their working time and those which help them to work better as members of a team.

Activity 23.2 – promotion for Bob?

Bob Parkis has been a very effective and popular line manager since he joined Whittakers. He knows he is good at his job and he feels that after six years he deserves a move upwards. Unfortunately, at the present time there are no vacancies higher up, although his boss, the present Distribution Manager, retires in two years time . . .

Study the range of development activities listed above.

1 Which of these of these would help Bob to get a promotion at Whittakers?

2 Which of these might help Bob to get a job elsewhere?

the use of national awards

The present Government is very keen to encourage organisations and their employees to invest time and money into training and development. Organisations can achieve the Investors in People Standard and National Training Awards. Employees can gain National Vocational Qualifications (NVQs).

LINCOLN STEFFENS
I have seen the future and it works

www.iipuk.co.uk

Investors in People

Investors in People is the national Standard which sets a level of good practice for training and development of people to achieve business goals. The Standard is already helping more than 26,000 organisations to succeed through their people.

The Standard consists of twelve indicators which help organisations to build a flexible, motivated and well-trained workforce that will have a positive impact on business success. There must be a regular review of the training and development needs of all employees. All employees should be given a clear idea of what the organisation is aiming to do and be encouraged to help to achieve that aim.

Real People,
Real Achievement

www.nationaltrainingawards.com

National Training Awards

Businesses and their employees can be granted National Training Awards for achieving excellence and success through training. The awards are aimed at people who have decided to improve their chances of success through learning new skills.

Visit www.nationaltrainingawards.com for details of winners of these awards.

National Vocational Qualifications (NVQs)

The aim of National Vocational Qualifications (NVQs) is to create a national system of approved skills-based qualifications for all employees. The Scottish equivalent is the SVQ.

These qualifications are workplace-based and they cover vocational areas such as Business Administration and Accounting. The basis of assessment is reaching a performance standard laid down by the industry concerned. Assessment is normally 'on the job' where the employee normally works.

Most Further Education colleges in the UK offer NVQ courses to back up the workplace assessment.

Activity 23.3 – training awards

Log onto the website of an organisation involved in encouraging excellence in training, for example: www.iipuk.co.uk or www.nationaltrainingawards.com

Look on the site for a Case Study or news item about one organisation that has achieved an award and make brief notes on what it does and how it achieved its success.

Nutshell summary

- Training and development are vitally important for the overall efficiency and competitiveness of an organisation.

- There are several types of training and development designed to fulfil a variety of organisational needs.

- All training is either 'on the job' or 'off the job' and both are equally valuable.

- Some skills and competences learnt in the workplace are non-transferable and others are transferable.

- Employee development helps both the organisation and the employee that is being developed.

- All organisations must regularly assess through the appraisal process the performance of their employees to make sure that they are being developed properly.

- The UK Government encourages organisations and their employees to develop training and development through various awards, including Investors in People (IIP) and National Training Awards.

- The UK Government has established a framework of National Vocational Qualifications (NVQs) to develop skills-based assessment in the workplace.

Key terms

Training
Learning knowledge and skills which can be used in employment.

Transferable skills
Skills which can be used in a wide variety of jobs.

Non-transferable skills
Skills which only apply to one type of job.

Development
Helping the employee by setting targets for improving performance, and arranging the necessary training.

Appraisal
An examination of an employee's performance over a period of time.

Investors in People
An organisation which upholds national standards for excellence in training and development.

National Training Awards
Awards made for achieving excellence and success through training.

NVQs
A national system of skills-based qualifications.

24

Sorting out disagreements

the pay rise

Whittakers PLC has done well this year. The company has increased its profits by 9% and, as a result, all the employees who own shares in the company have been paid a generous share dividend (a share of the company profits). About 220 employees own shares in the company.

The 420 employees at Whittakers are represented by the Transport and General Workers Union (known as the 'T & G'), Britain's second largest **Trade Union**. About 310 employees belong to the T & G. These are led by a senior **shop steward** who was chosen to do this by his workmates. He is Gareth Lewis, a 45 year-old man who works as a security officer.

The company has made an offer of a 2.5% pay increase this year. They are also offering two weeks paid parental leave for any employee who has had a child within the last five years. Gareth and the other members are angry that the company is being so mean about the pay rise after making so much profit. He believes that the Union should call for **industrial action** if the company will not make a better offer. This could mean an overtime ban or even a strike. Hopefully just the threat of these would get Whittakers to increase their offer. Before there is any kind of industrial action there has to be a ballot (a vote) of all the T & G members in the workplace and a one week 'cooling off period' during which the two sides try to sort out the problem.

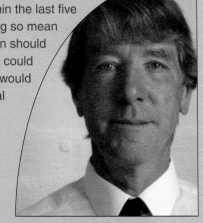

visit www.tgwu.org.uk

a point to think about . . .

There can only be industrial action of this type where there is Union representation in a business. This is not the case with all businesses.

disagreements at work

This chapter is about sorting out disagreements at work.
We will examine some examples of workplace problems and then look at ways of sorting them out.

There are two types of workplace disagreements:

- **collective** disagreements

  and

- **individual** disagreements

collective disagreements

Collective disagreements occur where there is a dispute between the employer and some or all of the employees.

causes of disputes

The most common causes of disagreement are:

- pay settlements – as in the Case Study
- redundancies – where an employer has to get rid of employees
- changes in ways of working – these may mean that employees have to work harder

possible Union action

a Unison (public sector Trade Union) picket line

Usually these problems are sorted out without any major dispute, but sometimes the Trade Union may have to put some pressure on the employer. This could take the form of:

- an **overtime ban** – this is a real nuisance in many organisations because employees rely on doing overtime for extra cash; an overtime ban means that businesses can be very badly hit and they may lose orders from customers
- a **strike** – again this causes big problems because of lost business

From an employee point of view an overtime ban is better than a strike because at least they still get their basic weekly pay. Employees on strike get absolutely nothing. This is one reason why strikes do not usually last very long. Many employees nowadays have big mortgages and heavy credit card bills – any action will make it very hard to keep up payments.

Activity 24.1 – to strike or not to strike?

You are at a meeting of the T & G union members at Whittakers. The purpose of the meeting is to decide whether to take strike action over the proposed 2.5% pay rise. Gareth recommends a strike because the threat will get the Whittakers management to increase their offer. Members make the following points at the meeting:

'I think we ought to call a strike – the management seem to think we are fair game by keeping pay low and increasing company profits and lining their own pockets!'

'But we did get a dividend on our shares, so we all benefit when the company does well.'

'Other workers in the Wakefield area are getting 3% rises or more. I think 2.5% stinks.'

'I reckon the two weeks paid parental leave they are offering is worth quite a bit.'

Hold a 'union' meeting in class and discuss the proposal to strike. Take a secret ballot (vote) on whether or not to strike.

staff associations

Out of 27 million employed people in the UK, only 8 million belong to trade unions. Most businesses do not have significant union representation (unlike Whittakers) and many employees are not interested in joining one.

In these cases the employer may discuss changes in pay and conditions with a **staff association**. This is a group of employees elected by the workforce to represent its interests. It has less power than an union representation and does not normally call strikes.

individual disagreements

Employees will sometimes have their own individual problems at work. There are two main areas where this can happen:

- **disciplinary problems** – where the employee is in trouble with the employer

- **grievance problems** – where the employee has a complaint about the employer for a variety of reasons

Both are dealt with by what are called **procedures**.

the disciplinary procedure

Imagine that the quality of an employee's work has been below the normal standard and has been reported by the supervisor to the manager. The poor work could be a result of the employee:

- being lazy

- not being properly trained

- being ill

- having problems at home

The stages in the disciplinary procedure are described below.

an informal discussion with the employee

At this stage the manager or supervisor will tell the employee that they are unhappy with the employee's work and ask the employee why this is so. The employee will be told to improve their work or further disciplinary action will be taken.

formal verbal warning

If there is no improvement in performance a formal verbal warning is given. This is officially recorded in the employee's records.

formal written warning

If the quality of the work has still not improved the employee will then get a letter from the Human Resources Department which will

---

disciplinary procedure

situation
the employer finds that the work of the employee is not up to standard

↓

informal discussion with the employee

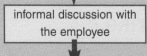

formal verbal warning if there is no improvement

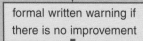

formal written warning if there is no improvement

↓

notice of dismissal if there is no improvement; the notice sets out:
- reasons for dismissal
- period of notice given

give details of their poor performance, stating what is wrong with it. The letter will say that if their work does not improve they could be sacked. Some employers give their employees a second and final written warning, but this is not legally required.

notice of dismissal

If the work has still not improved the employee will get a letter saying that they are dismissed 'with notice' (the notice period will be set out in the contract). The letter must, by law, give full details of the reasons why they have been sacked.

instant dismissal

If the disciplinary problem is extremely serious then it may be dealt with by the 'instant dismissal' of the employee concerned. This might be for theft from the workplace or for assaulting a workmate.

the grievance procedure

Employees sometimes have **grievances** – complaints – against the employer. Now that employment law (see Chapter 18) protects employees in so many areas, employees feel more confident about complaining. Grievances can include:

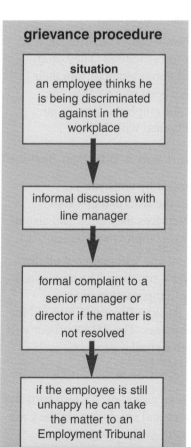

grievance procedure

situation
an employee thinks he is being discriminated against in the workplace

informal discussion with line manager

formal complaint to a senior manager or director if the matter is not resolved

if the employee is still unhappy he can take the matter to an Employment Tribunal

- unfair treatment by managers – for example, being passed over for promotion because of gender or race

- unfair pay – men paid more than women for the same work

- in an extreme case – unfair dismissal

grievance procedures

All employers should have a written **grievance procedure**.

This must be set down in writing and made available to all employees. It must state:

- The person to whom the employee must go to with their complaint. As with disciplinary procedures the process will be **informal** at first. Often a chat with the employee's line manager will be enough to sort matters out.

- If the employee is still not happy with the way they are being treated they will be allowed to make a **formal complaint** to a senior manager, or even a director.

- If the employee is still not happy with the result, they may then have to go outside the organisation and take the matter to an **Employment Tribunal** (an independent informal court)

If the employee is a Trade Union member, the Union will be able to give advice and support in every stage of the process. The Union will also give support in the case of a disciplinary procedure.

Activity 24.2 – grievance cases

Here is a list of typical grievances made by employees.

Which do you think could be sorted out informally? Which of them are more serious and will need more investigation by management? What laws could be used to support the more serious cases?

1 An able female employee, who has worked for the same company for twelve years, has never been promoted, whereas several male colleagues with far less service have been.

2 An employee complains that his office is poorly equipped so that he cannot do his job properly.

3 An employee complains that he is being picked on by other staff because he is from Pakistan.

4 An employee complains because he has been placed in the same section of the factory as his ex-wife.

resolving problems externally

employment tribunals

If an employee is not happy with the result of a disciplinary procedure or of a grievance procedure it will be possible for them to make an official claim to an Employment Tribunal.

An **Employment Tribunal** is an informal court consisting of a lawyer and employer and employee representatives. They offer employees the chance to win financial compensation from their employers or, in cases where they have been sacked, they can sometimes get their job back. Before the employee goes to an Employment Tribunal they will have to deal with ACAS . . .

ACAS (The Advisory, Conciliation and Arbitration Service)

The aim of **ACAS** (a public body funded by taxpayers) is 'preventing and resolving problems in the workplace'. (Visit www.acas.org.uk to see the range of services they offer, and also to find out about Trade Unions and general employment issues.)

An ACAS officer is totally independent and will point out all the weak and strong points of an employee's situation. The employee will be told if the chances of winning compensation in an Employment Tribunal are good. The ACAS officer will also tell the employee if the case is completely hopeless. The ACAS officer will also visit the employer and go through a similar process.

other roles of ACAS

Apart from dealing with these individual cases, ACAS also sorts out problems between groups of employees and employers. In the Case Study on page 200, if an overtime ban or strike looks likely at Whittakers, the company or the Union can call in ACAS to help.

An ACAS officer would, in this case, meet Ben Whittaker and Gareth Lewis to get a clear idea of what the problem is about. The officer will then suggest possible ways of ending the dispute.

European Court of Justice

If employees consider that they have been unfairly treated by an Employment Tribunal they have the option of taking the case to the European Court of Justice, in Luxembourg. This is an expensive option, but worth it if the employee has a strong case, and wins.

Nutshell summary

- In some organisations, employees are represented by Trade Unions. These organisations protect employees from unfair treatment by employers.

- Trade Unions also fight for better pay and working conditions and sometimes use measures such as strikes and bans on overtime working.

- Staff Associations within individual organisations are elected by the employees. These stand up for employee rights, but have less power than the Unions.

- A disciplinary case is where an employee gets into trouble with an employer. Reasons for this include sub-standard work or persistent lateness.

- A grievance case is where the employee has a complaint about the way in which the employer is treating them.

- Employers must have written disciplinary and grievance procedures so that employees are treated fairly. Trade Unions help employees by representing them in grievance and disciplinary hearings.

- If employees are not satisfied with the way they are treated at work they can make a claim to an Employment Tribunal to win compensation from their employer.

- ACAS, a public service, can be called in to help resolve disputes between employer and employee.

- If the case of an employee is rejected by an Employment Tribunal, the employee has the right to take the case to the European Court of Justice.

Key terms

Trade Union
An organisation which exists to protect the rights of its employee members.

Shop steward
The elected leader of a Trade Union membership in a workplace.

Industrial action
Action which is intended to force employers to do what their employees want.

Collective disagreement
Dispute between an employee group and the employer.

Individual disagreement
Dispute between a individual employee and the employer.

Procedures
Disciplinary and Grievance procedures are rules set down by an organisation for dealing with these two situations.

Employment tribunal
An informal court which deals with unfair dismissal and discrimination claims.

ACAS
A public organisation which aims to settle industrial disputes.

25

The importance of customers

Terry's face the music

Peter and Sarah Terry run a chain of CD and video shops in the East Midlands known as 'Terry's' Music'. Their biggest sales are chart CDs and videos but they also have a healthy trade in classical CDs.

Peter and Sarah believe that they offer a very high standard of customer service which makes them more appealing than the bigger, less friendly, high street chains.

Mike Smith came in to the Nottingham branch one Tuesday to collect a CD that he had ordered about a week before. It was a birthday present for his daughter. He was told that this had not been delivered because the shop had been very busy on the day Mike came in, and the order had been delayed. Gerry Marsden, the store manager, came and spoke to Mike about this problem . . .

'I am very sorry about your order, Mr Smith. We have been very short-staffed in the shop, so we have had a bit of a backlog in the ordering system. Anyway we have now put it right and I can assure you that the CD will be here for you by Friday.'

Mike replied, angrily: 'I am not satisfied with that excuse. Your shop guarantees to get CDs quickly and that is why I always come here. By Friday I will have waited two weeks and my daughter's birthday will have gone past. You can keep your CDs. I shall not be back here again.'

a point to think about . . .

The customer is always right, whatever the situation. The sign of a good business is that it can win back customers when things go wrong. What can Gerry do to win back Mike's custom?

why customers are important to a business

This chapter is all about customers and why it is important not to upset them as in this Case Study.

There are some basic home truths about customers:

customers provide income

no customers = no business

Any business that upsets people like Mike Smith will not be around for very long.

customers provide market share

Businesses have a share of the market for the product or service they provide. To keep that share, or to expand it, good customer service is very important.

New businesses can enter a product market and, by offering a better or cheaper service, can take customers from established businesses. This has happened in the short-haul airline business where new airlines such as easyJet and Ryanair have taken customers from the national airlines like British Airways and Lufthansa.

Activity 25.1 – getting your custom

Make a list of your favourite products – both goods and services, such as clothes and food, shops and clubs.

Now make a list of the factors that would make you change your loyalty and switch to another brand. You may need to look at your notes on competition and competitors. Discuss these factors in class.

contented customers come back to you

As Mike said, he was a regular customer. 'Regulars' provide a steady income which means that a business can plan ahead and invest to make the business even bigger. Remember that most businesses borrow from banks and the bank manager will be happier if there are plenty of regular customers.

Unfortunately, some customers do not come back. Why not ?

Market research has revealed the percentages . . .

why do customers go away?

1%	die
3%	leave the area
4%	naturally float between businesses – they have no loyalty to any business
5%	change because a friend tells them about other businesses which they say are better
9%	find the products or services are cheaper somewhere else
10%	are chronic complainers – they enjoy whinging!
	but the most important figure is . . .
68%	go elsewhere because they are unhappy with the service that they were given

customers tell their friends

Most people who are happy with a shop or a restaurant will want to tell their friends about it. Of course the opposite is true too. What will Mike say about his experience to his friends? Another statistic:

Research by the Ford Motor Company shows that a happy car buyer tells 8 friends but an unhappy car buyer tells 22 friends.

the importance of information

In the Case Study on page 206, management needs to **know** that problems sometimes occur with their ordering service. Businesses will not improve things if they do not know they need improving. It is essential that business owners keep in touch with what is happening on the 'shop floor'. Some larger service businesses send out their managers or senior executives as **mystery shoppers** to see exactly what is happening 'in the shop' or 'on the train'.

how can businesses keep their customers?

providing first class service and excellent products

Businesses achieve this by providing all staff with excellent training and making sure they are well paid and feel motivated in their work.

Businesses that provide quality products – which have a good image and reputation – have a big advantage over businesses which do not make quality so much of a priority.

Part of the task of providing an excellent product is giving excellent product information as well. Notice how supermarkets and fast food outlets supply glossy leaflets on nutritional information and recipes.

If you have a complaint, please speak to us. We'll do our best to put things right.

promotional leaflet from the Nationwide Building Society

dealing with customer complaints

Good businesses will give cards or leaflets asking for customers' opinions. Customers should also be given a reply-paid envelope to encourage them to complete these cards. As an alternative businesses can provide free phone lines (0800 numbers) so it is easy to ring in and complain.

Good businesses will contact customers regularly to find out if they are happy with the service or product they have purchased. For example, a car dealer should ring a customer 3 to 4 weeks after they have had their new car, to see how they are getting on with it.

sorting out complaints quickly

Customers like complaints to be sorted out quickly and efficiently. Any delay will add to their frustration. Having a complaint properly handled makes the customer feel special.

making sure problems do not happen again

In the Case Study, Gerry must make sure that orders do not slip back again because of staff shortages. If the same thing happened again, more customers would be likely to go elsewhere.

> British Airways reckons that customers who have a complaint which is dealt with properly and speedily are 10 times more likely to come back than customers who never complained at all.

 # Activity 25.2 – sorting the complaints

Read again the Case Study at the start of this chapter. If you were Gerry, the manager, what would you do to:

1   make things up with Mike Smith?

2   ensure that a similar situation did not arise again?

 # Nutshell summary

■ Customers are vitally important for any business because they provide income and information about the quality of service provided.

■ Customers will recommend a good organisation to their friends.

■ To retain customers it is important to give them the opportunity to complain about the service and products that are being provided.

■ Complaints should be acted on quickly and as generously as possible.

■ Actions should be taken to try to ensure that a complaint does not happen again.

■ A good organisation will follow up its customers to make sure that they are happy with the service they were given.

 # Key terms

Customer
A person who buys goods or services from a business organisation.

Market share
The percentage of sales within a market which is made by a single product or business.

Customer service
The level of service provided to customers of an organisation.

Mystery shoppers
Managers or executives who pretend to be customers in order to get a more accurate idea of what kind of service is provided by their employees.

26
What do customers expect?

A slip-up at Terry's

Pauline Fowler is employed to clean the Nottingham shop of Terry's Music. On several occasions she left parts of the shop floor wet and slippery. Sometimes she had left the staff toilets dirty and had not replaced towels and soap, as she was required to do in her job description. Her other job is to tidy up the CDs and videos and give them a 'light dusting'.

Gerry Marsden, the shop manager, told her off about it and threatened her with the sack if it happened again. Pauline was a good deal older than Gerry, whom she thought was a big softy who had probably never sacked anyone in his life.

Then one day Bill, a male customer in his fifties, bought a Dido video for his daughter and as he left the shop he slipped on a wet patch on the floor. Bill had twisted his ankle so Gerry spent all that morning in the casualty department of Nottingham Hospital with him. He also had to pay over £25 for a taxi to take Bill home. Luckily the sprain was not serious and Bill was a forgiving kind of guy who told Gerry to forget the whole thing.

Gerry was less forgiving, and certainly not a big softy. Pauline was given a final written warning to improve, otherwise she would lose her job.

a point to think about . . .

All organisations have internal 'customers', like Gerry, and external customers. Which are more important?

internal customers

In effect Gerry is an 'internal customer' of Pauline, as they are both employed by Terry's music. What does this mean?

An internal customer is an employee of an organisation who relies on the service of another employee.

Gerry in the Case Study relies on Pauline:

- keeping the shop clean so that it looks more attractive to customers
- keeping the toilets clean and properly stocked up with soap and towels

- keeping the shop clean so it looks good when Peter or Sarah Terry pay a visit – sometimes they come into the shop unannounced to check up on customer service standards

Gerry cannot afford to allow Pauline to do a poor job. If she does not do better in the future, Gerry will have to get rid of her. To achieve this improvement he must give her a specific set of standards, in writing.

Bill, on the other hand, is an **external customer** of Terry's music shop and is affected, in a dramatic way, by Pauline's 'service'.

external customers

Most employees dealing with external customers will meet examples of many different types of customer from time to time:

- customers who need information
- customers with complaints
- customers needing a special level of care – for example, children and customers with special needs

customers who need information

Customers either need specific information or they need help. Accurate and helpful information can:

- convince a person who is already thinking of buying a product that it really is what they want

  or

- persuade a person who has no real idea what they want that the product might be worth looking at

Clearly, if businesses really want these customers to buy anything, employees must know their products very well.

customers with complaints

customers with complaints

Employees may have to deal with complaints face to face or, increasingly, by telephone. Over 500,000 people in the UK work in call centres and it is certain that many of the calls they have to deal with will be complaints.

'Face to face' or 'phone to phone' a few key rules should be followed by all employees:

- **listen to the complaint** – let the person explain the problem, be sympathetic, but if they are very rude ask them to leave or cut them off the phone (call centre staff often have special 'cut off' buttons for this specific purpose)

call centres take many complaints

- be **detached** – this means the employee should never get involved and side with the complainer – the employee should remain cool and 'professional'
- consider if **help** is needed with the complaint – will it be necessary to call a a manager?
- take action, eg a refund, replacement, compensation

customers who need special care – children

Employees need certain special skills and the right kind of personality when dealing with children, whether as the children of customers or as customers themselves.

Children pose certain problems including:

- being a nuisance – they can be noisy and, if allowed to, may damage goods on display
- they can unintentionally 'steal' items by picking them up
- they can get lost

For very young children a good investment for a business – especially in larger shops – is a crèche. It keeps children amused and safe while parents get on with the serious job of shopping.

a child needs special care

customers with special needs

Dealing with special needs customers calls for a special type of care:

customers with physical disabilities

Customers with physical disabilities will need special facilities and staff will have to be very helpful to them. They may need lifts and ramps if they are in wheelchairs.

Remember that if they cannot get to parts of the business because there are no lifts (or the lift entrances are too narrow) this may be an offence under the Disability Discrimination Act 1998.

customers with learning difficulties

People who are slower than normal in carrying out simple transactions or who cannot understand simple instructions need a lot of help and support.

a lift for wheelchairs in a shop

the hearing-impaired and the visually-impaired

Some customers will be completely or partially deaf, so employees should speak clearly and face to face (so that the customer can read their lips).

Blind people and their guide dogs will often need help. Employees may be asked to accompany a blind person round a large store because they will not know the layout.

Activity 26.1 – are you good with customers?

If you already have a part time job in a shop you may already know how good you are at dealing with customers. Try this questionnaire to see how good you really are.

The maximum mark is 50. If you get over 40 it shows that you have the right attitude to deal directly with customers. 25 to 40 means that you may have a few problems dealing with customers but you can overcome them. Under 25 indicates that you should probably consider a job which does not involve much direct contact with customers!

To get your score, choose the number to show how far you agree or disagree with these statements, and then add up the numbers you have chosen.

	AGREE				DISAGREE
There is nothing wrong with a job serving other people.	5	4	3	2	1
I can always be cheerful with customers, regardless of their age or appearance.	5	4	3	2	1
Even when nothing is going right for me I am still always cheerful with customers.	5	4	3	2	1
The higher the standard of service I provide, the happier I am.	5	4	3	2	1
Dealing with problem customers does not put me off this kind of work.	5	4	3	2	1
When people compliment me on the service I provide it gives me a lot of pleasure.	5	4	3	2	1
Doing well in all aspects of my job is very important to me.	5	4	3	2	1
I am always enthusiastic about my job.	5	4	3	2	1
I like to think that I am a professional when it comes to customer contact.	5	4	3	2	1

levels of service expected by customers

Customers will normally expect all of these aspects of customer care . . .

good value products or services

Companies like Marks & Spencer provide good quality products at reasonable prices. They always require very high standards from their suppliers and they give them specific instructions as to what they require.

trained in customer care

enquiries are dealt with quickly and efficiently

Customers expect problems and enquiries to be handled quickly and by people who know what they are doing. Many shops pay a lot of attention to getting the right kind of staff who are bright, polite and friendly, have the right 'attitude' to customers, are prepared to train to get the right skills and are keen to learn about the products they are handling.

clear and honest information

Customers like to be told exactly what the real situation is. Many employees do not like being too honest with customers because they are frightened of how they will react. There have been cases, for example, of railway staff being physically assaulted when train delays rose to a high level.

information about suitable products

With simple products like food, staff do not really need a great deal of individual product knowledge, but for high quality technical products customers will expect staff to have a broad knowledge of all the technical detail.

In an electrical goods shop, staff will get questions like: what does this button do on a DVD recorder? What does an airport do in a PC? What is a firewire in a PC? How many pixels do you need to get a good photo off a digital camera?

Employers should always give good product training to staff selling high quality products. In practice, this does not always happen, and occasionally, shop staff do not know very much at all about their products. The problems created include

■ customers are sold the wrong items and have to come back for a refund or replacement – this creates bad feeling

■ customers get fed up with staff who do not know much, so they walk out without buying anything!

which button should I use?

after sales service

Customers will rightly expect that the service they get will continue after the sale is made. **After sales service** may start with delivery, which should be prompt and reasonably priced, if not free.

After sales service also covers anything that might go wrong with a product, whether it be a computer or a holiday. Employees should be away of customers' legal rights (see Chapter 28), so customers should be confident that if they take a product back within a reasonable period, either it will be replaced or mended, or they will get a refund.

They may be offered – for an extra payment – a guarantee scheme which provides 'at home' servicing for items like TVs and washing machines for 2 or 3 years. This does not, of course, replace any legal rights that the customer may have.

Activity 26.2 – levels of customer service

Choose a shop that you like going into and investigate the levels of types of customer service described on the two previous pages.

How do they compare with the levels of service offered by the business you are investigating for your Portfolio? Write a short report comparing the two, using the headings on the two previous pages.

Nutshell summary

- 'Customers' include internal customers (fellow-employees) and external customers who buy the products of a business.

- Employees dealing with external customers of many different types have to know what their needs are and they have to look after those needs. Types of customer include: enquirers, complainers, children, people with special needs.

- Customers have come to expect certain levels of service, including:
  - good value
  - a quick and efficient answer to enquiries
  - clear and honest information
  - after sales service

Key terms

Internal customer
An employee who relies on the services of another employee.

External customer
A person who buys the product of a business.

Special needs customers
Customers who have physical or mental disabilities.

After sales service
The service provided to a customer after a sale is made: eg delivery and guarantees.

27
Customer satisfaction

The customer is always right

Sarah Terry, one of the two directors of Terry's Music, looks after customer service in the company's four shops. She visits the shops at least one day every week and talks to regular customers.

As Sarah says, 'Younger customers expect staff to know what is going on in the contemporary music scene.' She also tries to make sure that at least one assistant in each shop knows about classical music.

On one visit to the newly appointed manager of the Derby shop, Ann Robinson, asked Sarah about using customer satisfaction surveys.

'You are really good on face-to-face customer service – all the staff know about the products and they are all friendly to the customers – but you really do need to measure customer satisfaction properly. In my last company this was really important.'

Every time Sarah heard Ann refer to her 'last company' her heart sank. She felt that other things were more important than measuring customer satisfaction. Ann kept telling her nothing was more important.

Sarah is very good at her job and has a good relationship with staff and customers. But she does not see why research into customer satisfaction is important.

a point to think about . . .

In the highly competitive retail business, measuring customer satisfaction is very important. How else can you tell whether you are keeping your customers happy and maintaining market share?

why measure customer satisfaction?

This chapter looks at why businesses need to measure **customer satisfaction**, how they do it and what they do to improve customer service.

Research into customer satisfaction involves using surveys and interviews to get **feedback** to find out what people really want.

Sarah thinks she knows what customers want. She has two teenage daughters who tell her what music they like and what the really popular DVDs are. This is useful information but it cannot replace proper research. Well-planned and well-designed customer satisfaction surveys will enable Sarah to find out what the strong and weak points of the business are.

how is customer satisfaction measured?

collection of statistics (data)

It is important to collect statistics (sometimes called 'data') to get an accurate picture of what customers think of customer service. Statistics can show businesses whether their customer service is good or bad . . .

if customer service is good there will be . . .

- an increase in the number of enquiries – enquiries show people are interested in a product or service
- an increase in the level of sales
- an increase in the number of customers – this will mean that existing customers are telling their friends, and also that advertising and marketing campaigns are working
- a fall in the number of complaints and returned products

if customer service is poor there will be . . .

- a decrease in sales
- an increase in complaints
- more items being brought back
- a fall in customer numbers – the word will be getting round just how bad the customer service is

the effect of customer service on sales

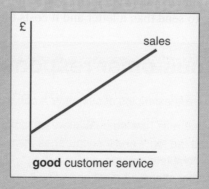

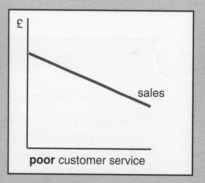

customer feedback – talking to customers

In our Case Study Sarah talks to customers' in the shops, using **on the spot questions**. This is a very useful way of getting a general impression of customer feedback, as is general **observation** of how customers behave and react.

customer feedback – questionnaires

In order to get a more thorough view, many businesses use customer service questionnaires. Well-organised businesses will provide attractive leaflets and forms for customers to complete.

These vary in design and layout but the key features will be:

- a free postage arrangement if the form is not handed in at the shop or service provider

- a manageable series of questions designed to collect as much data from customers as possible – too many questions will put people off

- questions are usually the 'tick in a box' type because they are much easier to fill in

- special offers may be made in return for completed questionnaires, eg '£1 off next purchase'

customer feedback – customer panels

Product manufacturers use panels – sometimes known as 'focus groups' – of customers to get their views on existing products and on new ones being developed. This book was designed with the help of a focus group of GCSE business students from Pershore High School, with the aim of making it 'student-friendly'.

customer feedback – websites and emails

Nowadays it is very easy for customers to enter their comments onto a feedback page on a company website. These are then sent as emails to the company Marketing Department. An email is far easier to send than a letter and it costs the customer virtually nothing.

 ## Case Study – customer response forms

On the next two pages there are examples of customer feedback forms.

The first, for Brewsters Restaurants (owned by Whitbread) looks friendly. It is in warm colours with a smiling bear at the top – and it encourages the customer to fill it in. Questions are very easy to complete and the card is not reply-paid, so customers are expected to fill it in immediately after their meal and hand it in at the bar.

The second feedback form is from the Nationwide Building Society. It is much simpler and humourous and can be folded up to form a reply-paid letter. It includes a page (not shown here) where customers can write their suggestions and comments.

Study the two forms and answer the questions in the Activity which follows.

Brewsters

from Brewers Fayre

TELL US WHAT YOU THINK.

Brewsters is committed to providing quality, value and fun in a relaxing environment.

We always aim to exceed your expectations, so it would be appreciated if you could spend two minutes answering these questions so we can make your eating out experience even better.

1. How often do you eat at Brewsters?

☐ First visit ☐ Once a week ☐ Once a fortnight

☐ Once a month ☐ Once every 3 months ☐ Less often

Would you visit again Yes ☐ No ☐
If not, why not

2. Which of the following describes the reason for your visit?

☐ Special occasion ☐ Business ☐ Family meal ☐ Casual

3. Please tell us the number in your party?

Adults (18 & over): **Children:**

4. Using the scale of 5-1, where 5 is excellent and 1 is poor, please rate the following:

	5	4	3	2	1
a) Your enjoyment	5	4	3	2	1
b) Your children's enjoyment	5	4	3	2	1
c) The quality of the food	5	4	3	2	1
d) The value for money	5	4	3	2	1
e) The friendliness of the staff	5	4	3	2	1
f) The service	5	4	3	2	1
g) The overall Brewsters experience	5	4	3	2	1

5. Did your server ask if you were fully satisfied with your meal?

Yes ☐ No ☐

6. Have you heard of Brewsters before?

NO ☐ YES ☐ if so, where?

RADIO ☐ PRESS ☐ LEAFLET ☐ WORD OF MOUTH ☐

7. Please add any other comments or suggestions that you would like to make.

questionnaire form from a Brewsters restaurant

Nationwide Building Society suggestion request

SERVICE

**Any suggestions?
Your view counts**

I wonder if...

**Any suggestions?
Your view counts**

Dear Member

At Nationwide, we want to give you the very best service every day. We'd really like your help to show us how we can do things better.

So, if you have a good idea about improving our service - whether it relates to your local branch, your postal account or our telephone service - please don't keep it to yourself. Share it with us by using this leaflet.

We promise to listen and to let you know if we put your idea into action.

Thank you for your help.

Activity 27.1 – getting customers to respond

1 Examine the Brewsters questionnaire form. What aspects of customer service is it interested in?

2 How could the answers in the Brewsters questionnaire help the company's Marketing Department?

3 In what ways is the Nationwide Building Society form different from the Brewsters form? What is the main aim of the form?

methods of improving customer service

Customer feedback may show that one or more of the areas listed below will need improving:

■ the product is not good value for money

■ the service or product is not up to the quality required

■ staff are not very friendly or helpful

■ services and products are not available when you want them

■ the exchanges and refunds system is not good enough

Activity 27.2 – customer service at Terry's

Read through the Case study on page 216 again.

Sarah has been thinking about what Ann Robinson has been saying about the need to get feedback from customers about the levels of customer service in their music stores. She has heard the following comments while walking around the Derby store:

'The stock here is a bit old – I would expect to see more new releases.'

'That shop assistant doesn't seem to know what she's talking about. I don't know what century she is living in!'

'I don't think I'll buy this album here, it's cheaper at HMV.'

'I'd come here more often, but the opening hours aren't so good.'

'I tried bringing a DVD back here the other day, but they wouldn't give me a refund.'

1   What areas of customer service need improving?
2   What methods could Sarah use to get more feedback from customers so that she can improve the level of customer service in the stores?

Nutshell summary

- It is extremely important for all organisations to research into customer satisfaction so that they can assess the strengths and weaknesses of their customer service.

- Statistics (data) can be collected in surveys which will analyse areas such as:
  - the trends in sales
  - the number of enquiries received
  - the number of customers
  - customer complaints

- Methods of obtaining feedback include:
  - observation and questioning by staff
  - questionnaires
  - customer 'panels' to discuss products and service
  - website and email responses

- Feedback on customer service problems makes it easier for the organisation to improve the level of service.

Key terms

Customer satisfaction
The level of positive response to an organisation's customer service.

Feedback
The information provided by customers on service and on product quality.

Customer questionnaire
A series of directed questions designed to produce data about levels of customer satisfaction.

Customer panels
Groups of customers who are asked by an organisation to comment on its products or services. These are also known as 'focus groups'.

28

Consumer protection

The old ones are the best!

Last week a customer came in to see Gerry Marsden, the manager of the Nottingham shop of Terry's Music. He'd bought a CD of 'Sixties' music at a bargain price of £2.99. It advertised hits by all the top Sixties groups on the cover. However, when he got it home and played it he discovered that the songs were not performed by the original artists.

He told Gerry that he wanted his money back because he had been 'conned'.

'You advertised this as Sixties music and it had all the song titles on the cover. Half of the singers on these tracks don't sound anything like the original artists. Frankly, this is a 'con' and I feel like reporting you to the local Trading Standards Department.'

Gerry had had a busy morning but he always tried to be polite.

'I am sorry, Sir, but it clearly says on the cover that these songs are not sung by the original artists. You could have asked any of my assistants if they would play it for you before you bought it – we are always happy to do that.

Would you like me to refund your £2.99 or swap the CD for something else? We are always happy to do that for any customer.'

The customer agreed to take the refund.

a point to think about . . .

The customer is nearly always right. Consumers have legal rights which can be enforced in a court of law. Gerry knows this, and so should anyone else dealing with customers.

consumer protection

A 'customer' is a person who buys goods and services.

A 'consumer' is a person who is the user of goods of services.

In the last few chapters we have discussed **customers**. In this chapter we look at the **legal protection** given to **consumers**, the end-users.

What and why the difference between the two?

Take the example of a parent who buys a cheap and shoddy teddy bear for a child, who then swallows one of its plastic eyes and ends up in hospital. The parent is the **customer**, who buys the product, but it is the child who is the **consumer**, the user, who needs protecting against dangerous products such as disintegrating teddies.

In this chapter we look at the laws which protect the consumer in the areas of:

- buying goods and services
- product labelling and product descriptions
- health and safety
- the misuse of information
- buying by mail order, by phone, digital TV or on the internet

Websites to visit:
www.tradingstandards.gov.uk
www.tradingstandards.net
www.oft.gov.uk

buying goods

The main law protecting consumers who buy goods is the **Sale of Goods Act 1979**. This states that goods should be sold:

'as described'

This means that the goods sold must be the same as in the description. You cannot sell someone a CD as 'Original Beatles Hits' when the CD was made by a group imitating them.

'of satisfactory quality'

The goods must be at least of satisfactory quality and meet the standard which a reasonable person would expect, given the price. In the Case Study the customer should not really expect a compilation of hits by original artists for £2.99, but he can expect (and did get) a CD of passable imitations.

'fit for the purpose for which they are intended'

A product should do what it is supposed to do.
A CD should play in a CD player, an umbrella should keep the rain off and a watch should keep time.

customer service desk – queries, returns and refunds

what to do if there is a problem

If any of these three above conditions is not met, the consumer is entitled to a full or a partial refund, depending on how soon the fault appears, how serious it is and how quickly the matter is taken up. Note also:

- the buyer can accept a replacement, but can also insist on a refund if a replacement is not wanted
- the buyer does not have to accept a credit note for spending on other purchases
- a shop is not entitled to put up a notice saying 'No Refunds!'

wrong!

buying services

The **Supply of Goods and Services Act 1982** protects the consumer when a service is provided by a business.

This Act states that anyone who supplies a service – a haircut, a train journey, a holiday – must carry out the work

- with 'reasonable' care and skill
- within a 'reasonable' time
- at a 'reasonable' price

the train must be reasonably punctual

The problem is, how do you decide what 'reasonable' is? Does a train have to arrive on time or just the same day? Does it matter if the holiday apartment is next to a building site?

The consumer is helped by standards laid down by various bodies: Trade Associations, professional bodies, or one of the official 'Watchdog' bodies which keep an eye on public services. Many service businesses that believe in customer care – railway companies, for example, operate compensation schemes when service s standards are not reached.

descriptions, prices and labels

The **Trade Descriptions Act 1968** makes it a criminal offence:

- to make false statements about goods offered for sale
- to make misleading statements about services

This Act affects false or misleading adverts, packaging and labels. For example:

- showing a picture of a juicy meat pie on packaging which bears little resemblance to the sad looking pasty inside
- making a misleading statement about a service, eg 'our dry cleaning is guaranteed to remove every stain' when it does not, or 'our apartments are within easy reach of the sea' when they are fifteen miles away
- 'clocking' a second-hand car which is for sale, eg changing the mileage indicator from 150,000 miles to 50,000 miles – unfortunately a widespread practice these days

wrong!

The **Weights and Measures Act 1986** requires that the weights and quantities of goods for sale should be clearly and accurately indicated. The Act makes it a criminal offence to label goods so that consumers do not receive the weight and quantity of goods that the labelling indicates. A trader who sells 'short' and who has inaccurate weighing equipment is breaking the law.

seatbelts are required by law

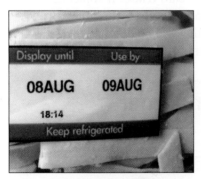

food safety for pasta

health and safety

We have already discussed the **Health and Safety at Work Act 1974** (page 158) which requires that an organisation maintains a healthy and safe working environment. In the case of a shop or business with public access, this law protects visiting consumers who might slip on a wet floor or be injured in some way.

There are two other laws which protect consumers from being harmed . . .

The first is the **Consumer Protection Act 1987** which makes it a criminal offence to supply unsafe goods. 'Unsafe' means goods which are in breach of the safety regulations which apply to those goods, for example:

- cosmetics should not contain lead or other materials harmful to health
- electrical equipment must have safe switches and insulation
- cars should have seat belts

Safety standards for products are regulated by the British Standards Institute (BSI) which issues its well-known 'kitemark'.

The Food Safety Act 1990 regulates the quality of food that is sold to consumers. The law requires that:

- food contents do not contain harmful substances
- food must be labelled with 'best by' and 'use by' dates and storage instructions and warnings about substances that could cause allergic reactions
- ingredients and additives must be listed
- hygiene in outlets such as restaurants and burger stalls must be controlled

control of information

The Data Protection Act 1998 regulates the use of personal information held by organisations on computer file and on paper records. Every time a consumer fills in a form from a business and gives personal details, you can be sure that the information will be used for marketing purposes. The problem for the consumer about information held is that:

- it may be incorrect and misleading
- it may be passed to other organisations without the consumer knowing

The Act requires that the information be kept securely and confidentially and that the 'subject' can have access to it, for a fee. Visit www.dataprotection.gov.uk for further information.

distance selling

Nowadays more and more goods and services are being bought from home – by mail order, telephone, digital TV and on the internet. This is known as **distance selling**. It is very convenient, but can be dangerous as the goods or services may not arrive, or they may be different from what was expected.

The **Consumer Protection (Distance Selling) Regulations 2000**, generally known as the **Distance Selling Regulations**, have been introduced to protect consumers who buy in this way. The Distance Selling Regulations require that:

- the seller must provide the buyer with **full information**, including: the name of the seller, the price, an accurate description of the goods or service, delivery arrangement, payment arrangements – all backed up with written confirmation

- the buyer has **the right to cancel the agreement**
    - for goods, seven working days after receipt – eg a TV
    - for services, seven working days after the agreement to buy the service, eg a holiday

There is also protection against credit card **fraud**. If someone fraudulently uses a credit card number in a distance selling transaction – eg over the internet – the card holder will get the money back, as long as the fraud is notified promptly.

Activity 28.1 – protecting the consumer

What are the consumer's rights in the following situations?

What should they say to the shop in each case?

Write down a summary of what you would advise, mentioning the law or set of regulations which is involved in each situation.

1 Jonni buys a CD of his favourite band. When he opens the box at home he finds a CD of Cliff Richard songs.

   The shop has run out of the CD he wants and offers him a credit note.

2 Kate buys a new pair of jeans and the next day finds that the zip is faulty. She takes them back to the shop, but the assistant points to a notice saying 'No refunds'.

3 Alex buys a new pair of shoes which are sold as 'leather effect'. A friend tells him that they are not real leather. He takes them back to the shop and demands a refund.

4 Jade buys a teddy bear for her young brother at Christmas from the local store, and gets a real bargain.

   On Boxing Day her brother is admitted to hospital having swallowed both the teddy's eyes.

5 Tim buys a jacket from an internet shop, but when he gets it, the colour is not quite what he thought it was. 'Tough luck,' says his brother Jack, 'you can't return it now! It was bought online.'

6 Sophie has bought some salmon from the corner shop. The label showing the sell-by date seemed to have been torn off, but the shopkeeper said, 'Its fine. You just need to cook it long enough. Anyway at that price I don't think you should complain.' Sophie's family eat the salmon and all go down with food poisoning.

 # Nutshell summary

- Customers and consumers are given a great deal of protection in law.

- When a customer buys goods, the goods should be 'as described … of satisfactory quality … fit for the purpose'. When a customer buys services, the service should be provided with 'reasonable' care, within a 'reasonable' time' and at a 'reasonable' price.

- Consumers are protected against false and misleading labels, packaging and pricing.

- Sellers are obliged in law to indicate weights and quantities clearly and accurately and to ensure that goods are safe to use. Food that is sold must be safe in date and free from harmful ingredients.

- Personal data held by organisations is controlled by law, and the 'subject' of the data can have access to it.

- Selling on the internet is strictly regulated and goods bought may be returned if the buyer wishes.

 # Key terms

Customer
The person who buys a product.

Consumer
The person who uses a product.

Legal protection
Know what these laws cover:
- Sales of Goods Act
- Supply of Goods & Services Act
- Trade Descriptions Act
- Weights and Measures Act
- Health & Safety at Work Act
- Consumer Protection Act
- Weights and Measures Act
- Food Safety Act
- Data Protection Act
- Distance Selling Regulations

Business Finance

This unit introduces you to the ways in which a business depends on the money which it receives and spends. Business finance – which is assessed by a written test – involves a number of different areas:

- the documents involved in financial transactions, the ways in which they are recorded, and the different methods of making payment

- the financial statements produced by a business which show how profitable it is and how much it is worth

- the need for a business to plan carefully so that it knows what its income and costs will be, and if it will break-even

- the planning needed so that a business can approach a lender and borrow money

- the use of computer programs to help with the 'number crunching' needed in business finance

Unit **3**

Chapters in this Unit...

29

The costs of starting a business

Webwise

Ella was the computer expert at work. Whenever anything went wrong she was asked to fix the problem. In her spare time at home she surfed the net and spent hours chatting and shopping online. She was often told by friends and people at work, 'I wish I could learn to use a computer properly'.

Then Ella won £150,000 on the Lottery. She had always fancied training people to operate computers and to access the internet. Now she had the money she needed to start up a business of her own.

Ella's plan was to set up a training centre in which she could train people to operate computers and also have a 'drop in' section where the public could come in and surf the net.

Ella had a brainstorming session with her friends and decided to call the business 'Webwise'.

But what was it all going to cost? Would she have enough money? Ella started to work out what her expenses were going to be. She soon realised that she needed expert help and so she visited her local bank to talk over her ideas with a business adviser. He pointed out that she needed to look at her start-up costs and her running costs.

a point to think about . . .

A good business idea is important, but careful planning and reliable advice are essential if that business idea is to succeed.

business revenue

Ella will need money to start her business. She has the Lottery money but this will not last for ever. Businesses raise their money from a number of different sources – the owners putting money in, banks making loans and money coming in when the business trades.

Revenue is the money received from the sale of the **products** of a business. Products can be haircuts, taxi rides, clothes, mobile phones or computer training courses. The sales revenue can make the difference between the success or failure of the business.

We will look in detail at revenue in later chapters of this book.

types of cost

When a business starts up for the first time, the owner needs to plan what he or she will need to get going.

There are two main types of cost:

- start-up costs
- running costs

make a note . . .

Start-up costs   are 'one-off' costs you have to pay when you start up a new business – for example buying a computer and furniture.

Running costs   are day-to-day costs you have to pay to run the business – for example wages and telephone bills.

Activity 29.1 – types of cost

1 Start-up costs and running costs have to be paid not only by businesses but also by individuals.

   Sort out which of the following are start-up costs and which are running costs.
   Write a list for each under the headings 'Start-up costs' and 'Running costs.'

   - buying a mobile phone
   - buying a phone 'top-up' voucher
   - buying a printer ink cartridge
   - buying a computer printer
   - buying a box of biros
   - buying a desk

2 Think of some more start-up costs and running costs and add them to your list.

3 The money a business receives from selling its products is its revenue. If you are starting up in business what costs do you think your revenue from sales will cover – start-up costs or running costs? Give a reason for your answer.

business start-up costs

There will be a number of start-up costs for a new business. These will, of course, vary with the type of business. A taxi firm will have different costs from a website designer. Start-up costs are explained on the next page.

premises to let

premises

Many new businesses will need premises, unless the business owner is working from home. Premises could be a new factory or workshop (for a manufactured product), a shop or an office (for a service).

But the owner of a business may not always be able to afford to buy premises. They can be rented, which will be cheaper.

Rent is not a start-up cost but a running cost.

machinery and equipment

A business is likely to need machinery and equipment of one sort or another when starting up. The term 'machinery and equipment' includes items such as production-line machinery, computers, photocopiers, fax machines and telephones.

Very often these items can also be rented or 'leased' – this will save on start-up costs.

fixtures and fittings

Another category of costs is described as 'fixtures and fittings.'

These are items which are 'fixed' and 'fitted' in the business premises. They include items such as carpets, lighting and furniture – all of which are needed in a new business and will need financing as a start-up-cost.

market research and advertising

A less obvious start-up cost is market research and advertising.

market research

There is no point in starting up a business if nobody is going to buy your product. There must be a demand for it. People must want it.

The successful business researches its market thoroughly and then promotes its product by means of advertising.

Market research can be carried out by an outside agency, or the business owner can draw up a questionnaire to find out what the public thinks of its product.

Advertising can then follow if the product seems to be what the market wants.

Market research and advertising can be expensive and are a significant start-up cost.

Activity 29.2 – Ella's start-up costs

Ella is estimating the costs of her new computer training business – Webwise.

She has won £150,000 on the Lottery but has not as yet thought about obtaining any further finance from elsewhere.

She has drawn up a 'shopping list' of start-up costs:

- Office premises — £125,000
- Computer equipment and software — £32,000
- Office furniture and fittings — £3,000
- Fee for market research — £2,500
- Adverts in local paper — £500
- Advertising leaflets — £2,000

1   What is the total of Ella's start-up costs?

2   Can you think of any other start-up costs she may have to pay?

3   Ella has seen an office for sale at £125,000. She would really like somewhere bigger than this, but bigger offices are more expensive. She is also worried about spending out so much of her winnings just on one item. How could she obtain bigger premises without having to spend so much money?

running costs for the new business

Running costs are day-to-day costs which a business has to pay.

It is important to know the difference between running costs and start-up costs. The difference applies to personal finance as well as business finance. For example, if you think about buying a new personal stereo, the start-up cost is the price of the machine, while the running costs are items like batteries which you buy from time to time to keep it playing.

types of running cost

You will know from your studies that there are a number of different functions in a business – sales and finance, for example. In a small business the owner is likely to do most of these himself or herself. In a larger business there will be separate departments for these functions. There are running costs for each of these areas. Look at the diagram on the next page.

business running costs

sales and marketing

The cost of making sure that the right products reach the right customers in the best possible way: advertising, providing customer care, getting customer feedback.

administration

The day-to-day costs of running the business: insurance, rent, rates, electricity, stationery, telephone bills, postage.

production

The cost of manufacturing a product or producing a service, eg sheet steel for a car manufacturer, goods bought by a shop to sell to its customers, air fares and hotel charges for a travel company, food for a restaurant.

human resources

The cost of employing staff, eg wages, recruitment costs, staff perks, training, Health & Safety (making sure people are safe at work).

finance

The financial cost of running the business: paying interest to the bank if money is borrowed, bank charges, paying accountancy fees.

Activity 29.3 - identifying running costs

1   Look at the business activities shown on the next page. Identify the manufacturing, retail and service businesses.

2   Make a list of the running costs each type of business is likely to have to pay.

3   What will be source of the sales revenue for each business?

4   How might a manufacturing company reduce its main running costs – the cost of labour and materials – if it finds its UK factories are becoming too expensive to run?

Activity 29.4 - Ella's running costs

Ella has now estimated her running costs for her computer training business for the first year. She has decided to rent premises rather than buy them. The list of the costs for the first year is as follows:

Office rental	£20,000
Training materials	£5,000
Advertising	£4,800
Wages	£30,000
Accountant's fees	£1,500
Bank charges	£440
Electricity bills	£450
Office insurance	£1,800
Office rates	£1,650
Telephone bills	£800
Stationery	£560

1   What is the total of Ella's running costs? Use a calculator if you need to.

2   Draw up a chart with six columns in the format shown on the next page.

Use an A4 piece of paper turned on its side, or, if you can, set up a suitable computer spreadsheet.

Make sure the left-hand column is about twice as wide as the other five. Head up the columns as shown.

Using Ella's running cost figures shown above, enter the type of running expense (eg advertising, staff wages, bank charges etc) in the left-hand column and the money amounts on the same row in the column which describes the type of expense. To give you a start, the figure for office rental is already entered in the 'office expenses' column.

Add up each money column and write the totals on the bottom line (or set up a formula if you are using a spreadsheet).

Add up the column totals and then check the total with your answer to 1 above. If the amounts are different you will need to check your workings.

Webwise					
type of expense	materials £	sales & marketing £	human resources £	finance £	office expenses £
office rental					20,000
TOTAL					

ICT and cost saving

There are many ways in which ICT (information and communication technology) can help save costs. The Activity that follows looks at a range of situations where computers and technology have helped businesses to become more efficient.

Activity 29.5 – saving costs with ICT

Look at the uses of ICT in the businesses shown below and then answer the questions that follow.

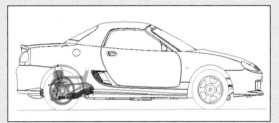

an MG sports car at the design stage

computer aided design (CAD)

Modern car design is made more efficient by computer simulations of car interiors and exteriors. This design used to be carried out by the use of expensive hand-made mock-ups using wood, metal and plastic.

CAD speeds up the design process and saves a lot of money.

bar codes and e-commerce

Bar codes are widely used in retailing. Each product has a unique bar code which can be scanned at the checkout. This sends data about the product sale to the shop's computer. As a result the business knows what stock it has got, what it has sold and what it needs to order. Orders for new stock can be placed direct with the supplier electronically from the shop's computer to the supplier's computer.

the barcode for this book

1   What costs does computer aided design (CAD) help to save?
    How could CAD also be useful for a car company in a very competitive market?

2   How do bar codes on products help a shop on a day-to-day basis?
    How does this help to save money?

3   What other examples can you find where applications of ICT in business help to reduce costs?

Nutshell summary

- Businesses are financed from a number of sources:
  - money from the owner
  - bank loans
  - sales revenue
- When businesses start up they will have to cover their costs in order to succeed.
- There are two main types of cost:
  - start-up costs
  - running costs
- Start-up costs have to be paid when a business starts up for the first time. They may include:
  - premises
  - machinery and equipment
  - fixtures and fittings
  - market research and advertising
- Running costs are the day-to-day costs a business pays in order to keep running. They include costs in the following areas:
  - sales and marketing
  - human resources
  - production
  - administration
  - finance
- Different types of business will have different categories of cost. The main types of business considered are
  - manufacturing
  - retail
  - service
- The introduction of ICT has helped many businesses save costs. Two significant ICT developments are:
  - computer aided design (CAD)
  - bar code scanning

Key terms

Revenue
Money received by a business from the sale of its products.

Product
A manufactured item or service sold by a business.

Start-up costs
One-off costs paid when a business starts up.

Running costs
Day-to-day costs which a business pays to run the business.

Manufacturing business
A business which makes a product which it sells to produce revenue.

Retail business
A business which buys a range of products to sell to the public to produce revenue.

Service business
A business which provides a service as its 'product' to produce sales revenue.

CAD
Computer aided design (CAD) allows a business to create designs on a computer screen.

30
Financing a business

Webwise

Ella plans to start up a computer training centre – Webwise. She has won £150,000 on the Lottery and intends to use some of the money to set up the business.

She has gone to the bank to talk to a business adviser. He has told her about her start-up costs and her running costs.

Her thoughts now turn to how she is going to finance the business. She knows that her £150,000 will more or less cover all her costs – but there is little to spare. She has wondered about buying a flat for herself, and she will need a deposit for that. She also wants to change her car and fancies taking her partner on a holiday to Barbados.

Should she borrow some money from the bank so that she can keep some of her own savings?

Are there any other ways of raising finance? Could she get a grant? Does she have to buy her business premises?

Does she have to buy computers, which will soon go out of date?

She decides to go for a further chat with the bank business adviser.

a point to think about . . .

Financing a business involves deciding how much you are going to invest yourself and how much you need to raise from outside sources.

financing start-up costs and running costs

A business adviser will point out a number of different sources of finance for a small business such as Ella's. Some finance is available straightaway; some finance will become available in the longer term.

finance available straightaway – for start-up costs

- the money – capital – put in by the owner
- bank loans
- grants from local and central Government

finance available in the longer term – for running costs

- profits made by the business that can be put back in the business
- a bank overdraft (loan) to cover day-to-day running expenses

This money will not be needed straightaway. The profit will be received and the overdraft borrowing taken as the business trades.

The diagram below shows the main sources of finance and how that finance is used for start-up costs and running costs.

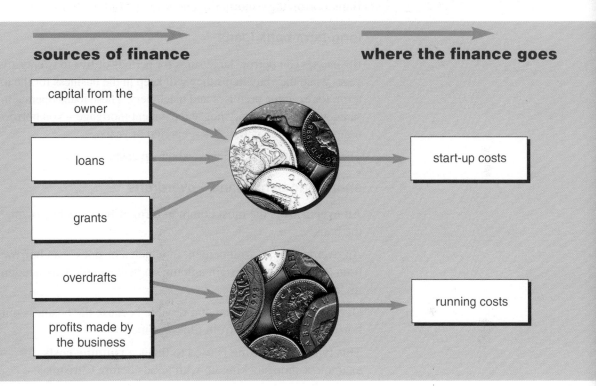

sources of finance

where the finance goes

- capital from the owner
- loans
- grants
- overdrafts
- profits made by the business

- start-up costs
- running costs

capital from the owner

A business starting up for the first time will always rely on the amount of money – the **capital** – invested by the owner.

Capital is the money investment of the owner of a business.

Capital is **internal finance** – it does not come from outside.

For a sole trader or partnership business the capital is the amount put in by the sole trader or the partners.

For a limited company the capital is the **share capital** – the money invested by the shareholders of the company.

Capital is paid in when a business starts up for the first time and can be 'topped up' by the owners when the business plans to expand.

Ella in the Case Study will have to decide how much of her £150,000 she will invest as capital.

loan finance

Many businesses rely on borrowing from the bank when they start up and also when they have a short-term need for money. Borrowing from the bank is **external finance**.

When businesses borrow they have to pay **interest** to the bank on the amount that they borrow – this is another running cost of the business.

Bank borrowing is normally either long-term or short-term.

long-term bank loans

Businesses can borrow large sums for periods of five to twenty-five years when they buy items they will keep in the business for the long-term, for example premises and machinery. These loans operate in the same way as an ordinary house repayment mortgage – you borrow a lump sum and repay it over a set period of years.

These loans are used to finance **start-up costs**.

short-term bank loans – overdrafts

An **overdraft** is the most common form of business borrowing from the bank.

An overdraft is an arrangement in which a business can borrow from time to time up to a certain amount on its business bank account – its 'current account.'

Overdrafts are convenient and flexible because the business only borrows what it needs from time-to-time.

This type of borrowing is used to finance **running costs**, for example a shop stocking up with goods before Christmas.

loans from family and friends

People starting up in business are sometimes helped by their family and friends who may be willing to lend them money. This may be a cheaper form of borrowing because the interest rate may be lower, or even zero!

make a note . . .

Interest calculation

The interest on a loan is calculated by using the formula:

$$\frac{\text{amount of loan} \ \times \ \text{interest rate} \ \times \ \text{number of years of loan}}{100}$$

If you borrow £1,000 at 5% for one year you will pay during that year:

$$\frac{£1,000 \ \times \ 5 \ \times \ 1}{100} \qquad = \quad £50 \ interest$$

Activities 30.1 – the cost of Ella's loans

The bank adviser suggests to Ella that she might consider taking out a bank loan for £10,000 to finance some of her start-up costs. The bank loan interest rate is 10% per year.

Ella goes home and her Uncle Matt says that he will lend her the same amount, but at an interest rate of 5%.

1   Calculate the amount of interest Ella will pay on the bank loan for the first year.

2   Calculate the amount of interest Ella will pay on her uncle's loan for the first year.

3   If Ella has the £10,000 anyway, what would be the cost to her personally of investing it in the business as capital?

grants

Businesses can apply for grants from the Local Authority, from the Government and the European Union to provide money for projects which will benefit society and the economy. Grants are available, for example, for businesses which create jobs in areas of high unemployment and for businesses which invest in new technology.

Grants are normally used to finance **start-up costs**.

Case Study – Ella applies for a grant

Ella has found out from her business adviser that the Government is offering grants for businesses that develop the use of information technology and training.

Ella goes to her local Business Link office and they interview her and give her all the forms she needs to complete.

The forms then have to be sent off to the Department of Trade and Industry (DTI) who will consider her application for a grant of £5,000. They will let her know their decision in a few weeks' time.

Ella has decided that if she is successful she will use the £5,000 to help pay for her computer equipment.

leasing

Businesses can often avoid paying high levels of start-up costs by **leasing** assets (items owned) instead of buying them.

FOR SALE / TO LET

HIGH TECH BUSINESS UNITS

FROM 2050 SQ FT (191 SQ M)
TO 6150 SQ FT (572 SQ M)

property can be leased to cut down on start-up costs

A lease is an agreement where the business pays a regular amount – often monthly – to a leasing company for the use of items such as computers and cars. The items are in effect 'rented' from the leasing company for an extended period of time – often a number of years.

The leased items – eg computers and cars – belong to the leasing company and not to the business.

A lease is useful where the business needs the cars or computers but wants to replace them regularly because they either wear out or go out of date quickly.

In financial terms lease payments are **running costs**. A lease saves a business having to pay out on **start-up costs**.

financing from profit

Profit equals sales revenue minus running costs.

Profit is the difference between the money received from the sale of products and the money spent on running costs.

Profit is an important internal source of finance for the running costs of a business.

If a business makes a profit, the money can either be taken out by the owner for personal use or it can be left in the business to finance its day-to-day operations. Most owners leave a certain amount of profit in the business. In the diagram below, the owner leaves £20,000 profit in the business and takes out 'drawings' of £20,000.

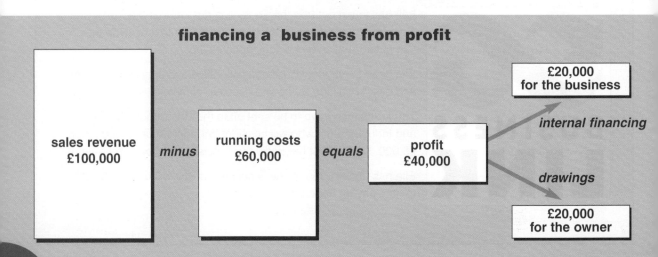

financing a business from profit

sales revenue £100,000 *minus* running costs £60,000 *equals* profit £40,000

£20,000 for the business — *internal financing*

drawings — £20,000 for the owner

Case Study – financial decisions for Ella

decisions to be made

Ella talks to the bank business adviser, who helps her to decide on the forms of finance she will need. He points out that she needs to answer a number of questions before she can come to a conclusion:

- 'How much money should I put in as capital?'
- 'How much of my own money do I need to keep to invest for myself or to spend on myself?'
- 'What are my business start-up costs?'
- 'What finance do I need for start-up costs?'
- 'What are my running costs for the first year?'
- 'What finance do I need for running costs?'

how much capital?

Ella has £150,000 from her Lottery win and has decided to keep £75,000 of this for her own use. She wants to put down a deposit on a flat, start a pension, buy a car and have a holiday.

So she has £75,000 to invest as capital to cover her business costs.

finance for start-up costs?

Ella has calculated that her start-up costs will be £50,000. But if she uses up £50,000 of her £75,000 capital on this, she will not have much left for paying her running costs. She decides therefore to raise £15,000 to help to pay for the computers (part of the start-up costs):

the loan from her uncle	£10,000
the grant through Business Link	£5,000

This will mean she will use £35,000 of her capital (£50,000 minus £15,000) on start-up costs. This will leave her £40,000 to contribute towards the first year's running costs.

finance for running costs?

Ella has worked out that her running costs for the year – including the office rental – will be £67,000. To this she decides to add £25,000 for her own living expenses (drawings). So in total she needs £92,000. But Ella also hopes that in the first year she will receive an income of £85,000 from selling her courses. Her forecast for the first year shows that she could need £7,000:

	Sales revenue from selling courses	£85,000
minus	Running costs for the year	£67,000
minus	Ella's living expenses	£25,000
equals	Shortfall which will need to be financed	– £7,000

the bank adviser's advice – the business plan

Where is the £7,000 going to come from? The bank adviser points out that Ella has £40,000 of her capital left which will comfortably cover the £7,000.

But he issues some warnings:

What would happen if she did not sell as many courses as she had hoped and her sales revenue was a lot lower?

What would happen if her costs were higher than she had calculated?

Ella has two possible courses of action:

- Use up more of her capital (if there is enough).

- Arrange an overdraft loan with the bank. This will enable her to borrow money when she needs to. She will repay it as and when the money comes in from sales revenue.

Before the bank can consider Ella for an overdraft loan, she will have to draw up a business plan. This is a document which gives a full picture of what the business does, what money it needs and what money it expects to make from its sales. The business plan is explained in full in Chapter 38.

conclusion

Ella can leave the meeting with the adviser reasonably confident that she has enough capital to cover her start-up costs and running costs. Her main worry is that she may not be able to sell as many courses as she had planned, in which case she could arrange a bank overdraft to keep her going.

limited company financing

Ella's 'Webwise' business is a sole trader business. She invests the capital herself and takes the profit. If she takes in a partner, the partner will invest further capital and they will share the profits. The financing of a limited company, however, is very different.

limited company share capital

The owners of a limited company are the **shareholders** who are issued shares in return for their investment.

Some limited company shares can be bought and sold on the Stock Markets. These are the larger 'PLCs' (public limited companies) which are often household names – Dixons and Tesco, for example.

But most limited companies are smaller. Their shares are normally owned by the directors of the company and are not for public sale.

financing expansion

financing a limited company

Many limited companies are expanding – opening up abroad, buying other companies, introducing new products and so on.

They need finance in order to do this. This can be achieved in a number of ways:

- selling parts of the business to raise cash, for example selling a chain of shops

- issuing new shares to existing and new shareholders to raise additional money

venture capital

Companies – particularly smaller new companies – may issue shares to **venture capital** companies. These are specialist investment businesses who will buy shares in new companies, providing them with capital and expecting them to grow and be a source of profit. Venture capital companies normally expect to 'sell out' – ie to sell the shares at a profit – in a number of years time.

Case Study – venture capital finance

Biostat Limited is a new medical research company which is being formed by a group of researchers to develop a cure for degenerative diseases such as AIDS.

Biostat Limited knows that if it finds a cure its shares will be very valuable.

The company has been given the financing it needs by a venture capital company, Ceres Developments Limited.

Ceres is investing £1 million in return for 50,000 Biostat shares and the appointment of a director on the board of Biostat Limited.

Ceres knows that if Biostat is successful it will be able eventually to sell its 50,000 shares at a substantial profit. In the meantime the director appointed by Ceres Developments will be able to keep an eye on the development of Biostat Limited.

Activities 30.2 – finance for costs

1 Use the following words and phrases in the gapped sentences below.

internal	lease	start-up	grants	venture capital
long-term loan	running	bank overdraft	external	

Business profit is an .... form of finance, but a business loan is an .... form of finance.

Businesses can .... a computer rather than buy it. This will result in a .... cost rather than a .... cost.

A .... is a form of finance for running costs, but a .... is a form of finance for a start-up cost.

.... companies invest in the shares of other companies that need financing.

Businesses can sometimes obtain .... if they provide jobs in areas of high unemployment.

2 Viv Oliver is starting a new business as a website designer. She intends to open up a small office in the town, where she will employ a designer and a programmer. She herself will do most of the marketing and selling.

She has a total of £20,000 from an inheritance which she is investing as capital.

She hopes to receive fee income of £100,000 in the first year.

She has estimated the following costs: new computers £10,000, office costs for the year £55,000, start-up advertising £2,500, wages for the year £40,000, her own living expenses for the year £25,000, furniture and equipment for the office £2,500.

(a) What are her running costs, start-up costs and total costs for the first year?

(b) Will she cover her costs? If not, what extra money does she need?

(c) Suggest <u>one</u> suitable form of finance for her start-up costs and <u>one</u> suitable form of finance for her running costs.

Nutshell summary

- The start-up costs of a business may be financed from a number of sources:
  - money (capital) from the owner
  - bank loans
  - grants from local and central government
- The running costs of a business may be financed from a number of sources:
  - profits made by the business
  - a bank overdraft (short-term loan)
- Businesses are financed *internally* by the capital invested by the owner.
- Businesses also raise finance *externally* from banks. This finance can be in the form of:
  - loans for start-up costs
  - overdrafts for running costs
- Businesses have to pay interest on money borrowed. Interest is calculated as:

$$\frac{amount\ of\ loan\ \times\ interest\ rate\ \times\ number\ of\ years}{100}$$

- Business owners can also raise loans from friends and family. These can have the advantage of a low rate of interest.
- Businesses can also apply for Government grants.
- Businesses can avoid high set-up costs by leasing items such as cars and computers. Leasing involves paying regular amounts for the use of the items.
- The capital of a limited company is in the form of shares issued to the shareholders of the company.
- Limited companies can finance expansion by selling parts of the business to raise cash or by issuing new shares.
- Limited companies starting up for the first time can finance the business by entering into an arrangement with a venture capital company, which will buy its shares and help to manage it.

Key terms

Capital
Money invested in the business by its owner.

Internal finance
Financing of a business by its owner or from profits made.

External finance
Financing of a business from outside sources, eg banks.

Overdraft
Flexible borrowing by a business on its bank account.

Share capital
Money invested by the shareholders of a company.

Shareholders
The owners of a limited company who hold shares.

Interest
Money charged on lending, normally as a percentage.

Leasing
An arrangement where a business 'rents' items rather than buying them.

Profit
Sales revenue minus the running costs of a business.

Venture capital
Company financing in the form of shares bought by a specialist investment company.

31

Budgeting and planning

a trip to Barbados

Budgeting in business, like personal budgeting, involves making plans to achieve objectives – something that you want. It involves planning and control.

Ella, who has won £150,000 on the Lottery, is planning the holiday of a lifetime for her partner and herself in the Caribbean island of Barbados.

First of all Ella must look at her income – how much money has she got and what can she afford to spend on the holiday? She reckons she can afford about £5,000 for a fortnight for two people. This is her *income budget*. As in business, if she wanted to spend more than she had available, she could always finance the holiday by means of a loan.

Then Ella must look at her expenditure. She writes down headings and costs such as 'flights', 'hotel', 'entertainment money', 'visits', and 'emergencies'. She adds them up and find that they come to about £4,000. This is her *expenses budget*.

When she is on holiday she must monitor her spending and make sure she is not running out of money. This is the *control process* of budgeting.

a point to think about . . .

Businesses, like holidays, never go exactly to plan. The important factor is to keep an eye on what is happening and take action when things turn out differently.

what is a business budget?

As a business plans ahead, it will set targets for income and costs – normally over the period of a year:

- a **sales budget** will estimate the number of products a business plans to sell and the amount of sales revenue it will receive

- a **production budget** will estimate the number of products a business will make or provide and the cost of producing those items

- **departmental budgets** will estimate the running costs of different areas of the business

Set out below is an example of a sales revenue budget of a business with three departments. Six months' figures are shown. Budgets can (and often do) show the figures for the whole year.

sales revenue budget (extract)

	January	February	March	April	May	June	Total
	£	£	£	£	£	£	£
Department A	1,000	1,000	1,000	1,000	1,000	1,000	6,000
Department B	1,500	1,500	1,500	1,500	1,500	1,500	9,000
Department C	2,500	2,500	2,500	2,500	2,500	2,500	15,000
Total Sales	5,000	5,000	5,000	5,000	5,000	5,000	30,000

The diagram below shows how the income and costs budgets work together and link into the **cash budget.** The cash budget estimates the money flowing in and out of the bank account each month.

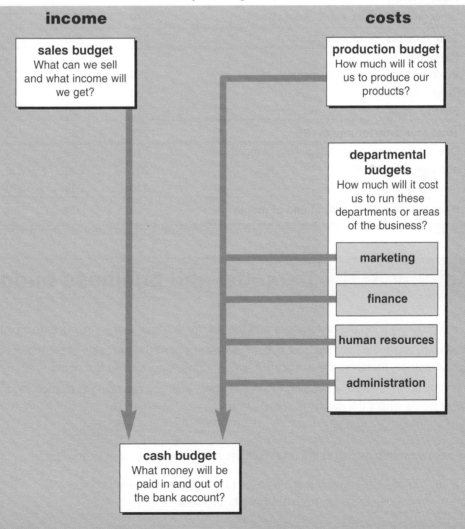

income

sales budget
What can we sell and what income will we get?

costs

production budget
How much will it cost us to produce our products?

departmental budgets
How much will it cost us to run these departments or areas of the business?

marketing

finance

human resources

administration

cash budget
What money will be paid in and out of the bank account?

cash budget

The **cash budget**, also known as the **cash-flow forecast** links all the other budgets together. It estimates the amounts of money received into the bank account and paid out of the bank account each month.

A typical cash budget shows sales revenue, start-up costs and running costs.

The 'bottom line' of each monthly column shows the forecast bank balance at the end of that month.

Study the format shown below. The calculations contained in it will be explained in detail in the next chapter.

CASH BUDGET	Jan £000	Feb £000	Mar £000	Apr £000
Receipts				
Sales revenue	150	150	161	170
Other receipts (loans, capital from owner)	70	80	75	80
Total receipts for month (A)	220	230	236	250
Payments				
Purchases of raw materials or stock	160	165	170	170
Running costs	50	50	50	60
Start-up costs		50		
Total payments for month (B)	210	265	220	230
Opening bank balance at beginning of month	10	20	(15)	1
add total receipts (A)	220	230	236	250
minus total payments (B)	210	265	220	230
Bank balance (overdraft) at end of month	20	(15)	1	21

Activity 31.1 – personal and business budgets

1   You are planning a trip out somewhere with friends, for example to the cinema or to a club.

Write down, under the heading 'cost budget', estimates of all the the costs of the trip, for example any new clothes, transport there, entrance tickets, drink, food, shared taxi home.

Then write down, under the heading 'income budget', how you are going to finance the trip – in other words where the money is coming from.

This is your personal budget.

2   Now write down the names of the main budgets that businesses have to draw up.

3   Will a car manufacturer have the same range of budgets as a holiday company? Explain why budgets can vary from business to business.

monitoring the budgets

Setting a budget in the first place is only half the story. It certainly helps with planning personal activities and business activities. But what if circumstances change? What if something goes wrong?

It is essential that budgets are monitored – in other words the figures that have been projected have to be checked against what actually happens. This is known as **monitoring**.

There are three main stages in budgeting:

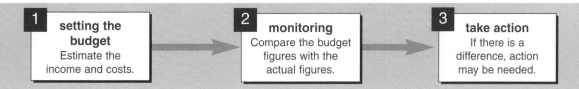

| 1 | **setting the budget** Estimate the income and costs. | → | 2 | **monitoring** Compare the budget figures with the actual figures. | → | 3 | **take action** If there is a difference, action may be needed. |

monitoring business budgets

When businesses monitor their budgets the process is more formal and carried out in a **budget report**.

In the example below the three columns with figures represent (from the left) the budgeted figures, the actual figures and the **variance**. The variance is the the actual figure *minus* the budgeted figure.

SALES BUDGET REPORT
Month October   **Date**   7 November

	budget	actual	variance
Product A	£60,000	£55,000	– £5,000
Product B	£75,000	£65,000	– £10,000
Product C	£80,000	£85,000	+ £5,000
Total	£215,000	£205,000	– £10,000

the estimated sales figures   the actual sales figures   the difference between the actual and budgeted figures

is action needed?

A minus sign for the Sales variance means that Sales are below target – the Sales Force will need consulting and sales will have to improve. If there is a plus sign for a Costs variance (eg Production) it means that costs are over target and will have to be cut.

Activity 31.2 – understanding business budgets

You are on a work experience placement in the Finance Department of Peakwear, a mail order company that sells its own brand of outdoor clothing, largely through catalogues and its website.

You have been shown some budgets for the first six months of the year . . .

SALES BUDGET

	January £	February £	March £	April £	May £	June £	Total £
Clothing Sales	120,000	140,000	150,000	150,000	170,000	190,000	920,000

PRODUCTION BUDGET

	January £	February £	March £	April £	May £	June £	Total £
Clothing Costs	60,000	70,000	75,000	75,000	85,000	95,000	460,000

You have been told by the Finance Manager that the *actual* results for June were:

Sales	£175,000
Production	£110,000

He points out that the 'actual' and 'variance' columns in the Budget Report are incomplete . . .

BUDGET REPORT

Month June   **Date** 7 July

	budget	actual	variance
Sales	£190,000		
Production	£95,000		

1 What are the missing figures? Remember to include a '+' or '–' sign in front of the variance.

2 What does the Sales variance mean for the business? Is it a good or bad result?

3 What does the Production variance mean for the business? Is it good or bad?
   Think about this carefully, remembering that Sales is an income but Production is a cost.

4 If you were part of the Management Team of Peakwear, what suggestions might you make about improving the performance shown in the Budget Report for June?

Nutshell summary

- Personal budgeting and business budgeting have many features in common.

- Budgeting involves making plans for income and costs to achieve certain targets.

- A business budget normally covers a period of a year and estimates figures on a monthly basis.

- The main income budget is the Sales Budget which estimates the number of products a business will produce and the amount of sales revenue which will be received. A 'product' can include a service provided, or an item sold by a shop.

- The costs of a business are covered by the Production Budget (which estimates the cost of the product) and Departmental Budgets which cover areas including:
  - marketing
  - finance
  - human resources
  - administration

- The Cash Budget – also known as the 'cash-flow forecast' – estimates the money received and paid out of the bank account of the business each month. It links all the other budgets together because all the income and costs from the other budgets will pass through the bank account

  The cash budget is the main feature of the next chapter.

- Monitoring is an important part of budgeting. This involves comparing the budgeted figures with the actual figures, month by month on a form known as a Budget Report.

  The budgeted figure is deducted from the actual figure each month to show what the difference is. This difference is known as the variance.

- The business may need to investigate and take action if the difference (variance) is a cause of worry.

  For example, a rise in costs or a fall in sales would need looking into. The business might then need to cut costs and to increase the sales effort.

Key terms

Budgeting
A plan which sets targets for income and costs, normally over the period of a year.

Sales budget
An estimate of the sales revenue a business will receive.

Production budget
An estimate of the cost to a business of producing a product.

Departmental budget
An estimate of the cost of running a business department or area of activity.

Cash budget
An estimate of the amount of money paid in and out of the business bank account month by month. Also known as a 'cash-flow forecast.'

Monitoring
Checking the figures of the budgets against the actual figures as they become available and taking any action which becomes necessary.

Budget report
A form which compares budgeted and actual figures.

Variance
The difference between budgeted and actual figures.

32

Cash flow forecasts

the importance of cash

Ella has been recommended by her business adviser at the bank to set up a cash-flow forecast for her first year of trading as Webwise. This, he says, is possibly the single most important piece of financial planning she can do.

Ella asks why.

He replies that cash in a business is like blood in a body – it must be there and it must reach the parts that need it. It has to pay the wages and the bills. It has to be available to pay all the running costs on time.

A cash-flow forecast (also known as a cash budget) estimates the amount of money coming into the business bank account each month and the amount of money being paid out each month.

Money coming in will be from sales revenue and capital, loans and grants. Money being paid out will be start-up costs and running costs.

A cash-flow forecast estimates the amount of money that will be left in the bank account at the end of each month. It will help to highlight whether the business needs to borrow from the bank.

a point to think about . . .

A cash-flow forecast is like any forecast. It is only an estimate. Only time will tell if it is correct or not. The important thing is that it should, like any budget, be checked regularly and changed if the need arises.

	12000	12000
3000		
3000		
3500		
2500		
1000	1000	1000
drawings	2000	2000	2000
costs	1500	1500	1500
costs	1500	1500	1500
vertising	1500	1500	1500
TOTAL PAYMENTS	36500	19500	19500

the importance of cash in the bank account

a central record of business transactions

You can see from the diagram shown on the next page that all the money coming in and out of the business passes through the bank account.

The boxes on the left represent the sources of money. The boxes on the right show that all the money passes through the bank account and is used to pay the start-up and running costs of the business.

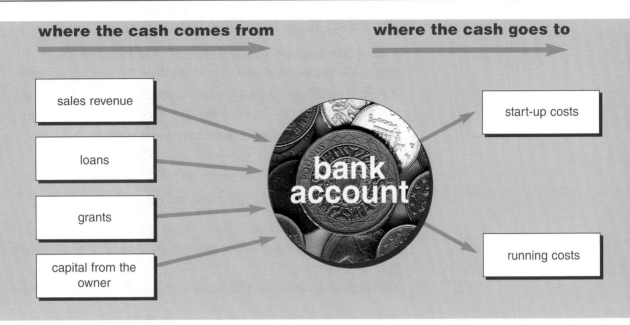

where the cash comes from → **where the cash goes to** →

- sales revenue
- loans
- grants
- capital from the owner

bank account

- start-up costs
- running costs

the importance of sales revenue

Once the business is up and running and the start-up costs have been paid, the most important of the sources of money is the **sales revenue**. This money will feed into the bank account and pay the running costs of the business.

why estimates must be realistic

The estimates of sales revenue and costs entered on the cash-flow forecast must be realistic, as this will enable the business to decide whether or not the product will be profitable.

If the sales revenue is less than forecast and the costs greater than forecast, the business may run out of money and go **bankrupt.**

Case Study – running out of cash

FOR SALE!

Car Alarm Business

Detached House in desirable area

Henry has started up a business selling car alarms. He has raised a £50,000 loan from the bank for his start-up costs, using his house as security for the borrowing

He has budgeted for monthly sales of £25,000 and running costs of £15,000 which should make him a clear £10,000 a month. He has put all these figures on a cash-flow forecast. But has he been realistic?

After six months he has only made sales of £75,000 and his costs have shot up to £100,000. He cannot repay his debts to the bank. They demand that he repays the loan. But how? He has run out of cash. He now faces the prospect of the bank demanding the money and selling his house.

the cash-flow forecast format

A **cash-flow forecast** is a table which estimates the amounts of money coming into and going out of the bank account each month.

A typical cash-flow forecast – which normally estimates figures for a whole year – sets out in a column for each month:

- a totalled up summary of the money coming into the bank account (A)

- a totalled up summary of payments out of the bank account (B)

- the bank balance at the beginning and the end of the month

The cash-flow forecast extract below shows only one column of figures; the remaining eleven monthly columns will normally extend off to the right.

The business shown here is Principal Designs, a graphic design business.

the heading includes the name of the business and the period of the cash- flow forecast

the total of the amounts paid into the bank account during the month (A)

the total of the amounts paid out of the bank account during the month (B)

the estimated bank balance at the end of the month

PRINCIPAL DESIGNS CASH-FLOW FORECAST 12 months ending 31 December	
	January £
Receipts	
Sales	10,000
Capital introduced	100,000
Loan	50,000
Grant	10,000
Other income	1,000
TOTAL RECEIPTS FOR MONTH (A)	171,000
Payments	
Premises	100,000
Equipment	45,000
Materials	2,000
Marketing	1,000
Other running costs	6,000
TOTAL PAYMENTS FOR MONTH (B)	154,000
Bank balance at the beginning of the month	zero
ADD total receipts (A)	171,000
LESS total payments (B)	154,000
BANK BALANCE AT END OF MONTH	17,000

working out the monthly bank balances

The bank account balances are worked out at the bottom of the cash-flow forecast. The formula is:

bank balance at the beginning of the month **add** *total receipts for the month* **minus** *total payments for the month* **equals** *bank balance at the end of the month*

The calculation for January (which starts with a zero balance) is:

zero **add** *£171,000* **minus** *£154,000* **equals** *£17,000*

Each month the **bank balance** at the end of the month is entered in the next column as the bank balance at the beginning of the next month. This is indicated here by the red arrows.

If a bank balance is negative it is shown in brackets. This means that the business is borrowing this money from the bank by means of an **overdraft**. This is quite usual – as long as the bank has agreed it!

PRINCIPAL DESIGNS
CASH FLOW FORECAST
12 months ending 31 December

	January £	February £	March £
Receipts			
Sales	10,000	10,000	10,000
Capital introduced	100,000		
Loan	50,000		
Grant	10,000		
Other income	1,000	1,000	1,000
TOTAL RECEIPTS FOR MONTH (A)	171,000	11,000	11,000
Payments			
Premises	100,000		
Equipment	45,000		30,000
Materials	2,000	2,000	3,000
Marketing	1,000		
Other running costs	6,000	5,000	4,000
TOTAL PAYMENTS FOR MONTH (B)	154,000	7,000	37,000
Bank balance at the beginning of the month	zero	17,000	21,000
ADD total receipts (A)	171,000	11,000	11,000
LESS total payments (B)	154,000	7,000	37,000
BANK BALANCE AT END OF MONTH	17,000	21,000	(5,000)

Activity 32.1 – working out the bank balance

You have been given figures for the estimated bank receipts and bank payments for three businesses for the months of January and February.

You have also been given the opening bank balances for January for each of the three businesses.

Remember that a bank balance in brackets is a minus figure – the business in this case will be borrowing from the bank on an overdraft.

JANUARY FIGURES

	Aztec Ltd	Brown & Co	Everard & Co
	£	£	£
Total Receipts	10,000	20,000	32,000
Total Payments	5,000	12,000	30,000
Opening Bank Balance	zero	3,000	(3,500)

FEBRUARY FIGURES

	Aztec Ltd	Brown & Co	Everard & Co
	£	£	£
Total Receipts	10,000	20,000	32,000
Total Payments	8,000	13,000	15,000

1 Draw up a cash-flow forecast for each of the three businesses for the two months. Use the format shown on the next page to calculate the bank balances at the end of January and February.

2 Write down in a few sentences an explanation of what has happened to the bank balance of Everard & Co during January and February.

What could this mean for the future of Everard & Co?

AZTEC LIMITED   CASH-FLOW FORECAST

	January £	February £
Total Receipts for Month (A)		
Total Payments for Month (B)		
Opening Bank Balance		
ADD Total Receipts for Month (A)		
LESS Total Payments for Month (B)		
Bank Balance at end of Month		

BROWN & CO   CASH-FLOW FORECAST

	January £	February £
Total Receipts for Month (A)		
Total Payments for Month (B)		
Opening Bank Balance		
ADD Total Receipts for Month (A)		
LESS Total Payments for Month (B)		
Bank Balance at end of Month		

EVERARD & CO   CASH-FLOW FORECAST

	January £	February £
Total Receipts for Month (A)		
Total Payments for Month (B)		
Opening Bank Balance		
ADD Total Receipts for Month (A)		
LESS Total Payments for Month (B)		
Bank Balance at end of Month		

Case Study – cash flow forecast

business start-up

Flick Moran is starting a mail order company in January to sell specialist CDs.

She will work from a rented office and will employ two part-time staff to help her. She will buy a computer and other essential mailing equipment.

finance

Flick has £15,000 of capital to invest herself, and her father is lending her £2,000 to be repaid at the end of five years. She has also been given a Government grant of £1,000.

sales revenue and running costs

As far as sales are concerned she reckons she will sell £20,000 of CDs a month; these will cost her £12,000 a month. She will pay for the stock in the month in which she receives it. She will also have to pay monthly office running costs.

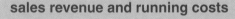

preparing for the cash-flow forecast

Flick has been asked by her accountant to draw up projected figures for the first twelve months of trading so that he can prepare a cash-flow forecast.

The accountant stresses that these figures, particularly the sales and running expenses will only be estimates. They will, however, help her to see if she will need a bank overdraft in the first year.

She has opened up a business bank account which has a zero balance.

The figures she writes down are shown on the next page

FLICK MORAN: ESTIMATED CASH-FLOW FIGURES

Receipts

	£
Capital provided by Flick Moran in January	15,000
Loan from father given in January	2,000
Government grant received in January	1,000
Forecast monthly sales from January	20,000

Start-up costs

Computer equipment paid for in January	8,000
Mailing equipment paid for in January	3,000
Other office start-up costs paid for in January	3,500
Marketing campaign paid for in January	2,500

Running costs – paid monthly from January

Stocks of CDs purchased	12,000
Wages of part-time staff	1,000
Flick's drawings (her living expenses)	2,000
Mailing costs	1,500
Office running costs	1,500
Advertising costs	1,500

The cash flow forecast set up by Flick's accountant is shown on the next two pages.

Study it carefully and then answer the questions which follow on page 266.

Case Study – cash flow forecast

business name   period of cash flow forecast

CASH FLOW FORECAST

Business: **Flick Moran**

Period: January - December

	Jan £	Feb £	Mar £	Apr £	May £	Jun £	Jul £
RECEIPTS							
Sales of CDs	20000	20000	20000	20000	20000	20000	20000
Capital	15000						
Loan	2000						
Grant	1000						
TOTAL RECEIPTS	38000	20000	20000	20000	20000	20000	20000
PAYMENTS							
CD purchases	12000	12000	12000	12000	12000	12000	12000
Computers	8000						
Mailing equipment	3000						
Office equipment	3500						
Marketing	2500						
Wages	1000	1000	1000	1000	1000	1000	1000
Owner's drawings	2000	2000	2000	2000	2000	2000	2000
Mailing costs	1500	1500	1500	1500	1500	1500	1500
Office costs	1500	1500	1500	1500	1500	1500	1500
Advertising	1500	1500	1500	1500	1500	1500	1500
TOTAL PAYMENTS	36500	19500	19500	19500	19500	19500	19500
Opening Bank	0	1500	2000	2500	3000	3500	4000
Add Receipts	38000	20000	20000	20000	20000	20000	20000
Less Payments	36500	19500	19500	19500	19500	19500	19500
Closing Bank	1500	2000	2500	3000	3500	4000	4500

Aug £	Sep £	Oct £	Nov £	Dec £	TOTAL £	
						totals column for all receipts and payments for the 12 months from January to December
20000	20000	20000	20000	20000	240000	CD sales of £20,000 a month total £240,000 for the year
					15000	
					2000	
					1000	
					0	
					0	
20000	20000	20000	20000	20000	258000	total receipts
12000	12000	12000	12000	12000	144000	
					8000	
					3000	
					3500	
					2500	
1000	1000	1000	1000	1000	12000	
2000	2000	2000	2000	2000	24000	total payments
1500	1500	1500	1500	1500	18000	
1500	1500	1500	1500	1500	18000	
1500	1500	1500	1500	1500	18000	
19500	19500	19500	19500	19500	251000	
4500	5000	5500	6000	6500	0	opening bank balance
20000	20000	20000	20000	20000	258000	total receipts
19500	19500	19500	19500	19500	251000	total payments
5000	5500	6000	6500	7000	7000	closing bank balance

bank calculation

Activity 32.2 – questions on the Case Study

Show that you understand the cash-flow forecast on the last two pages by answering these questions.

1   What is the period covered by the cash-flow forecast?

2   What does the column on the extreme right-hand side of the cash-flow forecast represent?

3   Is the bank account increasing or decreasing each month?

4   By what amount is the bank account increasing or decreasing each month?

5   Does this mean the business is likely to be making a profit or a loss?

6   What would happen to the end-of-month bank balance if Flick's sales projections were wrong and she sold £25,000 worth of CDs each month?

7   What would happen to the end-of-month bank balance if Flick's sales projections were wrong and she sold £15,000 worth of CDs each month?

8   Your answers to 6 and 7 should highlight the main advantage of using a cash-flow forecast when planning a new business. What does it tell you about the possible future of the business?

9   If you were Flick and the business started to go badly what steps could you take to improve the situation?

10 The cash-flow forecast in this Case Study is drawn up on a computer spreadsheet. From your experience so far of constructing cash-flow forecasts, what would be the advantages of using a computer in this way?

The use of a computer spreadsheet to construct a cash-flow statement is covered in the next chapter.

	Jan £	Feb £	Mar £	Apr £	May £	Jun £
RECEIPTS						
Sales of CDs	20000	20000	20000	20000	20000	20000
Capital	15000					
Loan	2000					
Grant	1000					
TOTAL RECEIPTS	38000	20000	20000	20000	20000	20000
PAYMENTS						
CD purchases	12000	12000	12000	12000	12000	12000
Computers	8000					
Mailing equipment	3000					
Office equipment	3500					
Marketing	2500					
Wages	1000	1000	1000	1000	1000	1000
Owner's drawings	2000	2000	2000	2000	2000	2000
Mailing costs	1500	1500	1500	1500	1500	1500
Office costs	1500	1500	1500	1500	1500	1500
Advertising	1500	1500	1500	1500	1500	1500
TOTAL PAYMENTS	36500	19500	19500	19500	19500	19500
Opening Bank	0	1500	2000	2500	3000	3500
Add Receipts	38000	20000	20000	20000	20000	20000
Less Payments	36500	19500	19500	19500	19500	19500
Closing Bank	1500	2000	2500	3000	3500	4000

Activity 32.3 – constructing cash flow forecasts

You have been asked to help two businesses draw up a cash flow forecast for a six month period.

R & R Opticians is starting up for the first time.

H H Sports has been trading for some time.

The figures you have been given are as follows:

R & R OPTICIANS

	Jan £	Feb £	March £	April £	May £	June £
Receipts						
Capital	10,000					
Loan	5,000					
Sales	10,000	10,000	10,000	10,000	10,000	10,000
Payments						
Equipment	15,000					
Stock	5,000	5,000	5,000	5,000	5,000	5,000
Other expenses	2,000	2,000	2,500	2,000	2,000	2,000
Opening bank balance	zero					

H H SPORTS

	Jan £	Feb £	March £	April £	May £	June £
Receipts						
Sales	20,000	20,000	20,000	20,000	20,000	20,000
Payments						
Stock	15,000	15,000	15,000	15,000	15,000	15,000
Other expenses	3,000	3,000	3,000	3,000	3,000	3,000
Computer equipment purchase						15,000
Opening bank balance	1,000					

1   Using the format shown on the next page, draw up cash flow forecasts for the two businesses for the six months from January to June. Remember that a negative bank balance is shown in brackets.

2   Write a brief explanation of the bank balance of H H Sports as it stands at the end of June.

NAME OF BUSINESS.....................

CASH-FLOW FORECAST

PERIOD..........................

Receipts	January £	February £	March £	April £	May £	June £	Total £
Sales							
Capital introduced							
Loan							
Grant							
Other income							
TOTAL RECEIPTS FOR MONTH (A)							
Payments							
Premises							
Equipment							
Materials							
Marketing							
Other running costs							
TOTAL PAYMENTS FOR MONTH (B)							
Bank balance at the beginning of the month							
ADD total receipts (A)							
LESS total payments (B)							
BANK BALANCE AT END OF MONTH							

Nutshell summary

- The cash-flow forecast – sometimes known as the cash budget – is an important part of business planning. It estimates the amount of money paid in and out of the business bank account month by month.

  The cash-flow forecast normally covers a period of six or twelve months.

- The cash-flow forecast is also important because it estimates the amount left in the bank account at the end of each month.

- The cash-flow forecast is constructed in the form of a table with columns for each of the months.

- The cash-flow forecast contains three sets of figures down the columns:
  - money received (eg sales revenue, capital, loans, grants)
  - money paid out (start-up costs and running costs)
  - a calculation of the bank balance at the end of the month; the formula for this is:

    Bank balance at the beginning of the month

    add   *Total Receipts*

    minus   *Total Payments*

    equals   *Bank balance at the end of the month*

- If the bank account balance figure shown at the bottom of the cash-flow forecast is positive, it means there is money in the bank.

- If the bank account balance figure shown at the bottom of the cash-flow forecast is negative (usually shown in brackets), it means the business needs to borrow from the bank in the form of an overdraft.

- The cash-flow forecast will tell the business owner whether or not the business will make enough money to keep it going. If the cash runs out, the business may go bankrupt.

- The figures in the cash-flow forecast should be altered if circumstances change as the months pass. A computer spreadsheet is therefore very useful in setting out a cash-flow forecast.

 # Key terms

Cash-flow forecast
A budget which estimates the amount of money paid in and out of the business bank account month by month.

The cash-flow forecast also estimates the amount of money left in the bank account at the end of each month.

Sales revenue
Money received by a business from the sale of its products.

Bankrupt
A person who does not have enough money to repay debts when they are due.

Bank balance
The amount of money in the bank account.

Overdraft
A negative (minus) bank balance – where money is being borrowed from the bank. A negative figure on the cash-flow forecast is normally shown in brackets.

33

Cash flow forecasts on a spreadsheet

the importance of ICT in business

Ella's business 'Webwise' has been set up to provide training in ICT (Information and Communication Technology).

When she launched the business Ella gave an interview to the local press who printed the following article:

Ella nets a Lottery fortune

Local girl Ella Webster has made good with a Lottery win of £150,000. Instead of splashing out with her money she has set up a computer training business called Webwise.

Ella commented 'I have always been interested in computers, and some people do seem scared of using them.

Webwise will help them set up computer systems and access the internet. This will save them so much money in producing letters, storing data and number crunching.'

a point to think about . . .

Businesses are using ICT more and more in everyday procedures. What aspects of ICT can you see at work in a business like a supermarket or travel company? How does this save the business money?

using a spreadsheet for a cash-flow forecast

the benefits of a spreadsheet program

The calculations on a cash-flow forecast are not particularly difficult, but they do take a long time if you are tackling the task with only pencil, paper, rubber and calculator.

The task is, of course, made simple when you have input the worksheet onto a computer spreadsheet program.

what is a computer spreadsheet program?

A computer spreadsheet is an automatic calculation table set up on a computer file.

A computer spreadsheet is a commonly used program. One of the most popular spreadsheets is Microsoft Excel.

If you are not familiar with a spreadsheet you should read through the rest of this page as it will explain its format and terminology.

The example shown below is based on Ella's start-up business 'Webwise'.

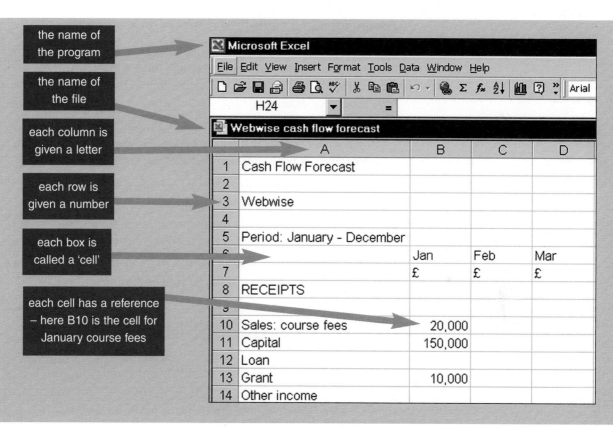

the name of the program

the name of the file

each column is given a letter

each row is given a number

each box is called a 'cell'

each cell has a reference – here B10 is the cell for January course fees

spreadsheet format

A spreadsheet is a table divided into **rows** and **columns**.

Each row has a number and each column has a letter.

The boxes into which data can be entered are known as **cells**.

Each cell has a **reference** which is made up of the column letter and row number, for example the name of Ella's business is in A3.

You can input text into a cell or you can input numbers.

You can perform a calculation by inputting a **formula** into a cell (see the next page for more on formulas).

formulas

Formulas enable you to add ranges of cells, subtract, divide and multiply They also enable you to transfer a figure from one cell to another.

Formulas will vary slightly from spreadsheet to spreadsheet.

Formulas will use the references of the cells which contain the numbers they need for the calculation.

You normally set up a formula by typing a '=' in the cell where you want the calculation done.

advantages of a cash-flow forecast on a spreadsheet

The big advantage of a computer spreadsheet is that you will be able to change any figure you have input, and the computer will recalculate all the figures for you, according to the formulas you have input. For example . . .

■ if you want to change the estimated figure for sales revenue, to see what happens if sales are better than expected, or more importantly, what happens if the sales are worse than expected

■ if you want to change the start-up costs, eg if computer equipment costs more than you expected

■ if you want to change the running costs, eg if the monthly wages bill goes up

In each case you will be able to see the effect on the important figure of the closing bank balance at the bottom of the spreadsheet.

Case Study – using spreadsheet formulas

background to Case Study

In the Case Study in the last chapter Flick Moran set up a twelve month cash-flow Forecast. This is shown on pages 264 and 265.

This was quite a complicated table and involved a number of formulas. This Case Study will take you through the formulas used by Flick.

formulas in Column C

cash-flow forecasts often need to add together ranges of cells – Receipts, for example, and Payments.

Each cell is given the reference of the column (the letter) and the row (the number). The formulas for the Flick Moran spreadsheet are illustrated on the next two pages

You will need to check your computer manual or refer to a technician to find the formula to use for your own program. The formula used here is =Sum(C8..C14) where all the cells between C8 and C14 are added together. (Note that Excel uses : instead of ..). Some of these rows are empty; they are included in the formula in case Flick needs to add extra types of income.

The formulas for column C are as follows:

- Total Receipts — Rows 15 and 32 — =Sum(C8..C14)
- Total Payments — Rows 29 and 33 — =Sum(C18..C28)
- Opening Bank — Row 31 — =B34*
- Closing Bank — Row 34 — =C31+C32−C33

* Note that B34 is the January closing bank balance and so is transferred by the simple '=' formula to C31 which is the opening balance for February – the figure is, of course, the same.

	A	B	C	D	E
1	CASH FLOW FORECAST				
2	Business: Flick Moran				
3	Period: January - December				
4					
5		Jan	Feb	Mar	Apr
6		£	£	£	£
7	RECEIPTS				
8					
9	Sales of CDs	20000	20000	20000	20000
10	Capital	15000			
11	Loan	2000			
12	Grant	1000			
13					
14					
15	TOTAL RECEIPTS	=SUM(B8..B14)	=SUM(C8..C14)	=SUM(D8..D14)	=SUM(E8..E14)
16					
17	PAYMENTS				
18	CD purchases	12000	12000	12000	12000
19	Computers	8000			
20	Mailing equipment	3000			
21	Office equipment	3500			
22	Marketing	2500			
23	Wages	1000	1000	1000	1000
24	Owner's drawings	2000	2000	2000	2000
25	Mailing costs	1500	1500	1500	1500
26	Office costs	1500	1500	1500	1500
27	Advertising	1500	1500	1500	1500
28					
29	TOTAL PAYMENTS	=SUM(B18..B28)	=SUM(C18..C28)	=SUM(D18..D28)	=SUM(E18..E28)
30					
31	Opening Bank	0	=B34	=C34	=D34
32	Add Receipts	=SUM(B8..B14)	=SUM(C8..C14)	=SUM(D8..D14)	=SUM(E8..E14)
33	Less Payments	=SUM(B18..B28)	=SUM(C18..C28)	=SUM(D18..D28)	=SUM(E18..E28)
34	Closing Bank	=B31+B32-B33	=C31+C32-C33	=D31+D32-D33	=E31+E32-E33

working out the totals in the final column (Column N)

Each row is totalled, eg cell N9 is =Sum(B9..M9).

Column N is also totalled vertically, in the same way as the other columns, except that

- cell N31 is =B31 . . . this is the opening bank balance for January)
- cell N34 is =M34 . . . (this is the closing bank balance for December)
- cell N32 is =Sum(B32..M32) . . . this is the total of all the Receipts for the year
- cell N33 is =Sum(B33..M33) . . . this is the total of all the Payments for the year

	K	L	M	N
1				
2	.			
3				
4				
5	Oct	Nov	Dec	TOTAL
6	£	£	£	£
7				
8				
9	20000	20000	20000	=SUM(B9..M9)
10				=SUM(B10..M10)
11				=SUM(B11..M11)
12				=SUM(B12..M12)
13				=SUM(B13..M13)
14				=SUM(B14..M14)
15	=SUM(K8..K14)	=SUM(L8..L14)	=SUM(M8..M14)	=SUM(N8..N14)
16				
17				
18	12000	12000	12000	=SUM(B18..M18)
19				=SUM(B19..M19)
20				=SUM(B20..M20)
21				=SUM(B21..M21)
22				=SUM(B22..M22)
23	1000	1000	1000	=SUM(B23..M23)
24	2000	2000	2000	=SUM(B24..M24)
25	1500	1500	1500	=SUM(B25..M25)
26	1500	1500	1500	=SUM(B26..M26)
27	1500	1500	1500	=SUM(B27..M27)
28				
29	=SUM(K18..K28)	=SUM(L18..L28)	=SUM(M18..M28)	=SUM(N18..N28)
30				
31	=J34	=K34	=L34	=B31
32	=SUM(K8..K14)	=SUM(L8..L14)	=SUM(M8..M14)	=SUM(B32..M32)
33	=SUM(K18..K28)	=SUM(L18..L28)	=SUM(M18..M28)	=SUM(B33..M33)
34	=K31+K32-K33	=L31+L32-L33	=M31+M32-M33	=M34

Note

This spreadsheet is shown to illustrate the formulas used. The months of May to September are not illustrated here, as space does not permit. The formulas in the columns for these months will mirror those of the other months.

Activity 33.1 – setting up a spreadsheet

Mike Moore is setting up a new fashion clothes shop in the town. The business will be called Ace Design.

Mike is the sole owner of the shop, which will open in January of next year.

His accountant has asked him to draw up some estimates of costs and income for the first year of trading.

The figures he produces are as follows:

ACE DESIGN: FINANCIAL PROJECTIONS

financing of business

Capital introduced by Mike in January	125,000
Bank loan given in January	15,000
Government grant given in January	5,000
Monthly rent received from tenant in office upstairs	900
Monthly sales revenue (estimate)	15,000

start-up costs (to be paid in January)

	£
Shop premises	100,000
Shop equipment	40,000
Market research	5,000

running costs (to be paid monthly)

Stock purchases	7,500
Wages	3,500
Other expenses	3,000

1   Using the spreadsheet format shown on pages 273 to 274 (or a similar computer spreadsheet file), draw up a cash-flow forecast for Ace Design for the twelve months from January to December.

Make sure that you have saved this spreadsheet and had it checked before going any further with this Activity.

2   Write down whether you think the business will be successful. Explain why you have come to this conclusion.

3   Mike's accountant says he should produce another cash-flow forecast showing the effect of increasing the estimated sales revenue by 20% to £18,000 a month.

Create a new spreadsheet for this task by saving the original spreadsheet with a different file name.

Now change the monthly sales revenue figure to £18,000 a month for all twelve months.

What effect does this have on the business cash-flow?

Explain what has happened to the month-end bank balances.

4   Mike's accountant now says that he should produce a spreadsheet decreasing the original sales estimate by 20% to £12,000 a month.

You are to create an additional spreadsheet file and change the monthly sales revenue figure to £12,000 a month for all twelve months.

What effect do the changes have on the business cash-flow?

Discuss what Mike might be able to do to rescue the situation.

5   The accountant says:

'Of course, these figures are only estimates. I doubt very much if the sales revenue will be the same figure each month. After all, it is a fashion shop and people will not buy the same amount of clothes each month.'

Suggest reasons why customers may buy at different times of year and cause the sales figures to fluctuate from month to month.

Nutshell summary

- The task of drawing up a cash-flow forecast is made a great deal easier in the long term if a computer spreadsheet is used.

- A computer spreadsheet is a table made up of boxes (cells) set out in columns and rows. The columns are referenced by letters and the rows by numbers.

- Each cell is referenced by the column letter and row number, eg A1, M5.

- Text and numbers can be entered in the cells.

- Cells can be set up to perform calculations – for example the cell below a column of figures can be set up as a Total cell which will automatically add up any figures which appear in the designated cells above.

- A calculation cell is set up by inputting a formula into that cell. A formula is a grouping of cell references and the appropriate mathematical function.

- A formula is entered in a cell by typing in the '=' sign and the appropriate cell references and mathematical function.

- The format of formulas will vary according to the computer program being used. Examples of common formulas include:

=C1+C2	adding two cells
=SUM(F5:F15)	adding the cells in a column between F5 and F15
=F5*G7	F5 multiplied by G7
=F5/K12	F5 divided by K12

- The great advantage of computer spreadsheets is that once they are set up you can change any figure within a calculation and the spreadsheet will automatically recalculate the total or totals.

- The advantage of using a spreadsheet for a cash-flow forecast is that any Receipt or Payment figure can be changed and the Bank Balances will automatically be recalculated. This is of great use when the business owner is planning ahead and needs to know the effect on the bank account of, for example, different levels of sales.

Key terms

Spreadsheet
An automatic calculation table set up on a computer file.

Cell
A field in a computer spreadsheet into which data is entered.

Column
A vertical series of spreadsheet cells, given a letter reference.

Row
A horizontal series of spreadsheet cells, given a number reference.

Cell reference
A reference to an individual cell made up of the column letter and row number.

Formula
A group of mathematical functions and cell references input into a cell which will make the spreadsheet perform a calculation and place the result in that cell.

34
Calculating break-even

the club trip – breaking even on transport

When a business is starting up or planning a new project it will want to know whether the income from the project will cover the running costs – in other words it will want to know if it will **break-even** and make a profit.

It is only likely to go ahead with the project if it is going to break-even.

A comparison on a personal level is a group of students planning a trip out to a nearby town to go to a well-known club.

They will need to hire a minibus and driver which will cost £120 for the evening. Everyone is prepared to pay £10 each maximum for the minibus.

How many people will need to come for them to break-even on the hire of the minibus and driver? If there are only ten who want to go, they will not manage it. Their income will only be 10 x £10 = £100 and the cost is £120. They are £20 short.

Simple arithmetic tells them they need at least twelve people (12 x £10 = £120) to cover the transport cost and to break-even.

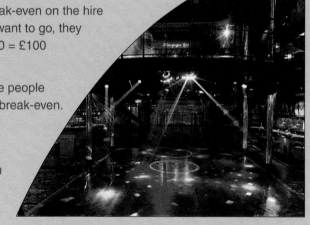

a point to think about . . .

What difference would it make to the cost per person if fifteen people wanted to come and there is room in the minibus for them all?

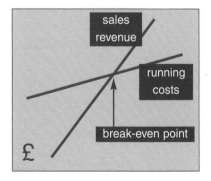

a definition of break-even

Turning again to businesses, the break-even point is the point at which running costs are covered by the income received (sales revenue) . . .

Break-even is the point at which sales revenue is equal to running costs.

Before that point the business is making a loss.

After that point the business is making a profit.

break-even involves running costs only

Note that the business costs involved in the break-even calculation are **running costs** only, eg wages, materials, and expenses such as insurance and rates. Start-up costs such as buying equipment are not included in the break-even calculation. If you think about it, they will already have been financed by the money (capital) the owner has put in or by loans from the bank

Activity 34.1 – calculating break-even

Calculate whether the following businesses have broken even or not. State in each case the amount of profit or loss they have made.

	revenue from sales (£)	running costs (£)
Business 1	45,000	35,000
Business 2	46,000	46,000
Business 3	47,000	48,000
Business 4	1,234,738	1,134,576
Business 5	2,983,472	2,983,524

types of running costs

Break-even is the point at which the sales revenue of a business over a given period equals its **running costs**.

In other words, at break-even all the running costs have been paid off by the money coming in from sales.

As we have already seen, running costs are the day-to-day expenses of a business.

A service business will pay for items such as wages and insurance.

A manufacturer will need to pay for the purchase of materials which it turns into its products.

A shop will purchase stock which is then sold as part of day-to-day trading.

But you might point out that not all of these costs work in the same way – some are fixed and have to be paid anyway, while others will vary with the number of items a business produces.

When calculating break-even you need to be able to tell the difference between two types of running costs: **fixed costs** and **variable costs.**

fixed costs

Fixed costs are running costs which do not vary in line with the number of items sold.

Fixed costs are running costs such as rent and insurance which have to be paid anyway, whatever the number of items sold by the business.

Even if the business closes down for two weeks' holiday and nothing is sold, the fixed costs still have to be paid.

Fixed costs can be shown in the form of a graph which shows the cost (£) and the number of items produced, 'the output'.

Remember that an item can be an item made in a factory, an item sold in a shop, or a service provided.

As you can see in the graph below, the fixed costs of a business remain at the same level, however many items are produced – the line on the graph is a horizontal straight line.

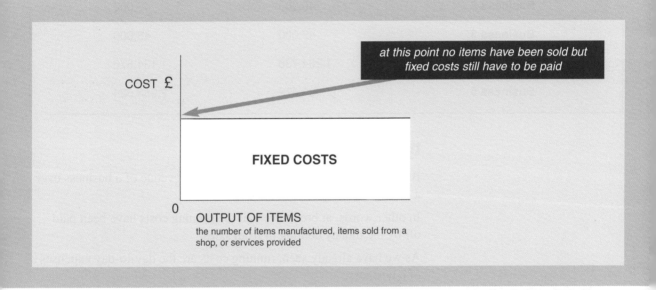

at this point no items have been sold but fixed costs still have to be paid

COST £

FIXED COSTS

0

OUTPUT OF ITEMS
the number of items manufactured, items sold from a shop, or services provided

variable costs

Variable costs are running costs which vary in line with the number of items produced.

Variable costs relate to the production of the item itself.

Variable costs include expenses such as purchases of materials, stock, and, in the case of a manufacturer, the wages paid to production line employees.

If the output is nil, variable costs will be zero, if the output increases, so does the total variable cost.

As you can see from the straight line on the graph below, total variable costs rise as the number of items produced rises.

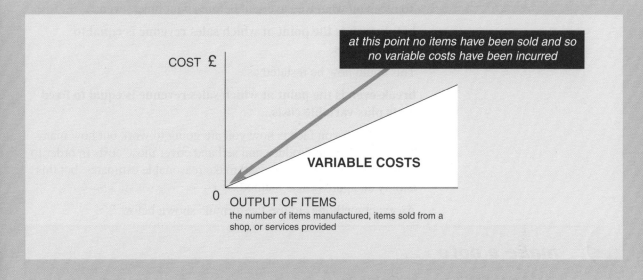

total cost = fixed costs + variable costs

As a business is likely to have to pay both fixed and variable costs, the two costs added together (the total cost) can also be shown in graph form:

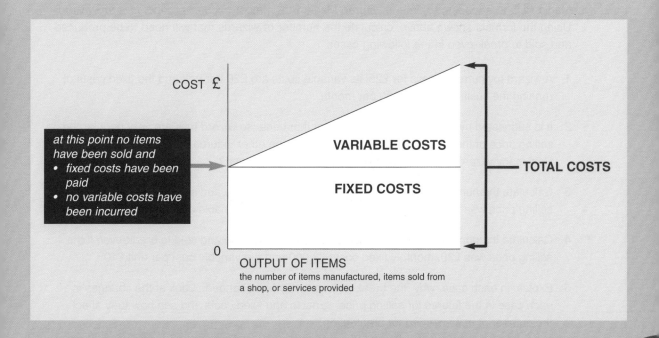

calculating the break-even point

the need for a formula

To recap on what we have said before about break-even:

break-even is the point at which sales revenue is equal to running costs.

This could now be restated as:

break-even is the point at which sales revenue is equal to fixed costs plus variable costs.

The problem you face is how you are going to work out how many items you need to produce and sell and cover those costs in order to break-even. You can guess and make reasonable estimates, but this is only an approximate method.

An exact method is to use the formula shown below.

make a note . . .

$$\text{Break-even (units)} \quad = \quad \frac{\textit{fixed costs (£)}}{\textit{selling price per unit (£)} \ \textbf{minus} \ \textit{variable cost per unit (£)}}$$

Activity 34.2 – using the break-even formula

Magic PLC is a leading toy manufacturer. Magic PLC's most popular product is a toy wizard. Using the formula shown above, calculate the number of wizards that will need to be produced and sold to break-even in the following cases:

1 A wizard toy currently sells for £25; its variable costs are £20 per unit and the fixed costs of running the business are £5,000 per month.

2 It is suggested by the Marketing Department that because wizard toys are very popular the selling price of the wizard could be raised to £30, the other figures staying the same. How many wizards would then have to be sold to break-even?

3 Calculate the number of wizards that would need to be made and sold to break-even if the selling price was £30, monthly fixed costs £3,000 and the variable cost per unit £10.

4 Calculate the number of wizards that would need to be made and sold to break-even if the selling price was £20, monthly fixed costs £3,000 and the variable cost per unit £10.

5 Explain in each case why the break-even quantity has changed. Look at the changes in each case in the figures for selling price, variable and fixed costs and see how they affect the number of units needed for break-even.

the break-even graph

The management of Magic PLC, the toy manufacturer on the previous page, will find the calculation by formula useful, but will point out its limitations. The management might ask questions like:

'How much profit will we make if we sell 200 more wizards per month than the break-even amount?'

The answer is to be found in the construction of a break-even table and graph. We have already seen a graph (page 281) showing fixed and variable costs. If a sales income line is added to this, a break-even point can be plotted.

Case Study – break-even graph

The management of Magic PLC has decided to construct a break-even graph so that it can have a better idea of the profits it could make.

Before a break-even graph can be constructed, a table will have to be drawn up setting out the income and costs for different numbers of units. A table for wizards is shown below.

The data used is: selling price per unit £20, variable cost per unit £10, fixed costs per month £5,000.

units of production (wizards)	fixed costs A	variable costs B	total cost C A + B	sales revenue D	profit/(loss) E D – C
	£	£	£	£	£
100	5,000	1,000	6,000	2,000	(4,000)
200	5,000	2,000	7,000	4,000	(3,000)
300	5,000	3,000	8,000	6,000	(2 000)
400	5,000	4,000	9,000	8,000	(1,000)
500	5,000	5,000	10,000	10,000	nil
600	5,000	6,000	11,000	12,000	1,000
700	5,000	7,000	12,000	14,000	2,000

Note that:

■ fixed costs (Column A) are fixed at £5,000

■ fixed costs (Column A) and variable costs (Column B) are added together to produce the total cost figure (Column C)

■ total cost (Column C) is deducted from the sales revenue figure (Column D) to produce in Column E either a positive figure (a profit) or a loss (a negative figure, in brackets)

As you can see, break-even occurs at 500 units, a result already worked out by the formula calculation you have already done (see the first task in the Activity on the previous page).

construction of the break-even graph

A graph can now be constructed from this table. The figures used are:

■ the total cost line (Column C)

■ the sales income line (Column D)

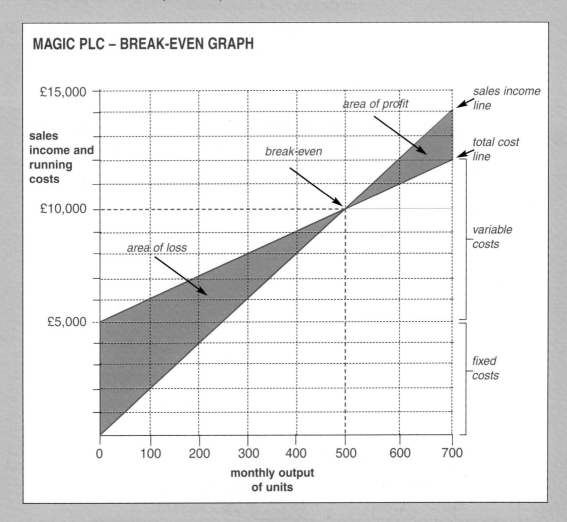

MAGIC PLC – BREAK-EVEN GRAPH

notes on the break even graph

■ The fixed costs of £5,000 are the same at all levels of output.

■ Total cost is made up of fixed costs and variable costs.

■ The total costs line starts, not at zero, but at £5,000. This is because if the output is zero, the business still has to pay the £5,000 fixed costs.

■ The point at which the total costs and sales income lines cross is the break-even point.

■ From the graph you can read off the break-even point both in terms of units of output (500 units on the horizontal axis) and also in sales income value (£10,000 on the vertical axis).

reading the graph

working out profit and loss from the graph

If you look at the graph on the opposite page you will see two blue shaded areas. On the left of the break-even point is an **area of loss** and on the right of the break-even point is an **area of profit**. This means that for levels of output to the left of the break-even point (ie fewer than 500 units) the business will make a loss and for levels of output to the right of the break-even point, the business will make a profit.

If you read off the vertical distance (in £) between the sales income line and the total cost line (ie down the shaded area) you will find the exact amount of profit and loss for any level of output on the graph. Note that each dotted 'box' on the graph represents £1,000 from top to bottom. For example, at an output level of zero you will make a loss of £5,000 (this is the fixed costs figure) and at an output level of 700 units you will make a profit of £2,000.

Activity 34.3 – reading the break-even graph

Study this graph and then answer the questions at the top of the next page.

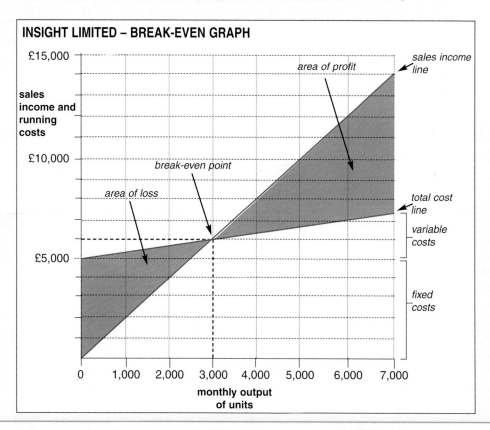

1 How many units does Insight Limited have to produce to break even?

2 What are the fixed costs at the break-even point?

3 What are the variable costs at the break-even point?

4 What loss does Insight Limited make when output is zero units?

5 Why is this loss made?

6 What profit is made by Insight Limited when the output is 6,000 units?

dealing with changes in costs and revenue

Business owners and managers often like to look at 'what if' situations, for example:

'What if we put the price of the product up by 20%? How many would we have to sell to break-even? How would it affect our profit?'

You could either use the formula (see page 282) or, better still, set up a computer spreadsheet to show you a range of possibilities.

break-even on a computer spreadsheet

The break-even table used in this chapter (see page 283) can easily be set up on a computer spreadsheet. Study the spreadsheet below.

The formulas to set it up are shown on the next page. All you have to do is to input the data as indicated on the diagram.
The spreadsheet then automatically does the calculations.

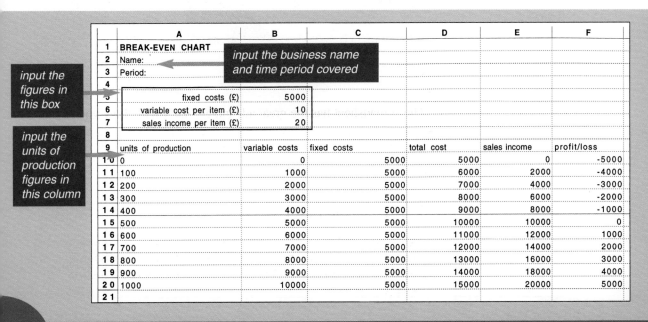

	A	B	C	D	E	F
1	BREAK-EVEN CHART					
2	Name:					
3	Period:					
4						
5	fixed costs (£)	5000				
6	variable cost per item (£)	10				
7	sales income per item (£)	20				
8						
9	units of production	variable costs	fixed costs	total cost	sales income	profit/loss
10	0	0	5000	5000	0	-5000
11	100	1000	5000	6000	2000	-4000
12	200	2000	5000	7000	4000	-3000
13	300	3000	5000	8000	6000	-2000
14	400	4000	5000	9000	8000	-1000
15	500	5000	5000	10000	10000	0
16	600	6000	5000	11000	12000	1000
17	700	7000	5000	12000	14000	2000
18	800	8000	5000	13000	16000	3000
19	900	9000	5000	14000	18000	4000
20	1000	10000	5000	15000	20000	5000
21						

input the business name and time period covered

input the figures in this box

input the units of production figures in this column

formulas for setting up a break-even table on a spreadsheet

	A	B	C	D	E	F
1	BREAK-EVEN CHART					
2	Name:					
3	Period:					
4						
5	fixed costs (£)	5000				
6	variable cost per item (£)	10				
7	sales income per item (£)	20				
8						
9	units of production	variable costs	fixed costs	total cost	sales income	profit/loss
10	0	=B6*A10	=B5	=B10+C10	=B7*A10	=E10-D10
11	100	=B6*A11	=B5	=B11+C11	=B7*A11	=E11-D11
12	200	=B6*A12	=B5	=B12+C12	=B7*A12	=E12-D12
13	300	=B6*A13	=B5	=B13+C13	=B7*A13	=E13-D13
14	400	=B6*A14	=B5	=B14+C14	=B7*A14	=E14-D14
15	500	=B6*A15	=B5	=B15+C15	=B7*A15	=E15-D15
16	600	=B6*A16	=B5	=B16+C16	=B7*A16	=E16-D16
17	700	=B6*A17	=B5	=B17+C17	=B7*A17	=E17-D17
18	800	=B6*A18	=B5	=B18+C18	=B7*A18	=E18-D18
19	900	=B6*A19	=B5	=B19+C19	=B7*A19	=E19-D19
20	1000	=B6*A20	=B5	=B20+C20	=B7*A20	=E20-D20
21						

the data you need for input

All you have to do is to head up the table with the name of the business and time period, and then input:

- units of production in Column A
- the fixed and variable costs and sales income (selling price) in the box at the top

The spreadsheet does the rest. If your spreadsheet program has a charting facility, you may be able to use the data to produce a break-even graph. This can be a bit tricky and you will probably need help with it.

using the spreadsheet to change data

The spreadsheet has the great advantage that it will allow you to change the data and will calculate the figures for you. You might, for example, want to see the effect on the break-even point of:

- changing the selling price of the unit
- increasing the fixed costs
- decreasing the variable costs

This would be useful in a business situation where you wanted to bring, the break-even point down and so increase profitability by, for example, increasing the selling price of the product or reducing the fixed costs.

Activity 34.4 – break-even on a spreadsheet

> **practical note**
> This Activity *can* be tackled if a computer spreadsheet is not available. It will, obviously, take longer to complete.

the business

Jim Nevinson has a business which imports shirts from Italy and sells them to retail stores in the UK.

His current monthly income and expense figures are:

Fixed costs per month	£10,000
Variable costs per item	£10
Sales income per item	£30

the tasks

1 Draw up a break-even chart on a computer spreadsheet. Input units sold in multiples of 100 from zero up to 1,000 per month.

How many shirts does Jim have to sell to break-even?

What profit will he make if he sells 1,000 shirts a month?

2 Six months have passed and trading conditions have worsened for Jim and he is having to change the way he operates. He is forced to make a decision between:

- importing shirts that are better quality – and so increasing his variable costs to £20 per item, or

- keeping his variable costs at £10 but employing more sales staff – this will increase his fixed costs by £8,000 to £18,000 per month

Which option should he choose? You are to produce spreadsheet files for both options (save them as separate files). Recommend to Jim the choice which provides an earlier break-even point and greater profit.

3 *Note: it is advisable to have your answer to Task 2 checked before carrying out this Task.*
Jim is not happy with the profitability projected in Task 2. He suggests putting his selling price up to £40 per item.

Produce a new spreadsheet file based on the recommended choice from Task 2 and a new selling price of £40 per unit. How many shirts does Jim now have to sell to break-even? What profit will he make if he sells 1,000 shirts a month?

4 Explain to Jim the problems he might encounter in raising his selling price to £40 per item. Calculate for him the percentage price increase involved.

Nutshell summary

- When businesses plan ahead they need to know that their products are going to be profitable.

- Businesses can calculate whether or not their products are going to break-even – in other words whether the money received from sales is going to cover running costs.

- Once the break-even point is reached and sales revenue covers running costs, the product will start to provide a profit.

- There are two types of running cost that have to be covered by sales revenue: fixed costs and variable costs.

- Fixed costs are running costs which do not vary in line with the number of items sold, eg insurance cover.

  Variable costs are costs which vary in line with the number of items sold, eg raw materials purchased by a manufacturer, stock purchased by a shop.

- The break-even point may be calculated in a number of ways: by formula, by table and by creating a break-even graph.

- The break-even formula calculates the number of items (units) that need to be sold to break-even as:

$$\frac{\text{fixed costs (£)}}{\text{selling price per unit (£) } \textbf{minus} \text{ variable cost per unit (£)}}$$

- A table can be drawn up to work out the break-even point and profit (or loss) of a product at different levels of production. This can be input onto a computer spreadsheet.

- A graph can also be drawn up (or produced on the computer) to work out the break-even point and show the areas of profit or loss of a product at different levels of production.

- The advantage of using a computer spreadsheet for break-even calculations is that the business owner or manager can alter the revenue and cost figures and produce break-even calculations automatically.

 # Key terms

Break-even
The point at which revenue from sales equals the running costs of a business.

Also . . .

The point at which revenue from sales equals fixed costs plus variable costs.

Running costs
Day-to-day costs which a business pays to 'run' the business.

Fixed costs
Running costs which do not vary in line with the number of items sold.

Variable costs
Running costs which vary in line with the number of items sold.

Area of loss
The area on a break-even graph to the left of the break-even point between the sales income line and the total cost line. It shows the amount of loss made.

Area of profit
The area on a break-even graph to the right of the break-even point between the sales income line and the total cost line. It shows the amount of profit made.

35 Calculating profit and loss

Who profits from business?

Flick Moran, who set up a CD mail order business in Chapter 32, drew up a cash-flow forecast (pages 264 and 265) to estimate monthly inflows and outflows of cash and likely bank balances.

She kept her accounts during the year. They show that she did well and finished up with a profit of £37,500, with which she was very pleased.

As a sole trader she has made the profit and it is hers to take and use.

Flick's brother **Seamus Moran** has bought shares in Tesco Plc. He receives a share of Tesco's profits (dividend payments) during the year, so he is also pleased.

James Morton is Flick's partner. He works for a large London bank. As an employee he receives a bonus payment every year from the large profits made by the bank. He is also delighted because he has bought a new Mercedes car with his money.

a point to think about . . .

The success of a business can be measured in terms of its profit, which can be good news for the owner, shareholder and employee.

But is profit made in this way such a good thing for overseas factory workers on low wages?

a definition of profit

profit or loss?

A business that sells a product or provides a service receives money from sales. It also has to pay running costs. If the sales income is greater than the running costs, the difference between these two figures is the **profit** made by the business:

*sales income **minus** running costs **equals** profit*

example

Sales income of £10,000 – running costs of £5,000 = £5,000 profit

What if the sales income is less than the running costs?
The difference between these two figures is the **loss** made by the business. For example:

sales income of £10,000 – running costs of £11,000 = £1,000 loss

It is common practice to show a loss in brackets, like this: (£1,000).

Activity 35.1 – calculating profit

Calculate the profit (or loss) made by the following businesses.
If a loss has been made, show the figure in your answer in brackets.

	Sales income	Running costs
	£	£
Business 1	10,000	6,000
Business 2	12,000	8,000
Business 3	10,000	12,000
Business 4	15,600	7,800
Business 5	13,900	15,100
Business 6	145,000	89,000
Business 7	1,200,000	987,650
Business 8	235,000	270,000
Business 9	78,000	45,000
Business 10	12,560	9,654

what costs are included in the calculation?

You will see that the profit calculation does *not* include:

- financing items such as capital from the owner, or grants or loans
- start-up costs such as the purchase of premises or equipment

The profit calculation involves only:

- income from day-to-day trading, for example sales of products and services
- running costs – these include the purchase of materials and stock which a business can then sell, and overheads – day-to-day expenses such as wages, telephone bills, rates and insurance

Activity 35.2 – sorting out the costs

Calculate the profit (or loss) made by the three businesses whose income and costs are shown below. If a loss has been made, show the figure in your answer in brackets.

Before working out the profit (or loss) you will need to decide which items are start-up costs or financing items (loans, capital) because you will not be able to include these in your calculation.

Business	Receipts		Payments	
		£		£
1 Travel Agent	Sales of services	45,000	Running costs	35,000
	Loan from bank	5,000	Computer	4,000
2 Manufacturer	Sales of product	62,000	Raw materials	30,000
	Loan from bank	150,000	Insurance	1,000
			Other running costs	20,000
			Premises purchase	100,000
			Machinery purchase	50,000
3 Shop	Sales of stock	100,000	Purchases of stock	50,000
	Capital	50,000	Wages	34,000
			Rates	4,500
			Other running costs	30,000

the profit and loss statement

At the end of a financial period – normally at the end of a year – a business will draw up a table of figures known as a **profit and loss statement**. This financial statement sets out the calculations you have been practising in this chapter:

*sales income **minus** running costs **equals** profit (or loss)*

Notice that the profit and loss statement looks back over the year and is very different from the cash-flow forecast which, as you saw in Chapter 32, looks forward. The profit and loss statement is an accurate record of the profit or loss that has been made; the cash flow forecast is only an estimate of the money that will come in and out of the bank account in the future.

A typical profit and loss statement for Joel Masters, a sole trader, is shown below. The arrows have been added to show the arithmetic. Note the following points . . .

heading

The statement is headed up with the words 'Profit and Loss Statement' followed by the name of the business and the financial period covered.

format

The statement is presented in two money columns: the expense items are shown on the left and their total is carried over to the right-hand column, as shown by the arrow.

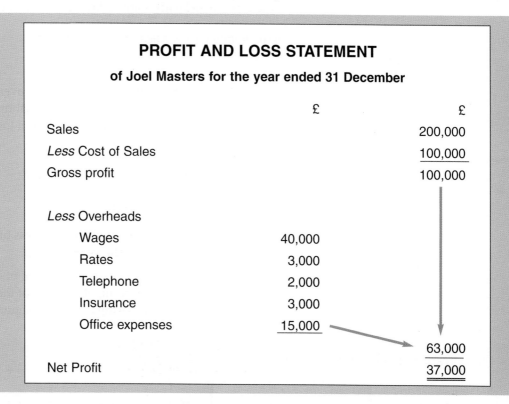

PROFIT AND LOSS STATEMENT

of Joel Masters for the year ended 31 December

	£	£
Sales		200,000
Less Cost of Sales		100,000
Gross profit		100,000
Less Overheads		
Wages	40,000	
Rates	3,000	
Telephone	2,000	
Insurance	3,000	
Office expenses	15,000	
		63,000
Net Profit		37,000

some terminology

cost of sales

The statement shown here is that of a business which makes or sells a product, ie a manufacturer or a shop. The item below the sales for the year is the cost of sales.

Cost of sales is the cost to the business of producing or buying in the goods that have actually been sold during the financial period of the profit and loss statement.

Cost of sales is normally more or less the same as the figure as the purchases of stock made by the business. It is usually adjusted for stock held at the beginning and the end of the year. In your studies you will not need to worry about these adjustments; as far as you are concerned:

*cost of sales **equals** purchases of stock and goods*

gross profit

Calculating cost of sales – the cost of what has actually been sold – enables the business to calculate profit accurately.

Gross profit is the profit to the business before the other running expenses – **overheads** – are deducted. The calculation is:

*sales **minus** cost of sales **equals** gross profit*

net profit

Net profit is the profit after the deduction of **overheads** such as wages, rates, telephone and so on – the normal running expenses of a business. If the figure is negative, it will be a loss and it will be shown in brackets. The formula is:

*gross profit **minus** overheads **equals** net profit*

what happens to the profit?

The net profit is the money that the business has earned for the owner (or owners) during the year.

If the owner is a sole trader or a partner, some of this net profit can be taken out by the owner during the course of the year in the form of payments known as **drawings**. See the diagram below.

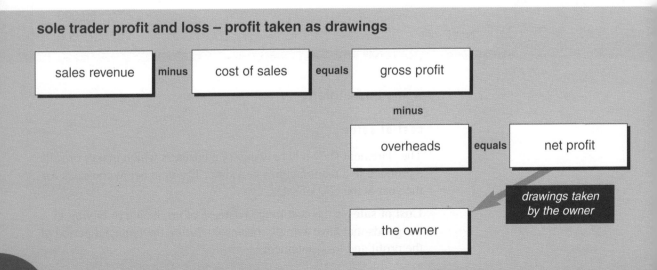

sole trader profit and loss – profit taken as drawings

sales revenue **minus** cost of sales **equals** gross profit

minus

overheads **equals** net profit

drawings taken by the owner

the owner

If the business is a limited company some of the net profit will be paid out to the owners – the shareholders – in the form of payments known as **dividends**.

It is sound business practice to keep some of the net profit in the business as savings or to buy more resources to help the business expand. Owners who take out all the profit are not helping the business.

Profit is not equal to money in the bank. Profit may have been earned during the year, but it may also have been spent.

limited company profit and loss – profit taken as dividends by shareholders

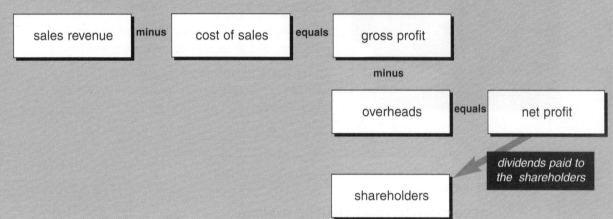

Activity 35.3 – defining profit

1 What is meant by 'cost of sales'?

2 What is gross profit and how is it calculated?

3 What would happen to gross profit if the cost of sales increased during the year more than sales revenue?

4 What is net profit and how is it calculated?

5 What profit can the owner (or owners) of a business take out – gross profit or net profit?

6 What is the difference between drawings and dividends?

7 Is it a good idea for the owner (or owners) of a business to take out all the profits of a business for themselves? Write down the reasons for your answer.

8 The gross profit of a jeweller is much higher in relation to its sales than the gross profit of a supermarket. Write down why you think this might be the case. Why are there not more jewellers?

Case Study – profit and loss statement

Flick's first year

In Chapter 32 we looked at the twelve month cash-flow forecast of Flick Moran who set up a CD mailing business (see pages 264 and 265). This forecast suggested that she would end up with £7,000 in the bank at the end of December.

But a cash-flow forecast is only an estimate. What was her actual profit for the year?

Her accounting records show that her sales did better than expected, but her costs were also higher.

Shown below are the actual figures which Flick took from her accounting records to use in her profit and loss statement.

FLICK MORAN

RESULTS FROM FIRST YEAR OF TRADING

	£
Sales	264,000
Purchases (cost of sales)	144,000
Wages	23,500
Mailing costs	15,000
Office costs	24,600
Advertising	19,400

Notice the items that Flick does **not** include in these figures:

- sources of money such as capital she has put in, loans or grants

- start-up costs such as computers and other equipment

A profit and loss statement only uses **sales figures** and **running costs**.

preparing the profit and loss statement

Flick passes these figures to her accountant who is drawing up her profit and loss statement. It will look like this:

PROFIT AND LOSS STATEMENT

of Flick Moran for the year ended 31 December

	£	£
Sales		264,000
Less Cost of Sales		144,000
Gross profit		120,000
Less Overheads		
Wages	23,500	
Mailing costs	15,000	
Office costs	24,600	
Advertising	19,400	
		82,500
Net Profit		37,500

---

some questions from Flick – and the answers

Flick then asks her accountant some questions :

1 'The net profit of £37,500 is far more than the amount I have got in the bank. Why is this?'

2 'What about the money I took out of the business to live on – the drawings of £24,000?'

Answers to these questions are:

1 Net profit is not the same as the money that you have left at the end of the financial period. You may have invested some of this and will have taken some out as living expenses.

2 Your living expenses – 'drawings' – never appear in the profit and loss statement. The net profit is the money that is available to you and the drawings will be deducted from it. You will know that profit needs to work for a business – you cannot take it all out as drawings. You have sensibly kept some money in the business.

profit and loss statement on a spreadsheet

spreadsheet format

You will see from the format of the profit and loss statement on page 297 that it can easily be set up on a computer spreadsheet.

Illustrated below is a sample spreadsheet file set up for a profit and loss statement. You will see that there are only two columns needed for numerical data.

It is a good idea to leave some extra rows clear in the overheads section in case you need to input extra items of expense.

spreadsheet formulas

On the opposite page is a copy of this spreadsheet showing the formulas used. You may need to consult your computer manual, teacher or technician to check the format of the formulas used on your program; they may differ from those used here.

profit and loss statement on a computer spreadsheet

	A	B	C
1	PROFIT AND LOSS STATEMENT		
2	Name:		
3	Period:		
4			
5		£	£
6			
7	Sales		150000
8	Cost of sales (Purchases)		55000
9			
10	Gross profit		95000
11	Less overheads:		
12			
13			
14	Wages	40000	
15	Rent	12000	
16	Rates	2500	
17	Insurance	3500	
18	Advertising	1500	
19	Other expenses	5000	
20			64500
21	Net profit		30500
22			

profit and loss statement – spreadsheet formulas

	A	B	C
1	PROFIT AND LOSS STATEMENT		
2	Name:		
3	Period:		
4			
5		£	£
6			
7	Sales		150000
8	Cost of sales (Purchases)		55000
9			
10	Gross profit		=C7-C8
11	Less overheads:		
12			
13			
14	Wages	40000	
15	Rent	12000	
16	Rates	2500	
17	Insurance	3500	
18	Advertising	1500	
19	Other expenses	5000	
20			=SUM(B14..B19)
21	Net profit		=C10-C20
22			

Activity 35.4 – profit and loss statements

practical note

If a computer spreadsheet is not available, complete question 1 only.

You have been given the figures for three separate businesses as at 31 December of this year.

1 Draw up profit and loss statements for each of the businesses on paper.

2 Set up a suitable spreadsheet file and input the figures from your paper-based originals. Use the spreadsheet to check your totals for accuracy.

Fairburn Foods

	£
Sales	175,000
Purchases	95,000
Wages	45,600
Rent	5,000
Rates	3,450
Insurance	2,300
Advertising	2,000
Other expenses	200

Grantley Garden Supplies

	£
Sales	250,900
Purchases	102,984
Wages	67,800
Rent	5,690
Rates	4,010
Insurance	4,560
Advertising	13,450
Other expenses	2,057

Hardy Hi-Fi

	£
Sales	65,000
Purchases	45,000
Wages	15,600
Rent	2,000
Rates	2,100
Insurance	1,950
Advertising	560
Other expenses	500

Nutshell summary

- Business owners rely on a business making a profit to provide them with money to live on.

- A profit is made when the sales revenue of a business is greater than its running expenses.

- If the running expenses are greater than the sales revenue, then the business makes a loss.

- The profit or loss of a business is calculated by means of a profit and loss statement.

- A profit and loss statement does not include items such as capital and loans or start-up costs. It deals only with income from sales revenue and running costs.

- There are two types of profit in a profit and loss statement: gross profit and net profit.

- Gross profit is calculated by deducting the cost of sales from the sales revenue.

- Net profit deducts the overheads (expenses) of the business from gross profit.

- Net profit is the best measure of how profitable a business is.

- Net profit is the money available to the owner (or owners) of a business for personal use.

- Net profit taken out by a sole trader or partner in a partnership is known as drawings.

- Most business owners will not take out all the net profit for personal use, but will leave money in the business to provide the finance for equipment and expansion.

- Shareholders of a limited company will receive a share of profits in the form of payments known as 'dividends'. The amount of the dividend will be decided by the management of the company.

- A profit and loss statement can easily be set up on a computer spreadsheet. This provides a quick and accurate way of calculating business profits and losses.

Key terms

Profit
The money made by a business over a period of time, calculated as sales income minus running costs.

Loss
The situation where the difference between sales revenue (income) and running costs is a negative amount.

Profit and loss statement
A table of figures which calculates the profit or loss of a business over a period of time.

Cost of sales
The cost to a business of producing or buying in the goods that have been sold during the financial period of the profit and loss statement.

Gross profit
The difference between sales revenue and the cost of sales, calculated before overheads have been deducted.

Net profit
The difference between gross profit and the overheads of the business.

Drawings
The money taken out of net profit by the business owner.

Dividends
Payments made out of net profit to shareholders of a limited company.

36

Business balance sheets

A 'snapshot' of a business

Financial statements are important for business owners such as Ella and Flick.

A cash-flow forecast looks forward over a year and a profit and loss statement looks back over a year.

But business owners such as Ella and Flick will also need to know what their businesses own at any one time and also what their businesses owe. In other words, what are they worth?

Their employees may also be interested and so will the bank, if it is lending them money.

The **business balance sheet** is the financial

statement which answers these questions. It is basically like a 'snapshot' of the business at one moment in time – which is often the end of the year. This balance sheet 'snapshot' shows how the business is financed and what the money has been spent on.

cash | premises | stock | computers | December 31 | loan | profits | overdraft | capital

a point to think about . . .

Will the figures in a business balance sheet be the same on 31 December as they were two weeks earlier? If not, why not?

what is a balance sheet?

A **balance sheet** contains figures taken from the accounting records of a business on a particular date – often the end of the year.

A **balance sheet** shows what a business owns – offices, computers and stock, for example – and the ways in which it has been financed: capital from the owner, profits it has made in the past, loans and overdrafts from the bank.

A balance sheet involves sets of figures from the accounts which balance – so we need to make a note of some accounting terms first.

definition of a balance sheet

A balance sheet is a financial statement which shows the assets, liabilities and capital of a business at a particular date.

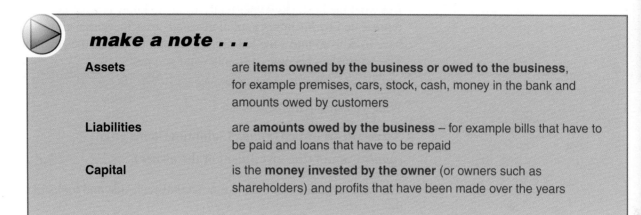

make a note . . .

Assets	are **items owned by the business or owed to the business**, for example premises, cars, stock, cash, money in the bank and amounts owed by customers
Liabilities	are **amounts owed by the business** – for example bills that have to be paid and loans that have to be repaid
Capital	is the **money invested by the owner** (or owners such as shareholders) and profits that have been made over the years

how does a balance sheet 'balance'?

If you borrow £10 and spend it on a CD you have a balance sheet which balances. In this case there is a balance of £10 on each side.

CD = an item you own = an asset £10	*financed by*	a loan = an item you owe = a liability £10

If you apply the same principle to a business you can see the same 'balance' between money spent on assets (items owned) and money raised (capital from the owner and loans from a bank).

Suppose a business starts up and . . .

- buys computer equipment for £7,000 and furniture for £3,000
- raises £2,000 from the bank and £8,000 capital from the owner

The 'balance' sheet looks like this:

assets		*financed by*	**liability**	
computers	£7,000		bank loan	£2,000
furniture	£3,000		**capital**	£8,000
total	£10,000		total	£10,000

the balance sheet equation

What we have said in the business balance sheet is

assets **equals** *capital* **plus** *liabilities*

But what the business owner really wants to know is what is represented by his or her capital invested. To achieve this all you have to do is to move the liabilities to the other side of the equation. The 'plus' then becomes a 'minus' and you get:

assets **minus** *liabilities* **equals** *capital*

What you are saying here is:

Assets (items owned) *minus* **Liabilities (items owed)**

equals **Capital (the investment of the owner).**

The balance sheet now balances at £8,000 each side and looks like this:

financed by

Activity 36.1 – balancing the balance sheet

Using the equation 'Assets minus Liabilities equals Capital' calculate the amount of capital invested by the owners of the following businesses. Show the workings to your answers.

1   Plastix Limited has assets of £10,000 and liabilities of £5,000.

2   Rubius Ltd has assets of £120,000 and liabilities of £65,000.

3   Gem Stones Ltd has assets of £123,000 and a bank loan of £50,000.

4   Britney & Co has assets of £155,000, an overdraft of £10,000 and a bank loan of £50,000.

5   Williams & Williams is setting up in business. It has bought:

■ premises for £150,000

■ equipment for £50,000

■ stock for £10,000

It has raised a bank loan for £75,000 to help finance the business.

more about capital in the balance sheet

You will remember that when we looked at profit and loss statements, some of the net profit earned by the business would normally be kept in the business. Capital – which is the owner's investment in the business – is therefore made up of two parts:

- the 'capital' originally invested by the business

- profit put back into the business by the owner (or owners) – this is known as 'retained profit' or 'profit and loss account' or 'reserves'

In the balance sheet the capital section looks like this:

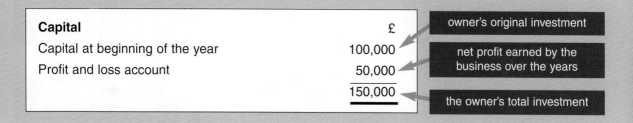

Capital	£	owner's original investment
Capital at beginning of the year	100,000	net profit earned by the business over the years
Profit and loss account	50,000	
	150,000	the owner's total investment

Note that in a limited company balance sheet the heading **Capital** is often replaced by the term **Shareholders Funds**.

assets and liabilities in the balance sheet

assets

The balance sheet splits assets (items owned) into two types – fixed assets and current assets:

- **fixed assets** are items owned which the business expects to keep for a long time – for example premises and computers

- **current assets** are items owned by the business or owed to the business in the short term – for example stock held by a shop, cash in the tills, amounts due from customers

liabilities

The balance sheet splits liabilities (money owed by the business) in the same way:

- **long-term liabilities** are amounts owed which are due to be repaid in more than a year's time, for example long-term loans

- **current liabilities** are amounts owed which are due to be repaid in less than a year's time to **creditors** (eg bills from suppliers)

Now study the balance sheet layout shown on the next two pages.

Case Study – balance sheet

the business

Hermione Grant Limited is a craft shop. It is a company set up and run by Hermione Grant.

financing

Hermione has invested £150,000 of her own money in the company as **capital**.

This capital is made up of 150,000 £1 shares.

Hermione has also borrowed a £75,000 long-term loan from the bank to help her set up the business. This is a **long-term liability**.

business assets

The company has bought shop premises for £200,000 and shop equipment for £40,000. These are its **fixed assets**.

The company also has **current assets** (short-term assets) which include stock (the cards), money owed by some trade customers (debtors), money in the bank and cash in the till.

business liabilities

The company owes money to its suppliers (its creditors). These are its **current liabilities** as they are short-term. The **long term liability** is the bank loan.

net assets

Assets minus *Liabilities* equals *Net Assets*. This £185,000 is Hermione's stake in the business and equals her Capital . . .

capital

The business is financed by Hermione's capital (the shareholder's funds). This is made up from her shares and the profits made by the business up to the date of the balance sheet.

how the balance sheet works . . .

balance sheet date
The balance sheet shows a 'snapshot' of the business on 31 December 2003.

fixed assets
These are the items owned by the business for the long-term.

current assets
These are the items owned by the business for the short-term. The 'debtors' figure is the amount owed by customers – so it represents money coming in soon.

current liabilities
These are the items owed by the business in the short-term (less than 12 months). Note that they are deducted from the current assets in the balance sheet.

long-term liabilities
These are the items owed by the business in the long-term (over 12 months) – here a bank loan.

net assets
This is all the assets minus all the liabilities.

financed by . . .
This shows how the business is financed and where the money has come from. In this case it is share capital (the owner's investment) and profits earned.

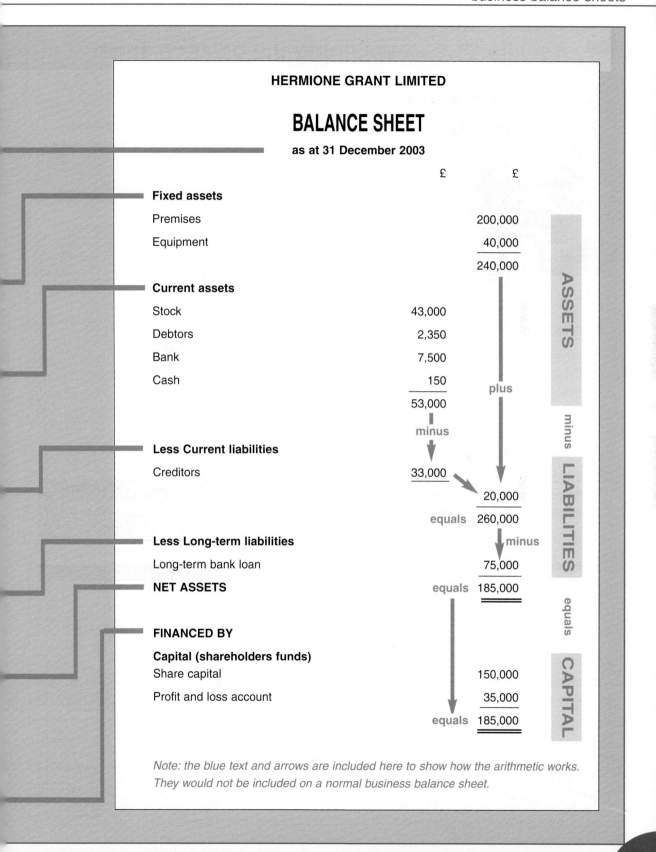

HERMIONE GRANT LIMITED

BALANCE SHEET

as at 31 December 2003

	£	£
Fixed assets		
Premises		200,000
Equipment		40,000
		240,000
Current assets		
Stock	43,000	
Debtors	2,350	
Bank	7,500	
Cash	150	plus
	53,000	
	minus	
Less Current liabilities		
Creditors	33,000	
		20,000
	equals	260,000
		minus
Less Long-term liabilities		
Long-term bank loan		75,000
NET ASSETS	equals	185,000
FINANCED BY		
Capital (shareholders funds)		
Share capital		150,000
Profit and loss account		35,000
	equals	185,000

ASSETS minus LIABILITIES equals CAPITAL

Note: the blue text and arrows are included here to show how the arithmetic works. They would not be included on a normal business balance sheet.

Activity 36.2 – explaining the balance sheet

the business

Axus Limited is a camera shop which sells to the general public and also to professional photographers. The company is has been set up by Sanjay Patel who owns 200,000 shares of £1.

Axus Limited has finished its first year of trading and Sanjay's accountant has prepared the balance sheet.

Sanjay is not used to the balance sheet format and has a number of questions for the accountant.

Write down your answers to Sanjay's questions.

Sanjay's questions

1 Where is the money that I invested in the company at the beginning of the year shown? How much was it?

2 What are 'fixed' assets? What are my fixed assets and what are they worth?

3 What are 'current' assets? How are they different to fixed assets? How much are mine worth?

4 What are debtors?

5 Explain the difference between current assets and current liabilities.

6 What are creditors?

7 Why is a long-term bank loan a long-term liability?

8 What two figures are the same? Why are they the same?

9 Why does the balance sheet have a particular date on it? Won't the figures be the same every day during the year?

10 How does the balance sheet differ from the profit and loss statement?

AXUS LIMITED
BALANCE SHEET
as at 31 December 2003

	£	£
Fixed assets		
Premises		165,000
Computer equipment		45,000
		210,000
Current assets		
Stock	110,000	
Debtors	50,100	
Bank	17,000	
Cash	218	
	177,318	
Less Current liabilities		
Creditors	85,700	
		91,618
		301,618
Less Long-term liabilities		
Long-term bank loan		50,000
NET ASSETS		251,618
FINANCED BY		
Capital (shareholders funds)		
Share capital		200,000
Profit and loss account		51,618
		251,618

Nutshell summary

- The balance sheet of a business is a 'snapshot' of that business. It shows what it owns, what it owes and the way in which it is financed on a particular date.

- The balance sheet is an important financial statement because it shows the owner what his or her investment has been used for and gives an idea of what the business is worth.

- The figures in a balance sheet are taken from the accounting records of the business – normally at the end of the financial year of the business.

- The balance sheet is a calculation which shows two figures which are equal – which 'balance'.

- In order to get to this 'balance' the balance sheet is constructed around an equation:

  assets **minus** *liabilities* **equals** *capital*

- Assets are the items that the owner's investment has been spent on. They can be long-term (fixed) assets like computers or they can be short-term (current) assets such as stock and cash in the tills.

- Liabilities, on the other hand, are items that the business will have to repay at some time and so have to be deducted from the assets to show the value of the owner's investment.

- Liabilities are long-term if they have to be repaid over more than twelve months and short-term (current) if they are due in less than twelve months' time.

- Current liabilities are deducted from current assets as part of the balance sheet calculation to show what money (and money coming in) the business has in the short-term.

- Net Assets is one of the 'balancing' figures of the balance sheet – it is all the assets minus all the liabilities.

- Capital (or Shareholders Funds in the case of a company) is the other balancing figure. This is made up of the investment of the owner and profits which the business has made.

Key terms

Balance sheet
A financial statement showing what a business owns and owes, and how it is financed.

Assets
Items owned by the business or owed to the business.

Fixed Assets
Items kept for the long-term.

Current Assets
Short-term assets.

Debtors
Money owed by customers of a business (a current asset)

Liabilities
Amounts owed by a business.

Long-term Liabilities
Liabilities due to be repaid over more than a year.

Current Liabilities
Liabilities due to be repaid in less than a year.

Creditors
Money owed by a business in the short-term (a current liability).

Capital
Money invested by the owner of a business.

Shareholders funds
Money invested by shareholders of a limited company and the profits they have earned.

37

Who needs financial statements?

Who is interested?

Financial statements such as the profit and loss statement and the balance sheet are very important to the owners of a business. But there are other people who are affected by what goes on in the profit and loss statement and balance sheet. Read through these newspaper headlines . . .

> **Dividend boost for shareholders as annual profits surge ahead**

> **Shareholders criticise big bonuses for managers following profit increase**

> **Company losses lead to massive lay-offs**

> **Banks threaten to call in loans as company losses mount**

> **Supermarket customers benefit from major investment in out-of-town stores**

a point to think about . . .

It is not just the owners of businesses who will be interested in the financial statements. There are many groups of people who will want to know how profitable or stable a business is – and their points of view may well conflict. What groups of people can you identify from these newspaper headlines?

stakeholders

The groups of people mentioned in the newspaper headlines are known as stakeholders.

Stakeholders are groups of people who have an interest in a business.

The diagram on the next page shows in more detail how stakeholders can have an interest in the financial performance of a business. Financial statements show the financial state of a business – how profitable it is, how strong it is and how much it is worth.

stakeholders of a business

shareholders
interested in the profit made and the dividend paid

employees
interested in whether the business will keep their jobs going

the business

managers
interested in the bonuses for helping to make a profit

banks
interested in the business being able to repay its loans

customers
interested in the success and stability of the business

'I am an employee of Dellsoft Computers. I always want to know if the company is making a profit. If it isn't, there may be cutbacks and I may lose my job. That's how I lost my last job. I got made redundant.'

'I am an Area Sales Manager at Dellsoft Computers. The sales and profit figures of the company are given to us each month. It matters to me because of my bonuses. Last year I got about £5,000, which paid for my annual holiday.'

shareholders

Shareholders are the owners of shares in a company. They have invested money in the company and expect to receive a **dividend** payment as their share of the profits. Shareholders will naturally be interested in the profit and loss statement.

employees

Employees depend on the business for their pay and their jobs, so they will want to have a profitable and stable employer. Some employers give their employees a profit-sharing bonus.

managers

Managers may also receive bonuses related to profit and so will be motivated to make the business successful.

'I am a lending officer at the National Bank. We are lending a total of £250,000 to Dellsoft Computers. We need to keep a regular check on the profit and balance sheet figures to make sure they can repay us.'

banks

Banks lend money and want to make sure it will be repaid. They will keep an eye on the profit levels of a business that borrows and also on the balance sheet to make sure that its liabilities are not too high.

'I work for Instil PLC which buys computers regularly from Dellsoft. We need to make sure that they are financially OK. If they are not, we could be in trouble for future supplies and maintenance contracts.'

customers

Customers will want to deal with a business that will be profitable and financially strong. This will ensure that they will not run short of the product or service that they buy from the business.

Activity 37.1 – stakeholder interests

Read through the newspaper headlines shown in the Case Study on page 310 and then answer the questions below.

1   Why should shareholders be interested in the level of profits made by a company?

2   What financial statement would provide them with this information?

3   Why should employees be interested in the level of profits made by a company?

4   What could happen to the workforce if the company they work for makes losses?

5   Why might the managers of a company be interested in the level of profits made by the company?

6   Why might the shareholders not be so keen if the directors and managers receive very large pay bonuses from the company?

7   A supermarket chain plans to build new out-of-town stores. Which stakeholders would directly benefit from this expansion, and why? Identify any other stakeholders who might be affected by this expansion and explain how they might benefit.

reading the financial statements

A stakeholder such as a shareholder or lender looking at a profit and loss statement or a balance sheet is like a doctor examining a patient. But instead of taking temperature, pulse or a blood test, a stakeholder will look at or compare key figures to make sure the business is healthy. Why? Read through the following examples and study the illustrations.

is the business profitable?

A business that is financially strong is one where:

- there is a good level of profits rather than a loss shown in the profit and loss statement

- the overheads (expenses) section in the profit and loss statement is not too high and does not result in a loss being made

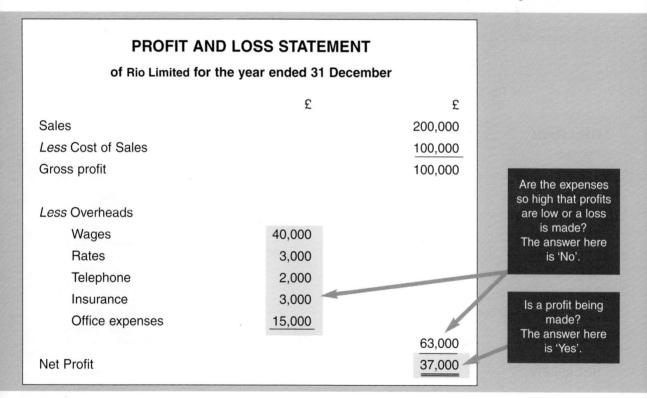

PROFIT AND LOSS STATEMENT

of Rio Limited for the year ended 31 December

	£	£
Sales		200,000
Less Cost of Sales		100,000
Gross profit		100,000
Less Overheads		
Wages	40,000	
Rates	3,000	
Telephone	2,000	
Insurance	3,000	
Office expenses	15,000	
		63,000
Net Profit		37,000

Are the expenses so high that profits are low or a loss is made? The answer here is 'No'.

Is a profit being made? The answer here is 'Yes'.

can the business repay its debts?

Businesses often owe money to stakeholders – to suppliers for goods supplied on credit (buy now, pay later) or to the bank for money borrowed. There is nothing wrong with owing money – the important thing is that the business can pay that money back.

The balance sheet will give these stakeholders an idea of the money available to repay debts. A business is said to be **solvent** when it can repay debts when they are due. **Solvency** is shown by calculating the money available for repaying short-term debt:

Current assets (what the business owns in the short term) minus Current Liabilities (what the business owes in the short term).

This is shown in the illustration below.

what is the business worth?

The Capital section in the balance sheet – which is equal to all the assets minus the liabilities – shows in basic terms how much the business is worth. The total of the Capital section is also the balancing figure (it also appears as the Net Assets). It is known as the **Net Worth** of the business. This is the figure the shareholders will be interested in – it represents their investment in the company.

This is also shown in the illustration below.

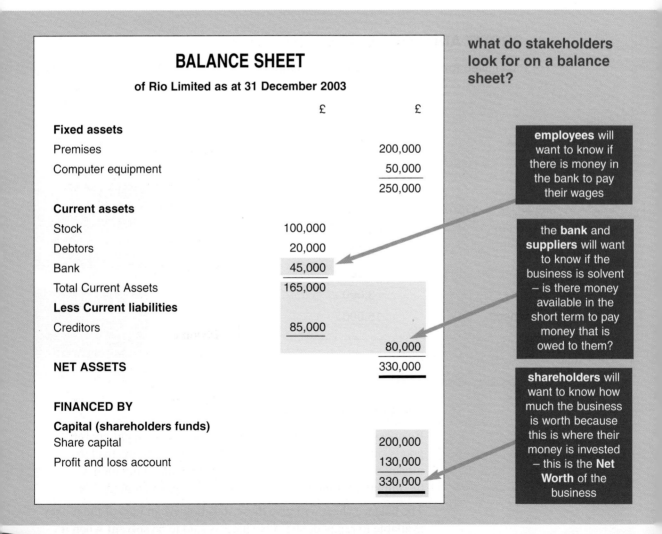

BALANCE SHEET

of Rio Limited as at 31 December 2003

	£	£
Fixed assets		
Premises		200,000
Computer equipment		50,000
		250,000
Current assets		
Stock	100,000	
Debtors	20,000	
Bank	45,000	
Total Current Assets	165,000	
Less Current liabilities		
Creditors	85,000	
		80,000
NET ASSETS		330,000
FINANCED BY		
Capital (shareholders funds)		
Share capital		200,000
Profit and loss account		130,000
		330,000

what do stakeholders look for on a balance sheet?

employees will want to know if there is money in the bank to pay their wages

the **bank** and **suppliers** will want to know if the business is solvent – is there money available in the short term to pay money that is owed to them?

shareholders will want to know how much the business is worth because this is where their money is invested – this is the **Net Worth** of the business

Activity 37.2 – reading financial statements

Study the diagrams of the profit and loss statement and the balance sheet on the previous two pages and answer these questions.

1   What is the Net Profit of Rio Limited? Would stakeholders be happy with this?

2   In the following year, total overheads (expenses) increased to £100,000 and Gross Profit dropped to £90,000. What is the Net Profit in this year, and how would stakeholders be affected by this?

3   What figure on the balance sheet of Rio Limited would be of interest to employees? Would they be happy with the figure shown here?

4   What resources are shown by the balance sheet of Rio Limited as being available in the short term for repaying debts? What stakeholders would be interested in this figure, and why?

5   What is the Net Assets and Net Worth (Capital) figure on the balance sheet of Rio Limited? What stakeholders would be interested in this figure, and why?

Nutshell summary

- The profit and loss statement of a business shows how profitable it is. The balance sheet shows how it is financed and what assets and liabilities it has.

- This information is of interest not only to the owner but also to other groups of people known as 'stakeholders'.

- Stakeholders such as shareholders and managers will be interested in the profit a business makes because they may receive some of it.

- Stakeholders such as lending banks need to know that they will get their money repaid. They will need to know about the profit made and the liabilities on the balance sheet.

- Employees and customers will need to know that the business is profitable enough to keep their jobs going and secure enough to deal with in the future.

- Stakeholders can interpret financial statements to see how well a business is able to repay its debts and what it is worth as an investment.

Key terms

Stakeholder
A person such as a shareholder or employee who has an interest in what a business does and how it performs.

Shareholders
Investors who have bought shares in limited companies.

Dividend
A share of a company's profits paid to a shareholder.

Solvency
The ability of a business to pay debts when they are due.

Net worth
The value of a business – normally the balancing figure on the balance sheet.

38

The business plan

Persuading the bank to lend

In earlier chapters we have seen how Ella has taken the first steps to setting up her computer training business 'Webwise'. She has worked out her start-up costs and running costs and has decided how to finance the business.

Ella has discussed her new business 'Webwise' with the bank adviser and the time has now come for her to set out her ideas in a formal 'Business Plan'. Most banks publish a range of leaflets and brochures containing advice and forms to fill in which will form the basis of the business plan. Many banks also provide information on their websites.

Ella reckons she may need to borrow up to £10,000 from the bank on an overdraft. The bank business adviser wants to be sure that she can repay this money and so asks her to draw up a formal written business plan.

The business plan itself is usually a ring-binder folder with forms and documents enclosed in it.

A smartly presented plan will impress the bank. The plan normally contains a number of sections, many of which involve answering questions.

a point to think about . . .

Good planning is essential if any business idea is to succeed. Writing a business plan is one of the best ways of 'thinking things through'.

what does a business plan contain?

A business plan is a formal written document which explains to an outsider such as a bank:

■ the business idea

■ the market

■ the finance

A business plan is written when a business is starting up for the first time and also when it starts a new project.

questions to be asked

A business plan involves providing the answers to a number of questions, many of which are shown below.

It involves the processes of budgeting and planning which we covered in Chapter 31.

The business plan

■ **The business idea**

What is the product going to be? What type of business ownership is involved? Sole trader? Partnership? Franchise? Why are you starting this business?

■ **The market**

Who are your customers? Are you aiming at a particular type of customer?

Who are your competitors? What do they charge?

■ **Who are you?**

If the bank is lending you money it will want to know about your background and how much money you have. Are you a safe bet for a loan? Do you have experience of what you want to do?

■ **Whom are you going to employ?**

You should list the staff you plan to take on. You should estimate what their wages will be.

■ **Marketing and sales**

How do your competitors promote their product? How are you going to promote your product? How will you reach your customers? What is your sales target?

■ **Pricing**

What are you going to charge for your product?

Are you going to try to undercut the competition?

■ **Equipment**

What equipment do you need if you are making a product? What computers and office machines do you need? How much will it all cost?

■ **Premises**

Will you need premises away from your home? Do you intend to buy premises? Or will you rent them? How much will they cost?

Activity 38.1 – the business plan

1   There will be a number of important questions that will be asked in a business plan.
    Write out ten questions which you think are important.

2   Which do you think is more important for a new business when it is writing a business plan:
    the market for its products or the equipment it needs?
    Give the reasons for your answer.

3   Ella's new business is setting up computer courses. Who do you think will be Ella's customers?
    How is Ella going to get those customers to sign up for her courses?

financial projections

One of the most important sections in a business plan contains the **financial projections**. These are calculations which show the business owner and the bank whether the business is likely to make a profit and survive. The most important calculations are contained in a:

■ forecast profit and loss statement

■ break-even calculation

■ cash-flow forecast

We have already covered the format of these financial statements in earlier chapters, so you should be familiar with them.

profit forecast

Profit is the difference between the money the business receives from selling its products and the money it has to pay out for running costs. The **profit forecast** shows how much money the business owner is likely to make out of the business.

break-even

Break-even is the point where income from sales covers all costs. It shows the number of items a business will have to sell to cover all its costs. The items can be products or services – cars or haircuts. If a business is not going to break-even it is likely to run into trouble from the start!

Profit Forecast

	£	
Income from sales		550,000
less cost of sales		250,000
Gross profit		300,000
less expenses		
Wages	80,000	
Office expenses	45,000	
Advertising	35,000	
Other expenses	28,500	
Total expenses		188,500
Net profit for the year		111,500

Profit   equals

Income from sales

minus

running costs

cash-flow Forecast

The **cash-flow forecast** sets out the amount of money the business expects to come in and out of the bank account each month.

The bottom line of the cash-flow forecast shows the amount of money in the bank at the end of each month

If more money goes out than comes in, the bottom line will eventually show a negative amount. This means the business will need to borrow that money from the bank.

Can the business sell enough to make a profit?

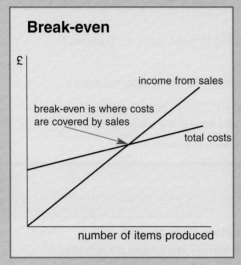

Break-even

£

income from sales

break-even is where costs are covered by sales

total costs

number of items produced

**Break-even =
The point where income from sales covers costs**

Will the business have to borrow from the bank?

Cash-flow forecast

	January £	February £
Receipts		
Sales	50,000	50,000
Other receipts	10,000	1,000
Total Receipts (A)	**60,000**	**51,000**
Payments		
Suppliers	20,000	22,000
Wages	9,000	9,000
Other payments	15,000	5,000
Total Payments (B)	**44,000**	**36,000**
Bank balance (beginning of month)	10,000	26,000
Add receipts (A)	60,000	51,000
Less payments (B)	44,000	36,000
Bank balance (end of month)	**26,000**	**41,000**

**Cash flow =
A projection of money paid into and out of the bank account, showing the monthly balance**

an interview with the bank – decision time

Does the business plan work?

The business plan – including all the financial projections – will show if the business has a chance of being successful.

If the business needs to borrow money, the next step is to send the plan in to the bank and to arrange an interview.

The bank lending officer will decide if the proposition is watertight – if the business can afford the repayments, the bank is more likely to lend the money.

Business plan summary

**questions
to be asked**

What is the product?	What staff will I need?
Who are my customers?	What will my costs be?
Who are my competitors?	What will my income be?
What price will I charge?	What money do I have?
What equipment will I need?	Do I need premises?

financial calculations

Profit forecast
What money am I going to make out of the business?

Break-even
How many items do I have to sell to cover my costs?

Cash-flow forecast
How much money will I have in the bank each month?

Will I have to borrow from the bank?

decisions to be made

The business – whether to go ahead?
Is the business idea viable? Will I make a living from it?

The business – will I need to borrow?
Is there enough money available or will a loan be needed?

The bank – will it want to lend the money?
Can the business make enough profit to repay the loan?

Activity 38.2 – financial projections

1 What are the three main financial projections in a business plan?

2 What will a forecast profit and loss statement tell the business owner?

3 What will a break-even calculation tell the business owner?

4 Ella is including a cash-flow forecast as part of her business plan. Why would this be of
particular importance to her bank?

Nutshell summary

- Good planning is essential if a business idea is to succeed.

- A business plan is a document put together by the business owner which sets out information about the way the business will operate.

- A business plan is drawn up when a business is starting up for the first time and also when it is expanding and undertaking new projects.

- The business plan consists of a number of areas which need to be considered when planning:
  - the business idea (the product)
  - the market it is being sold to (the customers)
  - details of the business owner (or owners)
  - the staff needed by the business
  - promoting the product
  - pricing the product
  - the equipment needed by the business
  - the premises needed by the business

- A business plan will also contain financial projections:
  - a profit forecast
  - a break-even calculation
  - a cash-flow forecast

  These will estimate the likely profit that will be made, the number of items that will need to be sold to make a profit and the cash needs of the business over the year.

- If a business plan indicates that the business idea is likely to work, it will be shown to a bank if the business needs to borrow money. The bank can then make up its mind whether or not to lend money to the business.

Key terms

Business plan
A presentation of information and financial projections for a new business or business project.

Financial projections
The section of the business plan which contains financial data including a profit forecast, a break-even calculation and a cash-flow forecast

Profit
The difference between income from sales and the running expenses of a business.

Break-even
Break-even is the point where income from sales covers the costs of a business.
It represents the number of items the business has to sell to cover all its costs.

Cash-flow forecast
An estimate of the amount of money coming into and out of the business bank account, month by month. If more money goes out than comes in, it is an indication that the business will need to borrow money from the bank.

39

Documents for buying and selling

Documents at 'Trends'

Trends is a town centre clothes store. It has a staff of five and is managed by its owner, Dan Signer.

Dan has been in the business for a few years now and so knows how to price his goods and also how to get the best deal from his suppliers.

He is good at managing his money – his cash flow. His customers pay over the counter for the goods by cash, cheque and plastic card. So he gets the money straightaway and it goes into the bank account.

He buys from his suppliers all over the country and pays them after he receives the goods – sometimes up to sixty days later. This buying 'on credit' is normal trade practice and so Dan is in a good position financially – he gets the money in from selling clothes before he has to pay for them.

Dan has to deal with and oversee a lot of financial documents and paperwork. There is the documentation to deal with when the shop takes payments over the counter – cheques, receipts, card authorisations and then all the money that has to be paid into the bank.

He also looks after all the documents for ordering goods from his suppliers – purchase orders, delivery paperwork, invoices, credit notes and payments.

a point to think about . . .

Documents need to be clear and accurate – mistakes lead to problems and problems can cost money!

cash and credit sales

Dan's shop sells goods over the counter and gets the money straightaway, but he pays his suppliers later.

- a **cash sale** is when payment is made straightaway
- a **credit sale** is when payment is made at a later date

The words 'cash sale' used in this way do not mean that just cash (notes and coins) is used – a 'cash sale' can be made using cash or a cheque or a plastic card. 'Cash' here means immediate payment.

cash sales and receipts

A receipt is a document issued by the seller when a cash sale is made.

When you buy something in a shop most cash tills or checkouts show on the screen the money amount of the purchase and also any change to be given.

The till or checkout will also issue a paper receipt for all purchases when cash, a cheque or a plastic card is used. In the example below, a customer has bought a pack of coloured paper and some disks from Everest Stationery. A receipt has been issued.

a till receipt

Everest Stationery		name of shop
15 High St Mereford		address
08 10 02 15.07		date and time of transaction
Salesperson Tina		salesperson
A4 paper (blue)	5.99	goods purchased
Disks	8.99	goods purchased
TOTAL	14.98	total due
CASH	20.00	£20 (probably a £20 note) given by the customer
CHANGE	5.02	change given
Thank you for your custom		personal message to help customer service
Please retain this receipt in case of any query		advice to retain receipt in case of a problem with the goods
VAT REG 373 2888 11		VAT Registration number

businesses buying for cash – petty cash

But it is not just the public that makes cash purchases. When someone makes a cash purchase for a business – for example going out to buy some stationery – it is important that they obtain a receipt. The business needs to record the fact that money has been spent on stationery – it is a running cost of the business and will have to go in the accounts.

Often the cash used for this type of purchase comes from a cash tin in the office known as the **petty cash**.

The person who looks after the cash will need the receipt for the accounts and will enter the details on a **petty cash voucher**.

In the example here, the business has bought some instant coffee for £4.95 cash. The receipt has been stapled to the petty cash voucher and the cost of the coffee entered on the petty cash voucher ready for entering in the accounts of the business. There is no VAT on coffee!

a petty cash voucher

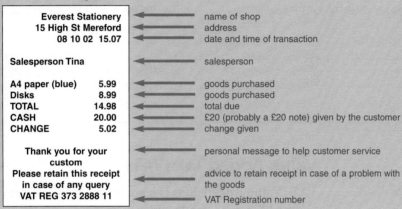

petty cash voucher			Number *PC022*
			date *6 Oct 2002*
description			amount
		£	p
Instant coffee		4	95
	VAT		
		4	95
signature *R Weasley*			
authorised *H Granger*			

handwritten receipts

Sometimes a business buying goods for cash will ask for a handwritten receipt which will provide more detail about the transaction, particularly where VAT (Value Added Tax) is concerned. Look at the example below.

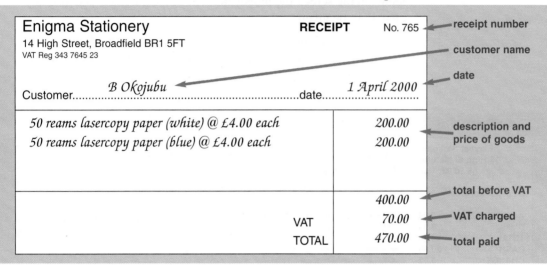

a hand-written receipt

Value Added Tax (VAT)

VAT (Value Added Tax) is a government tax on the selling price charged for most goods and services.

VAT is involved in a number of the financial documents you will be studying and you will need to know what it is and how it works.

charging Value Added Tax (VAT)

Most businesses register for VAT and charge VAT at the standard rate on the money value of the goods or services it sells. The VAT rate at the time of writing is 17.5%. The formula for working out the VAT charged on a sale is:

$$VAT\ charged\ =\ Sales\ amount\ \times\ \frac{17.5}{100}$$

For example, if a business sells goods or services for £200 it has to add on 17.5% of the £200 to the amount charged, ie

$$VAT\ =\ £200\ \times\ \frac{17.5}{100}\ =\ £35$$

The total amount the business receives will be £200 + £35 = £235

Please note, however, that receipts and invoices for purchases under £100 (see the receipt on the previous page) do not have to show the VAT amount separately – it is included in the final amount.

Activity 39.1 – receipts and VAT

1   Draw up or obtain two blank petty cash vouchers. Your business has made the following cash purchases during the week and you have been handed the till receipts:

   (a)   postage stamps costing £15.00 (there is no VAT charged on stamps)

   (b)   office stationery costing £4.00 plus 70p VAT = receipt total of £4.70

   Complete the two petty cash vouchers with the details of the purchases. Make up the dates and voucher numbers if you need to and sign the vouchers in your own name. Ask a fellow student to check and 'authorise' each voucher by signing it along the bottom.

2   Design and draw up your own receipt. It should be a receipt which you can fill in by hand. Use a computer package if you can. Invent your own business name and address for a fashion clothes shop. Use the receipt on the previous page as an example.

   Make (or print out) three copies of your receipt and enter the following sales transactions:

   (a)   2 T-shirts @ £13.99, plus 2 pairs of black tights @85p each, sold to Emmy James

   (b)   1 dress @ £149.95, plus one pair of white tights @ 99p, sold to Alex Bell

   (c)   2 tops @ £35.99 sold to Sam Fox

   Use today's date and add VAT at the current rate to the prices given.

   When calculating VAT, round it down to the nearest unit of pence.

3   VAT is not charged on all products. Write down any products you have come across on which you do not have to pay VAT. Will this affect a clothes shop at all?

buying on credit

financial documents for transactions 'on credit'

A credit sale is when payment is made at a later date

When a business buys goods or services on credit it orders the goods first and then pays later.

During this process a number of different financial documents will be issued by the seller and the buyer.

We will look in this chapter at a whole range of financial documents by means of a Case Study involving the purchase of fashion clothes by Dan's shop 'Trends'.

the more important financial documents

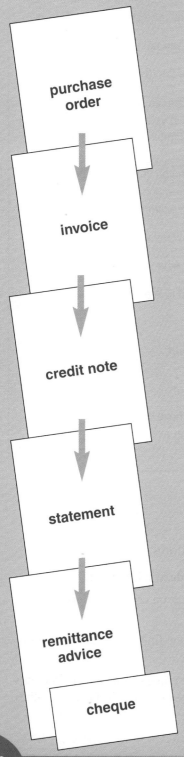

financial documents – what your studies require

You must bear in mind that not all purchases involve all the documents. Many purchases are for services, eg office cleaning, and do not involve goods being sent. The more important documents are shown on the left. It is important for your studies that:

■ you can recognise each of the documents

■ you know what they are for

■ you can complete a number of them

the documents

The financial documents explained here include:

■ the **purchase order** – the order the buyer sends to the seller

■ the **delivery note** which goes with the goods from the seller to the buyer

■ the **goods received note** which is sometimes completed by the buyer to record the actual amount of goods received

■ the **invoice**, which lists the goods and tells the buyer what is owed

■ the **credit note**, which is sent to the buyer if any refund is due

■ the **statement**, sent by the seller to remind the buyer what is owed

■ the **remittance advice**, sent by the buyer with the cheque when the goods are paid for

■ the **cheque** which is completed by the buyer to pay for the goods

the flow of documents

Before you read the Case Study, examine the diagram set out on the next page. Down the columns representing the buyer and the seller are various activities which lead to transactions, which in turn result in financial documents being sent.

Remember that not all the activities shown here happen every time – the order may be for services, the order may be placed by telephone, you may not get a delivery note, and a credit note is only used when a refund is needed . . . and so on . . .

the flow of documents in a credit sale

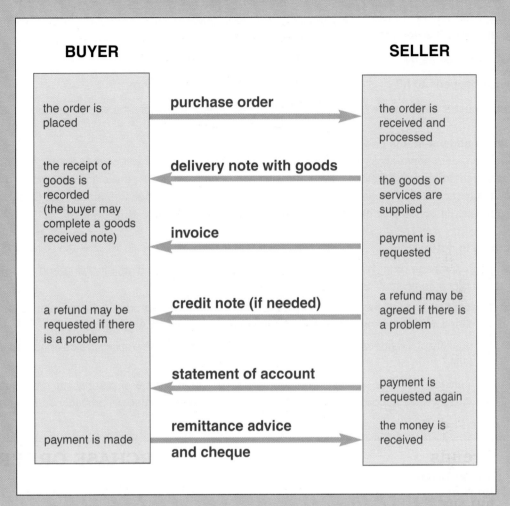

BUYER		SELLER
the order is placed	**purchase order** →	the order is received and processed
the receipt of goods is recorded (the buyer may complete a goods received note)	← **delivery note with goods**	the goods or services are supplied
	← **invoice**	payment is requested
a refund may be requested if there is a problem	← **credit note (if needed)**	a refund may be agreed if there is a problem
	← **statement of account**	payment is requested again
payment is made	**remittance advice and cheque** →	the money is received

Case Study – documents for selling on credit

Cool Socks Limited is a company which manufactures fashion socks in a variety of colours. It supplies a number of different customers, including Trends, a clothes shop in Broadfield.

In this Case Study we see an order for 100 pairs of socks placed by Trends with Cool Socks. The socks are delivered, but some are found to be faulty, so a refund has to be made. Finally, payment has to be made for the socks.

The Case Study looks in detail at the purchase and sales documents involved.

Now read on!

purchase order – the buyer orders the goods

purpose of the document	to order goods or services
who completes it?	the buyer of the goods or services
what happens to it?	it is sent by the buyer to the seller
why must it be accurate?	if it is not completed accurately the wrong products may be ordered

what happens in this case?

Trends orders some socks from Cool Socks. The buyer at Trends will post or fax the authorised purchase order shown below. The order will have been typed out in the office, or produced on a computer accounting program. The details of the socks will have been obtained from Cool Socks' catalogue, or possibly by means of a written or telephoned enquiry.

points to note:

- each purchase order has a specific reference number – this is useful for filing and quoting on later documents such as invoices and statements

- the product code of the goods required is stated in the product code column – this is like the number you write on the slip when ordering something from an Argos store

- the quantity of the goods required is stated in the quantity column – socks are obviously supplied in pairs!

- the purchase order is signed and dated by the person in charge of purchasing – without this authorisation the supplier is unlikely to supply the goods (the order will probably be returned!)

Trends   PURCHASE ORDER

4 Friar Street
Broadfield
BR1 3RF

Tel 01908 761234 Fax 01908 761987
VAT REG GB 0745 8383 56

Cool Socks Limited, Unit 45 Elgar Estate, Broadfield, BR7 4ER	purchase order no **47609** date **25 09 02**

product code	quantity	description
45B	100 pairs	Blue Toebar socks

AUTHORISED   signature.......*D Signer*..date...*25/09/02*...

delivery note – the goods are delivered

purpose of the document	it states what goods are being delivered
who completes it?	the seller of the goods
what happens to it?	it is sent by the seller to the buyer
why must it be accurate?	if the goods delivered do not tally with the description on the delivery note, the goods may be refused

what happens in this case?

The delivery note is despatched with the goods when the order is ready. It is normally typed in the office or printed out by a computer accounting program. In this case, the delivery note travels with the socks, and a copy will be signed by Trends on receipt.

points to note:

■ the delivery note has a numerical reference, useful for filing and later reference if there is a query

■ the delivery note quotes the purchase order number – this enables the buyer to 'tie up' the delivery with the original order

■ the details of the goods supplied – the quantity and the description – will be checked against the goods themselves

■ the delivery note will be signed and dated by the person receiving the goods

---

═══ DELIVERY NOTE ═══

COOL SOCKS LIMITED

Unit 45 Elgar Estate, Broadfield, BR7 4ER
Tel 01908 765314 Fax 01908 765951
VAT REG GB 0745 4672 76

Trends 4 Friar Street Broadfield BR1 3RF	delivery note no	68873
	delivery method	Lynx Parcels
	your order	47609
	date	02 10 02

product code	quantity	description
45B	100 pairs	Blue Toebar socks

Received

signature.......*V Williams*.......name (capitals)...*V WILLIAMS*....date.*5/10/02*...

goods received note – the buyer records receipt

purpose of the document   it records what goods have been delivered

who completes it?   the buyer of the goods

what happens to it?   it is kept by the buyer

why must it be accurate?   there will be a problem if an error in the delivery is not spotted when the goods arrive – eg wrong quantity, wrong goods

what happens in this case?

The goods received note (GRN) will be completed by the person in Trends who looks after the stock. In the case of this delivery, ten pairs of the socks have been received damaged – Trends will want a refund.

points to note:

■ details of the goods are noted on the form

■ the condition of the goods – the damage to the socks – is recorded and this fact will be notified on separate copies to the buyer, to Accounts and to the stockroom

■ a goods received note is not used by all businesses

Trends   **GOODS RECEIVED NOTE**

Supplier

| Cool Socks Limited,
Unit 45 Elgar Estate,
Broadfield,
BR7 4ER | GRN no   1871
date   05 10 02 |

quantity	description	order number
100 pairs	Blue Toebar socks	47609

carrier   Lynx Parcels   consignment no   **8479347**

received by   *V Williams*   checked by   *R Patel*

| **condition of goods**
(please tick and comment) | good condition
damaged ✓ (10 pairs)
shortages | **copies to**
Buyer ✓
Accounts ✓
Stockroom ✓ |

---

invoice – payment is requested by the seller

purpose of the document	it tells the buyer how much is owed and when it has to be paid
who completes it?	the seller of the goods
what happens to it?	it is sent by the seller to the buyer, who checks it carefully and keeps it on file for reference
why must it be accurate?	a mistake could result in the wrong amount being paid; a wrong address could delay payment

what happens in this case?

The invoice, like the delivery note, is prepared in the seller's office, and is either typed or produced on a computer printer using a computer accounting program. Invoices produced by different organisations will vary to some extent in terms of detail, but their basic layout will always be the same.

The invoice prepared by Cool Socks Ltd – illustrated on the next page – is typical of a modern typed or computer-printed document.

points to note:

addresses

The invoice shows the address:

- of the seller/supplier of the goods – Cool Socks Limited
- the place where the invoice should be sent – to Trends
- where the goods are to be sent – it may not always be the same as the invoice address; for example a supermarket ordering a container load of bananas will ask them to be delivered to a distribution warehouse, not to the Accounts Department!

references

There are a number of important references on the invoice:

- the numerical reference of the invoice itself – 787923
- the account number allocated to Trends by the seller – 3993 – for use in the seller's computer accounting program
- the original reference number on the purchase order sent by Trends – 47609 – which will enable the shop to 'tie up' the invoice with the original order

terms

The 'terms' are very important – they state when the invoice has to be paid.

Now look at the document and the explanations on the next two pages to find out what you have to check when you receive an invoice.

invoice – payment is requested by the seller

INVOICE
COOL SOCKS LIMITED
Unit 45 Elgar Estate, Broadfield, BR7 4ER
Tel 01908 765314 Fax 01908 765951
VAT REG GB 0745 4672 76

invoice to

| Trends |
| 4 Friar Street |
| Broadfield |
| BR1 3RF |

invoice no	787923
account	3993
your reference	47609

date/tax point   **02 10 02**

product code	description	quantity	price	unit	total	discount %	net
45B	Blue Toebar socks	100	2.36	pair	236.00	0.00	236.00

GOODS TOTAL	236.00
VAT	41.30
TOTAL	277.30

terms
30 days

points to note and check on the invoice . . .

You will need to check that the reference number quoted here ties up with your purchase order number.

The date here is normally the date on which the goods have been sent to you. It is known as the 'invoice date'. The date is important for calculating when the invoice is due to be paid. In this case the 'terms' (see the bottom left-hand corner of the invoice) are 30 days. This means the invoice is due to be paid within 30 days after the invoice date. The invoice date is 2 October, so it is due to be paid by 31 October.

The arithmetic and details in this line must be checked very carefully to make sure that you pay the correct amount for what you have ordered:

- *product code* – this is the catalogue number which appeared on the original purchase order and on the delivery note
- *description* – this must agree with the description on the purchase order
- *quantity* – this should agree with the quantity ordered
- *price* – this is the price of each unit shown in the next column
- *unit* is the way in which the unit is counted up and charged for, eg units (single items), pairs (as here), or 10s,100s and so on
- *total* is the unit price multiplied by the number of units
- *discount %* is the percentage allowance (known as trade discount) given to customers who regularly deal with the supplier, ie they receive a certain percentage (eg 10%) deducted from their bill
- *net* is the amount due to the seller after deduction of trade discount, and before VAT is added on

The Goods Total is the total of the column above it. It is the final amount due to the seller before VAT is added on.

Value Added Tax (VAT) is calculated and added on – here it is 17.5% of the Goods Total, ie £236.00 x $\frac{17.5}{100}$ = £41.30

The VAT is then added to the Goods Total to produce the actual amount owing: £236.00 + £41.30 = £277.30

The 'terms' explain the conditions on which the goods are supplied. Here '30 days' means that payment has to be made within 30 days of the invoice date.

credit note – the seller gives a refund

purpose of the document   a credit note is a 'refund' document which reduces the amount owed by the buyer – the format of a credit note is very similar to that of an invoice

who completes it?   the seller of the goods

what happens to it?   it is sent by the seller to the buyer, who checks it carefully and keeps it on file with the invoice

why must it be accurate?   a mistake could result in the wrong amount eventually being paid

what happens in this case?

Trends has received 10 damaged pairs of socks. These will be sent back to Cool Socks with a 'returns note' and a request for *credit* – ie a reduction in the bill for the 10 faulty pairs. Cool Socks will have to issue the credit note for £27.73 shown below.

points to note:

- a credit note can be issued for faulty goods, missing goods, or goods which are not needed
- the credit note quotes the invoice number and states why the credit (refund) is being given

---

CREDIT NOTE

COOL SOCKS LIMITED

Unit 45 Elgar Estate, Broadfield, BR7 4ER
Tel 01908 765314 Fax 01908 765951
VAT REG GB 0745 4672 76

to

Trends
4 Friar Street
Broadfield
BR1 3RF

credit note no	12157
account	3993
your reference	47609
our invoice	787923
date/tax point	10 10 02

product code	description	quantity	price	unit	total	discount %	net
45B	Blue Toebar socks	10	2.36	pair	23.60	0.00	23.60

Reason for credit
10 pairs of socks received damaged
(Your returns note no. R/N 2384)

GOODS TOTAL	23.60
VAT	4.13
TOTAL	27.73

statement – the seller requests payment

purpose of the document	a statement – which is normally issued at the end of every month – tells the buyer how much is owed
who completes it?	the seller of the goods
what happens to it?	it is sent by the seller to the buyer who checks it against the invoices and credit notes on file
why must it be accurate?	a mistake could result in the wrong amount being paid

what happens in this case?

A seller will not normally expect a buyer to pay each individual invoice as soon as it is received. Instead, a statement of account showing what is owed is sent by the seller to the buyer *at the end of the month.* It shows:

◼ invoices issued for goods supplied – the full amount due, including VAT

◼ refunds made on credit notes – including VAT

◼ payments received from the buyer (if any)

The statement issued by Cool Socks to Trends for the period covering the sale (the invoice) and refund (the credit note) is shown below. Trends now has to pay the £249.57 owing.

STATEMENT OF ACCOUNT

COOL SOCKS LIMITED

Unit 45 Elgar Estate, Broadfield, BR7 4ER
Tel 01908 765314 Fax 01908 765951
VAT REG GB 0745 4672 76

TO

```
Trends
4 Friar Street
Broadfield
BR1 3RF
```

account **3993**

date **31 10 02**

date	details	debit £	credit £	balance £
02 10 02	Invoice 787923	277.30		277.30
10 10 02	Credit note 12157		27.73	249.57
			AMOUNT NOW DUE	249.57

remittance advice – sent with the payment

purpose of the document	a remittance advice is a document sent by the buyer to the seller stating that payment is being made
who completes it?	the buyer
what happens to it?	it is sent by the buyer to the seller
why must it be accurate?	a mistake could result in the wrong amount being paid

what happens in this case?

Trends have completed a remittance advice listing the invoice that is being paid and the credit note which is being deducted from the amount owing. Trends will make out a cheque for the total amount of the remittance advice. This is shown on the next page. It will be attached to the remittance advice and will be posted to Cool Socks in November.

points to note:

■ the remittance advice quotes the account number (3993) allocated to Trends by Cool Socks – this will help Cool Socks to update their records when the payment is received

■ the documents are listed in the columns provided: 'your reference' describes the documents issued by Cool Socks and quotes their numbers; 'our reference' quotes the number of the Purchase Order originally issued by Trends

■ the amounts of the invoice and the credit note are entered in the right-hand column – note that the credit note amount is negative, so it is shown in brackets; the total payment amount is shown in the box at the bottom of the form – this will be the amount of the cheque issued

■ payment can alternatively be made by computer transfer between bank accounts (BACS); in this case a remittance advice is still sent, but no cheque

■ a 'tear-off' printed remittance advice listing all the items is sometimes attached to the statement sent by the seller; all the buyer has to do is to tick the items being paid, and pay!

TO   **REMITTANCE ADVICE** FROM

Cool Socks Limited
Unit 45 Elgar Estate,
Broadfield, BR7 4ER

Trends

4 Friar Street
Broadfield
BR1 3RF

Tel 01908 761234 Fax 01908 761987
VAT REG GB 0745 8383 56

Account 3993   5 November 2002

date	your reference	our reference	payment amount
02 10 02	INVOICE 787923	47609	277.30
10 10 02	CREDIT NOTE 12157	47609	(27.73)
		CHEQUE TOTAL	249.57

cheque – the buyer sends a payment

purpose of the document	a payment document which, when completed, can be paid into a bank account; it enables people to settle debts, for example a buyer paying money to a seller
who completes it?	the person who owes the money signs the cheque and writes the amount in words and figures, the name of the person who is to receive the money (the payee) and the date
what happens to it?	it is passed or posted by the buyer to the seller
why must it be accurate?	if the amount is wrong the seller could end up being underpaid or overpaid; also, any mistake on the cheque could result in the banks refusing to let it through the clearing system

what happens in this case?

Trends complete the details on the cheque – including the date, amount and signature – and send it to Cool Socks with the remittance advice.

points to note:

■ If a cheque is not completed correctly, it could be refused by the banks. Particular points to note are:
- the cheque should be signed – it is completely invalid without a signature
- the amount in words and figures must be the same
- lines should be drawn after the name of the payee and the amount to prevent fraud
- the current date should be written in – cheques become invalid after six months

■ The lines across the cheque are known as the 'crossing'. The words 'a/c payee only' are an important security measure because they mean that the cheque can only be paid into the bank account of the person named on the 'pay' line of the cheque.

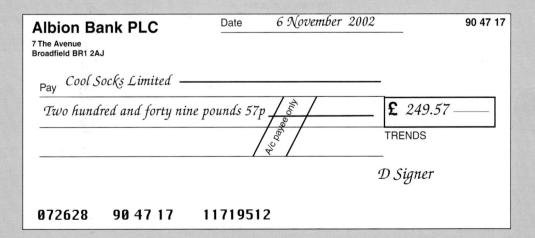

what to do with incorrect cheques

As we saw on the previous page, if you receive a cheque with a mistake, it may not be accepted by the bank you are paying it into. Alternatively it might be returned by the bank of the person paying the money because of a mistake, or because the person has not got any money in the account – it might 'bounce' (be returned by the bank), in which case you will not get your money. How do you avoid this situation?

correcting mistakes

If you receive a cheque with a mistake on it, you will need to get the mistake corrected and any correction initialled by the person writing out the cheque. If the person has posted the cheque to you, this means in most cases posting the cheque back again with a covering letter asking for the mistake to be corrected. The most common mistakes that occur are:

mistake	what you do to correct it
there is no signature	send it back asking for a signature
the amount in words and figures differs	send it back asking for it to be corrected and the correction initialled
the name on the 'pay' line is wrong	send it back asking for it to be corrected and the correction initialled
the date is more than six months ago	send it back and ask for the date to be changed and the correction initialled
the date is missing	you can write it in! – this is the one situation where you do not have to send it back

Activities – exercises with documents

Your course requires you to complete and check a series of financial documents.

The next chapter contains a series of activities which will put into practice what you have learnt about financial documents in this chapter.

Nutshell summary

- The buying and selling of goods and services by businesses involves a wide variety of financial documents.

- It is important that financial documents are completed accurately and are checked. Otherwise mistakes will occur – such as sending the wrong goods or charging the wrong amount. These waste time and money.

- Many financial documents will involve VAT (Value Added Tax), which is a tax on sales. It is important that you know how VAT is calculated.

- A cash sale is when someone buys something and pays straightaway. Payment for a 'cash' sale can be with notes and coins, cheque or plastic card. A receipt is normally issued when a cash sale is made.

- A credit sale is when someone buys something and pays at a later date. A credit sale can involve a variety of financial documents which 'flow' in a set order. The 'flow' of documents involves some or all of the following:

  - the buyer issues a purchase order

  - the seller sends the goods with a delivery note

  - the buyer issues a goods received note when the goods arrive

  - the seller sends an invoice to request payment and then a credit note if a refund is needed

  - the seller sends a statement as a reminder of what is due

  - the buyer settles up by sending a cheque together with a remittance advice

- It must be stressed that this 'flow' of documents can be varied to suit the trading relationship between the buyer and seller. For example, orders can be made by email or phone, goods received notes are not always used and payment need not be by cheque. Also, if services are supplied, delivery notes are not needed!

Key terms

Cash sale
A sale where payment is made straightaway.

Credit sale
A sale where payment is made at a later date.

Receipt
Document issued by the seller when a cash sale is made.

Petty cash
Cash kept in the office for small business purchases and recorded on a petty cash voucher.

VAT (Value Added Tax)
A tax on sales charged on most goods and services.

Purchase order
The written order sent by the buyer to the seller.

Delivery note
The document which accompanies the goods.

Goods received note
The document which records the arrival of the goods.

Invoice
The document which lists the goods and requests payment.

Credit note
A 'refund' document which reduces the amount due.

Statement
Sent by the seller to the buyer as a reminder of what is owed.

Remittance advice
Sent by the buyer with the cheque when payment is made.

40

Financial documents – practical exercises

In-tray exercise

In this chapter you will practise completing and checking the financial documents explained in the last chapter.

The documents used here are those used in a credit purchase.

If you need blank documents they should be available from your teacher and also in downloadable form on the Osborne Books website: www.osbornebooks.co.uk in the Free Resources section.

To remind you of the 'flow' of documents that normally takes place, study the diagram shown below.

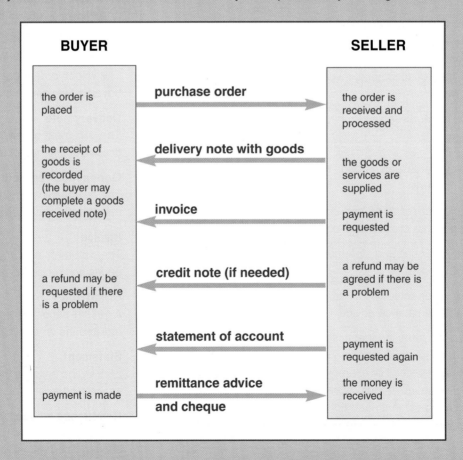

Activity 40.1 – making the purchase

task 1

You should work in pairs and play the roles of buyer and seller.

The buyer is a clothes shop, Oasis, 5 High Street, Mereford MR1 3GF.

The seller is a clothes importer, Fashions Imports Limited, Unit 4 Beech Industrial Estate, Salebury, Manchester, M62 5FG.

You will need copies of blank purchase orders and invoices (available for download from www.osbornebooks.co.uk). You should use today's date and the current VAT rate, but will need to make up the following details:

■ catalogue numbers

■ order numbers and invoice numbers

The buyer is to complete two separate purchase orders and the seller is to complete an invoice for each order. The orders are as follows:

(a)　100 pairs of tights (black) at £1.50 each

　　　25 sweatshirts (green) at £8 each

　　　50 T-shirts (black) at £3.50 each

(b)　25 fleeces (red) at £15 each

　　　30 pairs of jeans (black) at £17.50 each

　　　50 pairs of tights (black) at £1.50 each

There is no trade discount available to the buyer. Add VAT at the current rate and round it down to the nearest unit of pence.

task 2

You work for Deansway Trading Company, a wholesaler of office stationery, which trades from The Modern Office, 79 Deansway, Stourminster WR1 2EJ. A customer, The Stationery Store of 126 The Crescent, Marshall Green, WR4 5TX, orders the following on order number 9516:

(a)　50 boxes of assorted rubbers at 50p per box, catalogue no 26537

(b)　100 shorthand notebooks at £4 for a pack of 10, catalogue no 72625

(c)　250 ring binders (red) at £2.50p each, catalogue no 72698

VAT is to be charged at the current rate on all items, and a 5% trade discount is given to The Card Shop.

Prepare invoice number 8234, under today's date, to be sent to the customer.

Activity 40.2 – checking invoices

task 1

A colleague in the Accounts Department of Cool Socks has prepared this sales invoice.

You are to check it and state what is wrong with it.

You are then to draw up a new, correct, invoice with the same reference number and today's date. Assume the price quoted is correct.

INVOICE

COOL SOCKS LIMITED

Unit 45 Elgar Estate, Broadfield, BR7 4ER
Tel 01908 765314 Fax 01908 765951
VAT REG GB 0745 4672 76

invoice to

Oasis
5 High Street
Mereford
MR1 3GF

invoice no	876512
account	3461
your reference	87541

date/tax point

product code	description	quantity	price	unit	total	discount %	net
45R	Red Toebar socks	100	2.45	pair	254.00	10.00	279.40

GOODS TOTAL	279.40
VAT	48.89
TOTAL	230.51

terms: 30 days

task 2

You work in the Oasis clothes shop and have received this invoice in the post. You check it against the Purchase Order, the details of which are:

Order No 98372 for 50 pairs of dark blue Country trousers @ £12.45 a pair (code 234DB). You are normally given 10% trade discount.

The jeans were received, as ordered, on the same day as the invoice.

Check the invoice against the purchase order and if there are any problems contact the Sales Ledger Department of The Jeans Company by e-mail, fax or letter.

Draft out the text of your email, fax or letter, if possible on a word processing file.

INVOICE

The Jeans Company

Unit 6 Parry Trading Estate, Southfield, SF1 5LR
Tel 01901 333391 Fax 01901 333462 email Jeansco@goblin.com
VAT REG GB 8762 54 27

invoice to

Oasis
5 High Street
Mereford
MR1 3GF

invoice no	**942394**
account	**2141**
your reference	**98372**
date/tax point	**01 12 02**

product code	description	quantity	price	unit	total	discount %	net
234B	**Country trousers (black)**	**50**	**12.45**	**pair**	**622.50**	**5.00**	**591.38**

GOODS TOTAL	**591.38**
VAT	**103.49**
TOTAL	**694.87**

terms: 30 days

Activity 40.3 – goods received note

You work in an insurance broker's office and have just received a consignment of 50 reams of photocopy paper from Wintergreen Stationers. A ream is a packet of 500 sheets. The reams are packed in boxes of five. One of the boxes is badly dented at one end. The 5 reams of paper in this box are unusable as they will jam any photocopier or printer. The delivery note for the paper is shown below.

DELIVERY NOTE

WINTERGREEN STATIONERS

75 Holmes Street, Broadfield, BR2 6TF
Tel 01908 342281 Fax 01908 342538 Email WGreen@newserve.com
VAT REG GB 0822 2422 75

Uplands Insurance Brokers 8 Friar Street Broadfield BR1 3RF	delivery note no	68673
	delivery method	Parcelexpress
	your order	23423
	date	01 10 02

product code	quantity	description
A4PPW	50 reams	A4 photocopy paper, white, 80gsm

Received
signature...........*J Rutter*...........name (capitals)...*J RUTTER*...........date *5/10/02*

---

1   You are to complete a Goods Received Note. See the Osborne Books website: www.osbornebooks.co.uk for copies of blank documents.

The goods arrived by Parcelexpress, consignment number 7429472.

2   The damaged paper will be sent back to the supplier within the next few days. Write the text of a fax or an email to the supplier (if possible on a wordprocessor file), explaining the situation. Include all the references and details which you think will be needed. You should not at this stage ask for a credit note.

The following day the invoice for the goods arrives by post. This will be dealt with in the next Activity.

Activity 40.4 – requesting a credit note

The invoice for the photocopy paper delivered in the last Activity is shown below.

It should be checked carefully for errors. Uplands Insurance Brokers normally receives a 10% discount on goods supplied.

You are to write the text of a letter (if possible on a word processor) to the Accounts Department of Wintergreen Stationers requesting a credit note for the returned paper. The letter should include the money amount (including VAT) of the credit that is due.

INVOICE
WINTERGREEN STATIONERS

75 Holmes Street, Broadfield, BR2 6TF
Tel 01908 342281 Fax 01908 342538 Email WGreen@newserve.com
VAT REG GB 0822 2422 75

invoice to

Uplands Insurance Brokers
8 Friar Street
Broadfield
BR1 3RF

invoice no	**9384**
account	**3455**
your reference	**23423**
date/tax point	**01 10 02**

product code	description	quantity	price	unit	total	discount %	net
A4PPW	**A4 photocopy paper white, 80gsm**	**50**	**1.70**	**ream**	**85.00**	**10.00**	**76.50**

GOODS TOTAL	**76.50**
VAT	**13.38**
TOTAL	**89.88**

terms: 30 days

Activity 40.5 – issuing a credit note

When you have had your answer to Activity 40.4 checked you should complete the credit note issued by Wintergreen Stationers, the suppliers of the damaged paper. Do not forget the discount!

You will find a blank credit note in the Business Studies Resources section of the Osborne Books website: www.osbornebooks.co.uk

Activity 40.6 – sending statements

It is the end of the month of October in the Accounts Department of Wintergreen Stationers. You have been asked to prepare the statements for two of your customers. Their statements for last month (issued on 29 September) are illustrated on the next page – they will be needed for the starting balance for October. You will see how the starting balance (Balance b/f) is shown on the September statements.

The transactions on the two accounts for October are shown below.

Tiny Toys Limited

Date	Transaction	Amount (£)
10 10 02	Payment received	105.00
13 10 02	Invoice 9410	560.00
20 10 02	Invoice 9488	3450.50
26 10 02	Credit note 12180	230.50

R Patel Associates

Date	Transaction	Amount (£)
10 10 02	Payment received	4999.83
16 10 02	Invoice 9433	1098.50
22 10 02	Invoice 9501	678.35
26 10 02	Credit note 12183	670.00

You will find a blank statement in the Free Resources section of the Osborne Books website: www.osbornebooks.co.uk

STATEMENT OF ACCOUNT

WINTERGREEN STATIONERS

75 Holmes Street, Broadfield, BR2 6TF
Tel 01908 342281 Fax 01908 342538 Email WGreen@newserve.com
VAT REG GB 0822 2422 75

TO

Tiny Toys Limited
56 Broad Avenue
Brocknell
BK7 6CV

account   3001

date   29 09 02

date	details	debit £	credit £	balance £
01 09 02	Balance b/f			139.67
05 09 02	Payment received		139.67	nil
19 09 02	Invoice 9276	150.00		150.00
25 09 02	Credit note 12157		45.00	105.00

AMOUNT NOW DUE	105.00

STATEMENT OF ACCOUNT

WINTERGREEN STATIONERS

75 Holmes Street, Broadfield, BR2 6TF
Tel 01908 342281 Fax 01908 342538 Email WGreen@newserve.com
VAT REG GB 0822 2422 75

TO

R Patel Associates
78 Greenford Mansions
Mereford
MR3 8KJ

account   3067

date   29 09 02

date	details	debit £	credit £	balance £
01 09 02	Balance b/f			679.05
06 09 02	Payment received		679.05	nil
21 09 02	Invoice 9303	5345.50		5345.50
25 09 02	Credit note 12162		345.67	4999.83

AMOUNT NOW DUE	4999.83

Activity 40.7 – remittance advices and cheques

It is now the first week of November in the Accounts Department of Wintergreen Stationers. The October statements from suppliers are arriving in the post. Two are shown on the next page.

You are asked to make out a remittance advice and a cheque (ready for signing) to settle each account. Make up purchase order numbers.

A sample cheque is shown below. Blank remittance advices and cheques can be found in the Business Studies Resources Section of the Osborne Books website: www.osbornebooks.co.uk

You find the following note attached to the paperwork relating to the Hilliard & Brown Account.

NOTE TO FILE
19 October 2002

<u>Hilliard & Brown - disputed invoice</u>

Please note that we should not pay their invoice 3213 for £1,256.90 because the goods on the invoice have not been delivered. Please check each month when paying against their statement.

R Otter

Accounts Supervisor, Purchase Ledger

You check to see if the goods have arrived and find that they have not.

specimen cheque

Albion Bank PLC	Date _____	90 47 17

7 The Avenue
Broadfield BR1 2AJ

Pay _____

_____

A/c payee only   £

WINTERGREEN STATIONERY

123238   90 47 17   45195234

STATEMENT OF ACCOUNT
PRONTO SUPPLIES

Unit 17, Blakefield Estate, Broadfield, BR4 9TG
Tel 01908 482111 Fax 01908 482471 Email Pronto@imp.com
VAT REG GB4452 2411 21

TO

Wintergreen Stationers 75 Holmes Street Broadfield BK2 6TF	account	2343
	date	31 10 02

date	details	debit £	credit £	balance £
02 10 02	Balance b/f			234.75
05 10 02	Payment received		234.75	nil
19 10 02	Invoice 8717	290.75		290.75
22 10 02	Invoice 8734	654.10		944.85
25 10 02	Invoice 8766	125.00		1069.85

AMOUNT NOW DUE	1069.85

STATEMENT
HILLIARD & BROWN

99 Caxton Street, Norwich, NR2 7VB
Tel 01603 342281 Fax 01603 342538 Email Hillibrown@newserve.com
VAT REG GB 4532 1121 06

TO

Wintergreen Stationers 75 Holmes Street Broadfield BK2 6TF	account	2234
	date	31 10 02

date	details	debit £	credit £	balance £
02 10 02	Balance b/f			560.00
05 10 02	Payment received		560.00	nil
19 10 02	Invoice 3213	1256.90		1256.90
22 10 02	Invoice 3244	987.60		2244.50
25 10 02	Credit note 4501		135.00	2109.50

AMOUNT NOW DUE	2109.50

Activity 40.8 – checking cheques

You work in the accounts department of Morton Components Limited. The cheques shown here have been received in this morning's post. The date is 10 November 2002.

1   Examine the cheques and write down what is wrong with them.

2   State in each case what you would do to put matters right.

(a)

| **Albion Bank PLC** | Date | *5 November 2002* | 90 47 17 |

7 The Avenue
Broadfield BR1 2AJ

Pay   *Marton Computers Limited*

Two hundred and forty nine pounds 87p   A/c payee only   249.87

K J PLASTOW

K J Plastow

083772   90 47 17   11719881

(b)

| **WESTSIDE BANK PLC** | Date | *1 November 2002* | 78 37 17 |

22 Cornbury Street
Shelford SL1 2DC

Pay   *Morton Components Limited*

One hundred and sixty pounds only   A/c payee only   160.00

BACCHUS LIMITED

072628   78 37 17   23487611

(c)

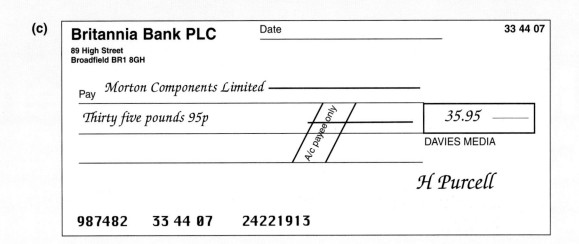

Britannia Bank PLC

89 High Street
Broadfield BR1 8GH

Date _____ 33 44 07

Pay *Morton Components Limited* _____

Thirty five pounds 95p

A/c payee only

35.95 ———

DAVIES MEDIA

H Purcell

987482   33 44 07   24221913

(d)

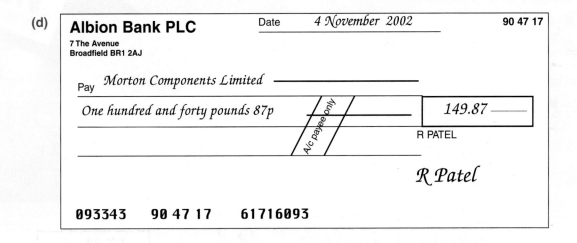

Albion Bank PLC

7 The Avenue
Broadfield BR1 2AJ

Date *4 November 2002* 90 47 17

Pay *Morton Components Limited* _____

One hundred and forty pounds 87p

A/c payee only

149.87 ———

R PATEL

R Patel

093343   90 47 17   61716093

41

Methods of payment

Payments by 'Trends'

'Trends' is the clothes shop which featured in Chapter 39, which dealt with financial documents.

As a shop, Trends accepts payments from customers over the counter in a number of forms:

- cash
- cheques
- debit cards
- credit cards

As a business, Trends also has to make payments in different ways:

- cash – for small purchases
- cheques – useful for paying suppliers through the post
- bank transfer (direct debit, standing order) – automatic payments to a bank account – useful for paying wages and regular bills

a point to think about . . .

The methods of payment are very varied. They mainly differ in what they cost and how long they take. A business should choose the method which best suits the type of payment being made.

cash payments

who uses cash?

Despite the growth in the use of plastic cards, **cash** is the most common way of paying for goods and services – newspapers, magazines, sandwiches, cans of drink, bus fares, stationery – the list is very long.

Customers use cash when shopping and paying for services such as a haircut and a bus fare.

Businesses use cash for making small purchases and also for paying wages, although nowadays more and more employees have their wages paid direct to their bank accounts.

the cost of paying by cash

Cash is easy for customers to use, but it can be expensive for businesses to handle:

- it has to be counted and checked by hand
- it has to be kept safe and secure in case of theft and it has to be insured
- in the case of cash wages it has to be collected from the bank

In fact, businesses would probably prefer not to deal in cash. They only do so because their customers insist on using it.

timescale

Cash is instant payment. As we saw in Chapter 39 the words 'cash payment' can mean 'payment straightaway'.

advantages of cash payments	disadvantages of cash payments
payment is made straightaway	cash has to be checked by hand
cash is ideal for small purchases	cash has to be locked up for security
cash is convenient to use	cash can be stolen

Activity 41.1 – making cash payments

1 For what type of payments is cash normally used?

2 Why can cash be expensive for a business to look after?

3 State two advantages of using cash as a way of paying for goods.

4 State two disadvantages of using cash as a way of paying for goods.

discussion point

Do you think people and businesses will ever stop using cash?

payments by cheque

Cheques are commonly used in business by customers paying for goods and services either over the counter or by post.

Cheques are also used by businesses paying bills and other amounts owing. They are very useful for making business payments by post.

what is a cheque?

A cheque (see below) is an instruction by the person writing the cheque to their bank to pay someone a sum of money. Cheques are normally provided by the banks for their customers in books with counterfoils. When the cheque has been written out, the details (amount, date and person being paid) are also recorded on the counterfoil and the cheque is torn out and given or sent to the person being paid.

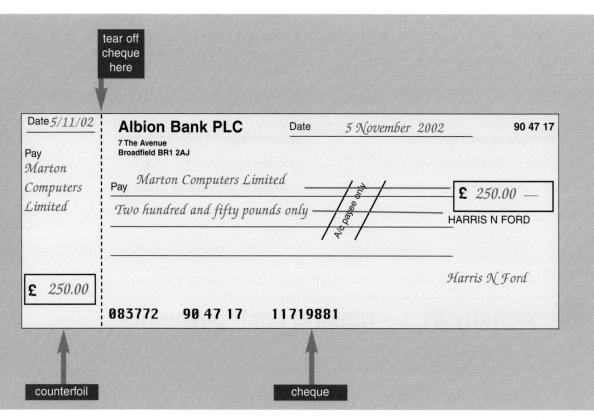

what happens to a cheque?

We will use as an example the cheque shown above. It is sent by Harris N Ford in payment for £250 owing to Marton Computers Limited for a computer printer which he has bought. What happens to the cheque? Look at the flowchart on the next page:

the cheque clearing system

Harris N Ford writes out a cheque for £250, dates it and signs it

the cheque is posted to Marton Computers Limited

the cheque is received by Marton Computers Limited

the cheque is paid in over the counter of Marton Computers Limited's bank

£250 will be added to the bank account of Marton Computers Limited

the cheque will be sent through a bank clearing system to Harris N Ford's bank – Albion Bank – and the £250 will be deducted from his account – three days after the cheque has been paid into Marton Computers' bank

three days for clearing the cheque

the cost of paying by cheque

Banks may charge for cheques written out and also when businesses pay in large numbers of cheques received from their customers. Cheques are otherwise cheaper to deal with than cash.

timescale

Cheques normally take three days to clear after they have been paid in. A business paying in a cheque for £100,000 received from its customer will have to wait three days before it can use that money.

problems with cheques

Cheques are more convenient than cash for larger payments, but things can go wrong . . .

bounced cheques

A business may be given a cheque when the person writing out the cheque has no money in his/her bank account. What happens? The cheque will not be paid, it will 'bounce' back to the bank where it was paid in, marked 'refer to drawer', and the money will be taken off the account of the business that paid it in. The 'drawer' is the person who wrote out the cheque.

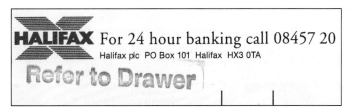

a 'refer to drawer' bounced cheque (extract)

advantages of cheque payments	disadvantages of cheque payments
safer than cash	a cheque takes three days to clear
better for large amounts	a cheque is not guaranteed payment – it can 'bounce'
cheaper than cash to operate	cheques with errors can be refused by the banks

Activity 41.2 – cash and cheque payments

1 Which is the better way of sending a payment by post – to send cash or to send a cheque? Give reasons for your answer.

2 What is the cheque counterfoil used for?

3 How long does it take for a cheque to clear when it has been paid in at the bank?

4 If you want your money quickly would you be better being paid in cash or by cheque? Give reasons for your answer.

5 If someone pays you by cheque are you as sure to get your money as if they had paid you using cash? Give reasons for your answer.

6 What is the cost to a business of using a cheque to make payment?

payments by debit card

what is a debit card?

A **debit card** – shown below – is a plastic card issued by a bank to its customer which enables him or her to make payment without having to write out a cheque. Payment can be made in this way over the counter, over the telephone or online. Common examples of debit cards include 'Switch' and 'Connect' cards.

how does a debit card work?

We will use as an example a customer wanting to buy clothes costing £39.95 from a small shop:

- the customer hands over the debit card and the goods at the till

- the shop assistant examines the card and then 'swipes' it through an electronic machine which automatically prints out a voucher slip

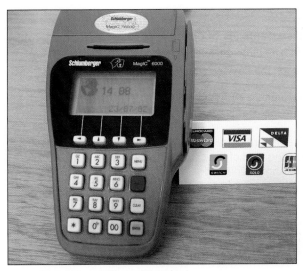

an electronic credit card terminal

- the customer signs the voucher slip

- £39.95 will be added to the bank account of the shop, normally electronically through the linked computers of the shop and the bank

- £39.95 will be taken off the customer's bank account, electronically through the linked computers of the shop and the banking system

Note that no cheque is issued – the whole transaction is carried out by an electronic link-up between the shop and the banks

A debit card payment is secure – it will not 'bounce' as a cheque might. Once the payment has gone through the till or terminal the business is sure of getting its money.

mail order and e-commerce payments

Debit cards can also be used to make purchases by telephone or with mail order companies. They are also accepted on many on-line shopping sites on the internet.

Instead of the customer signing a voucher slip, the mail order business or online shop takes the number of the card and processes it through an electronic terminal or through a secure link on the internet.

Some people do not like shopping like this because of the level of fraud – criminals can get hold of the card numbers and use them to pay for purchases.

the cost of paying by debit card

Customers of businesses who use them may have to pay bank charges each time they use the card, or the use of the card may be free – it all depends on the bank and the type of bank account.

Businesses who accept the cards have to pay a small charge, 30p for example, each time they accept a debit card payment. They are likely also to have to rent the till or terminal which processes the payment.

timescale

It takes three working days for a payment to get to the bank account of the business accepting the payment. If a customer pays for goods on Monday, the business gets the money in its account on Wednesday.

advantages of debit cards	disadvantages of debit cards
guaranteed payment	it takes three days for the money to reach the business bank account
useful for mail order and e-commerce	the charge for the card and the till or terminal that the business uses
cheaper than cash to handle	the danger of fraud through criminals getting hold of the card numbers and making on-line and telephone purchases

Activity 41.3 – debit card payments

1   Why would a business which sells goods prefer a customer to pay by debit card rather than by cheque?

2   What are the costs to a business of accepting debit card payments?

3   How long does it take for a debit card payment to get to the bank account of a business accepting payment through a terminal?

payments by credit card

what is a credit card?

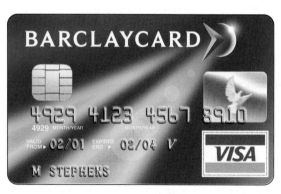

A **credit card** – as shown here – is a plastic card issued by a credit card company. Common examples of credit cards include Mastercard and Visa.

Issuers of cards include banks, building societies, shops and car manufacturers.

Credit cards are a means of payment used by customers who want to buy goods and services over the counter, by mail, by telephone, or over the internet and pay for them later.

Credit cards are also used by employees of businesses to pay for business expenses, eg travel and hotel bills.

how does a credit card work?

A customer wants to buy a personal stereo costing £69.95 from a branch of an electrical chain-store.

■   the customer hands over the credit card at the till

■   the shop assistant will examine the card and then 'swipe' it

an electronic till

through an electronic machine which will then automatically print out a voucher slip

- the customer then signs the voucher slip and takes the goods and a separate till receipt
- £69.95 will be added to the bank account of the shop, normally electronically through the linked computers of the shop and the bank

how does a credit card differ from a debit card?

- the customer does not pay straightaway
- the customer will receive a statement from the credit card company listing the £69.95 item together with other items bought on the card; the customer will be asked for payment within a few weeks
- the customer will make payment to the credit card company, normally by cheque, and often over a month after the purchase is made
- the payment can either be the full amount owing or a lower amount if the customer wants to pay the rest later

e-commerce and mail order shopping

Credit cards, like debit cards, may be accepted as a means of payment over the telephone, by mail order firms and by on-line shops on the internet. As with debit cards, there is the danger of fraud. Criminals may get hold of the credit card numbers and use them to obtain goods and services.

the cost of paying by credit card

Customers of businesses who use credit cards normally have to pay:

- an annual fee for using the card, £10 for example
- if the full amount owing is not settled by the date stated on the statement, interest will be charged on what is left owing

In other words, using a credit card is another way to borrow money. It can be an expensive way to borrow as the interest rate charged can be very high.

Businesses that accept credit cards have to pay a percentage on the amount of the transaction, 2.5% for example. In this case, if a business sells goods for £100 it will have to pay £2.50 to the credit card company. It may also have to rent the till or terminal which processes the payment.

timescale

It takes three working days for a credit card payment to get to the bank account of the business accepting the payment. If a customer pays for goods on Friday, the business gets the money on its account on Tuesday – three working days later.

The customer, on the other hand, has a major time advantage. Payment for the goods or services may be made over a month later.

advantages of credit cards	disadvantages of credit cards
guaranteed payment	it takes three days for the money to reach the business bank account
useful for mail order and e-commerce	the charge for the card and the till or terminal that the business uses
enables the card holder to borrow	an expensive form of borrowing for the card holder

Activity 41.4 – methods of payment

1   What are the costs to a business of accepting credit card payments from customers?

2   How long does it take for a credit card payment get to the bank account of the business accepting payment after it has been processed by the terminal?

3   Set up a table comparing the advantages and disadvantages to a business of accepting different methods of payment.

Use the format below if you wish, and set it out on an A4 page. Make sure that you explain the advantages and disadvantages as fully as you can.

payment method	advantages	disadvantages
CASH		
CHEQUE		
DEBIT CARD		
CREDIT CARD		

credit transfers

paper or computer payments?

There are two main ways of sending payments – **credit transfers** – through the banking system:

- by paper – using a **bank giro credit**
- by computer – using the bank system known as **BACS**

We will look at the paper-based system first.

bank giro credits

Suppose you have to pay a gas bill or a credit card bill. Your bill will normally have a paper slip at the bottom to enable you to pay. This is known as a **bank giro credit**.

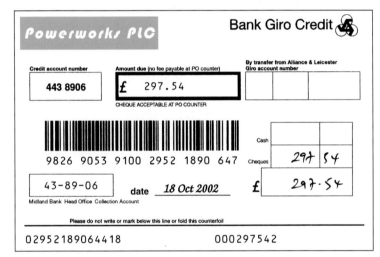

All you have to do is fill in the bank giro credit, take it to the bank with a cheque for the same amount and pay it over the counter. The bank will process the paper slip and arrange for the money to reach the power company or credit card company three working days later.

There is normally no charge for this service.

A bank giro credit is shown on the left. Note that most of the details are already filled in; all you have to do is to complete the amount to be paid and the date.

computer payment transfers – BACS

The banks' computers are all connected together. Because all the accounts are held on these computers, it is an easy matter to program the computers to send payments from one bank to another. This system is known as **BACS**, which is short for Bankers Automated Clearing Services.

BACS enables bank customers to send computer payments to each other.

For example:

- a **standing order** – regular payments made from one bank customer to another, eg making rent payments to a landlord
- a **direct debit** – where a business that receives many payments (eg an insurance company or the AA) takes the money from its customers' bank accounts on a regular basis

on-line direct debit

Standing orders and direct debits traditionally need the signature of the customer before the bank can make or take payments.

As customers deal more and more on the internet, signatures are becoming less commonly used.

The form on the left is the type of on-screen direct debit used by an insurance company to collect premiums from its customers. No signature is needed. It could be a bit of a problem for an online business!

bulk payments

The BACS payment transfer system is also used by businesses when they need to make **bulk payments**, for example paying wages to employees weekly or monthly or paying suppliers on a monthly basis.

The way this works is that the business supplies its own bank with the bank account details of the people who receive the payments. All that then happens is that when the payments are due, the business tells its bank the amounts that are due.

As with all BACS payments, the money takes three working days to get to its destination.

Activity 41.5 – credit transfers

Complete the sentences below with one of the following pairs of words:

standing order   paying wages   bank giro   direct debit

1 A BACS payment where the person receiving the money asks its bank to set up the transfer is known as a ....

2 A BACS payment where the person sending the money asks its bank to set up the transfer is known as a ....

3 A paper-based payment made through the banking system is known as a .... credit

4 A bank 'autopay' BACS system is useful for ....

recording payments – the cash book

Money paid in and out of the business bank account is often recorded in a **cash book**. This can take a number of different forms. The cash book described here is a format commonly used in business. It might be in paper form, or it might be set up as a computer spreadsheet.

A cash book when opened up has two sides:

■ money received 'in' is recorded on the left-hand page

■ money paid 'out' is recorded on the right-hand page

The cash book contains a number of columns for recording payments in and out – these are the same on both sides:

■ the date of the transaction

■ the description of the transaction

■ a 'cash' column for items of cash

■ a 'bank' column for items paid through the bank account

Any payment entered in the cash book will therefore appear in three columns, either as a receipt (money in) or as a payment (money out). Study the cash book and payment entries illustrated below. Note that the first entry is the 'balance brought forward' – the amounts in the cash fund and the bank account at the start of the period.

MONEY IN **MONEY OUT**

CASH BOOK

receipts | | | | payments

Date	Description	Cash £	Bank £	Date	Description	Cash £	Bank £
2002				2002			
11 Feb	Balance brought fwd.	100.00	850.00	12 Feb	Cheque (Gas bill)		160.00
12 Feb	Cheque (G Smith)		120.00	13 Feb	Cash wages (cleaner)	60.00	
13 Feb	Cheque (R Patel)		550.00	14 Feb	Cheque (B Jones)		220.85
14 Feb	Cash received (sales)	55.75		15 Feb	Standing order (Rent)		360.40
15 Feb	Cheque (B Davis)		275.00	15 Feb	Bank charges		79.00

cash held and money already in the bank

cash payments received

payments into the bank account

cash payment made

payments from the bank account

Activity 41.6 – recording payments

You are working in the Accounts Department of A Moody Limited and have been given a number of payments to enter in the business cash book.

The cash balance on 2 December 2002 is £250 and there is £960 in the bank on the same date.

1   Enter the cash and bank balances in the cash book, using 2 December 2002 as the date.

2   Enter the cash and cheques received and paid in the appropriate columns of the cash book below (or on a separate sheet or into a spreadsheet file set up for the purpose).

The transactions are:

		£
2 Dec	Cheque paid (telephone bill)	275.00
3 Dec	Direct debit paid (rates)	325.00
3 Dec	Cash received from sales	550.80
3 Dec	Cheque received from a customer V de Mort	890.65
4 Dec	Cheque paid to a supplier H Granger	499.00
4 Dec	Cash wages paid to cleaner	55.00
4 Dec	Cheque received from a customer S Fry	347.84
5 Dec	Cheque paid to a supplier W White	125.00
5 Dec	Standing order (rent received)	120.00
6 Dec	Cheque paid to a supplier D Dore	450.65
6 Dec	Cheque received from a customer B Crouch	400.00

receipts				CASH BOOK		payments		

Date	Description	Cash £	Bank £	Date	Description	Cash £	Bank £
2002				2002			

Nutshell summary

- Paying for goods and services using cash is still very common and convenient. It is also an instant method of payment.

- Businesses find cash expensive to store and handle as it can easily be stolen.

- Cheques are often used by consumers and businesses when paying for goods and services. They have the major advantage that they can safely be sent through the post.

- Cheques take three days to clear once they have been paid into the bank. They are not a guaranteed payment as they may then possibly 'bounce' and be returned with the result that the business then loses its money.

- Debit cards have replaced cheques to some extent as a means of payment. They have the advantage to the business accepting them that they guarantee payment. Debit cards can also be accepted as a means of payment over the internet.

- Credit cards are very popular as they enable the purchaser of goods or services to pay at a later date. Credit cards can also be accepted as a means of payment over the internet.

- There are many different ways of paying money – making credit transfers – through the banking system.

- Bank giro credits are a traditional paper-based method of making payments. They are very convenient for paying bills such as gas and electricity accounts.

- BACS computer-based payments are becoming increasingly popular as they are far cheaper than paper-based systems.

- There are a number of different forms of BACS payment, each suitable for a particular purpose:

  - standing orders for regular payments

  - direct debits for payments such as insurance premiums which may vary from time to time

  - bulk payments where payments have to be made to a number of different people.

Key terms

Cash
Notes and coins.

Cheque
An instruction in writing to a bank to pay a sum of money.

Debit card
A plastic card issued by a bank to its customer which enables payment to be made without the need for a cheque

Credit card
A plastic card issued by a credit card company which enables a customer to purchase products and pay for them at a later date.

Credit transfer
Payment through the banks.

Bank giro credit
Paper-based payment system.

BACS
Bankers Automated Clearing Services – the banks' computer payment system.

Standing order
Payments set up by the bank of the person paying.

Direct debit
Payments set up by the bank of the person receiving payment.

Bulk payment
Payments to a number of different people.

Cash book
Record of cash and cheque payments in a single book.

42

Computer accounting

Computer accounts for Pronto Supplies?

Pronto Supplies Limited is a limited company business owned by Alex Shaw. It sells stationery and has been in business for a year.

The financial records of Pronto Supplies Limited have been kept by Alex (with the help of a book-keeper) in a paper-based format. The records include:

■ a cash book which records payments in and out of the bank account

■ accounts for sales, expenses, assets (items owned) and liabilities (items owed)

■ accounts for customers who have bought on credit

■ accounts for suppliers from whom Pronto Supplies Limited buys on credit

Alex finds it a pain to have to write up the accounts all the time and to type out invoices and credit notes.

A friend suggests putting the accounts on a Sage computer accounting package called 'Line 50'. She says 'Once the system is set up, it will be so much easier to do your accounts. It will even print out your invoices for you.'

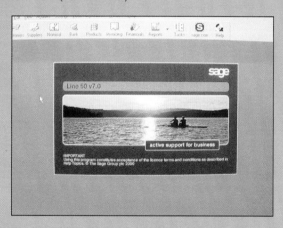

a point to think about . . .

A computer accounting package sounds like a good idea. But what if the computer crashes or is stolen?

deciding on a computer accounting program

what is a computer accounting program?

A **computer accounting program** is a program which enables a business owner such as Alex to:

■ enter data relating to **customers** and **suppliers** on a computer

■ enter financial transactions on a computer

■ print out financial documents

■ print out reports and other useful financial information

setting up the records

Alex first buys a new PC and then with the help of the **book-keeper:**

- sets up all the accounts for sales, expenses, assets and liabilities
- sets up the customer records
- sets up the supplier records

Study the computer screens which are shown below.

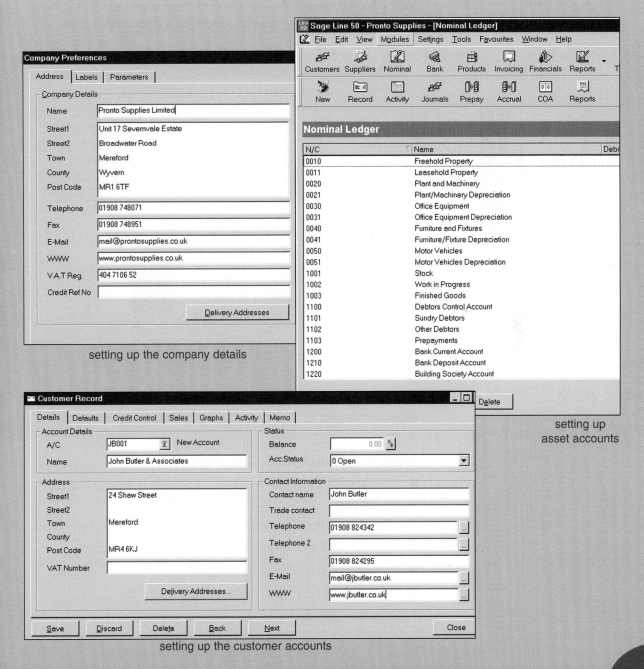

setting up the company details

setting up asset accounts

setting up the customer accounts

advantages of computer accounting systems

Using a computer accounting system provides Alex with a number of benefits:

- the system is accurate
- the system automates processes like printing invoices
- it saves time and money
- it provides useful information

Study the two screens shown below. On the right is an invoice input screen, on the left is an 'activity report' on a customer account.

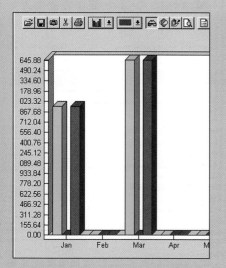

a report on customer activity
(goods bought) in graph form

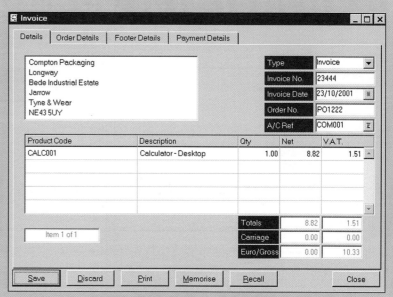

an invoice input screen

disadvantages of computer accounting systems

The benefits of using a computer accounting package have to outweigh the disadvantages. The main problems are:

- the system is expensive to set up – you have to buy and insure the computer
- people using the software will need training
- the data input will have to be backed up and kept securely
- computers can crash and be stolen
- computers can get viruses and the data can be lost

The fact that so many businesses now use computer accounting software shows that the benefits do outweigh the disadvantages.

Activity 42.1 – computer accounting

Alex has been using a Sage computer accounting program for three months and has been getting on well with it.

A friend, who is also in business, asks:

"Would it be worth it for me to set up my accounts on a computer accounting program? What do you think?"

Write down:

1   Four advantages to a business of setting up accounts on a computer accounting program.

2   Four disadvantages to a business of setting up accounts on a computer accounting program.

Nutshell summary

- A computerised accounting system means that the computer can
  - hold data relating to customers and suppliers
  - process financial transactions
  - print out financial documents
  - produce reports for the business owner

- Setting up a computer accounting program can be a lengthy process, but once it has been done it makes life easier for the business:
  - the financial records will be accurate
  - invoices can be printed out automatically
  - information about customer and supplier accounts is easy to get hold of

- The data held on computer accounting programs needs to be backed up and kept secure. Computers can easily go wrong and are frequent targets for thieves.

Key terms

Computer accounting program
A computer program which holds and processes financial data held by a business.

Customers
People to whom a business sells goods or services on credit.

Suppliers
People from whom a business buys goods or services on credit.

Book-keeper
A person who enters the financial transactions of a business in 'the books'.

Web Directory

business websites for investigation

Websites of organisations which you might want to investigate for your Portfolio work for Units 1 and 2:

www.amazon.co.uk – an online bookshop

www.bbc.co.uk – the public sector broadcasting corporation

www.bized.ac.uk – an educational site with much business information

www.co-op.co.uk – the site of the Co-op group

www.easyjet.com – the 'low price' airline

www.mcdonalds.co.uk – big Macs and more

www.mg-rover.com – the UK car manufacturer

www.osbornebooks.co.uk – the publisher of this book

www.richersounds.com – the hi-fi retailer

www.tesco.com – the supermarket chain

www.volvocars.co.uk – the car site where you can 'design' your own car

www.unilever.co.uk – a large company whose brands include Walls and Persil

websites for background information

Websites which provide background information to help your investigations:

www.bankofengland.co.uk – information about inflation, interest rates, and other statistics

www.british-franchise.org.uk – information about franchises

www.dti.gov.uk – the Department of Trade and Industry site with much business information

www.environment-agency.gov.uk – environmental issues

www.greenpeace.org.uk – an environmental protection group

www.statistics.gov.uk – a useful source of Government statistics

www.streetmap.co.uk – maps of your locality, based on postcodes

www.tca.org.uk – the site of the Telework Association

websites for Human Resources information

Websites which provide background information to help your investigations for Unit 2:

www.acas.org.uk – site of the Advisory, Conciliation and Arbitration Service

www.unison.org.uk – the Trade Union for public sector workers

www.tgwu.org.uk – the 'T & G', a major private sector Trade Union

www.eoc.org.uk – the Equal Opportunities Commission

www.disability.gov.uk – rights for the disabled in the community

www.hse.gov.uk – the Health & Safety Executive

www.dti.gov.uk/lowpay – information about low pay

www.jobsite.co.uk – an online recruitment agency

www.iipuk.co.uk – Investors in People

www.nationaltrainingawards.com – National Training Awards

websites for consumer protection issues

Websites for information about customer service requirements to help your investigations for Unit 2:

www.dataprotection.gov.uk – protection of personal information about individuals

www.tradingstandards.gov.uk – general consumer protection information

www.tradingstandards.net – specific issues relating to consumer protection

www.oft.gov.uk – the Office of Fair Trading, which regulates consumer affairs

search engine websites

Websites in which you can enter key words such as 'franchise' or 'co-operative' to help you with your investigations:

www.google.co.uk

www.yahoo.co.uk

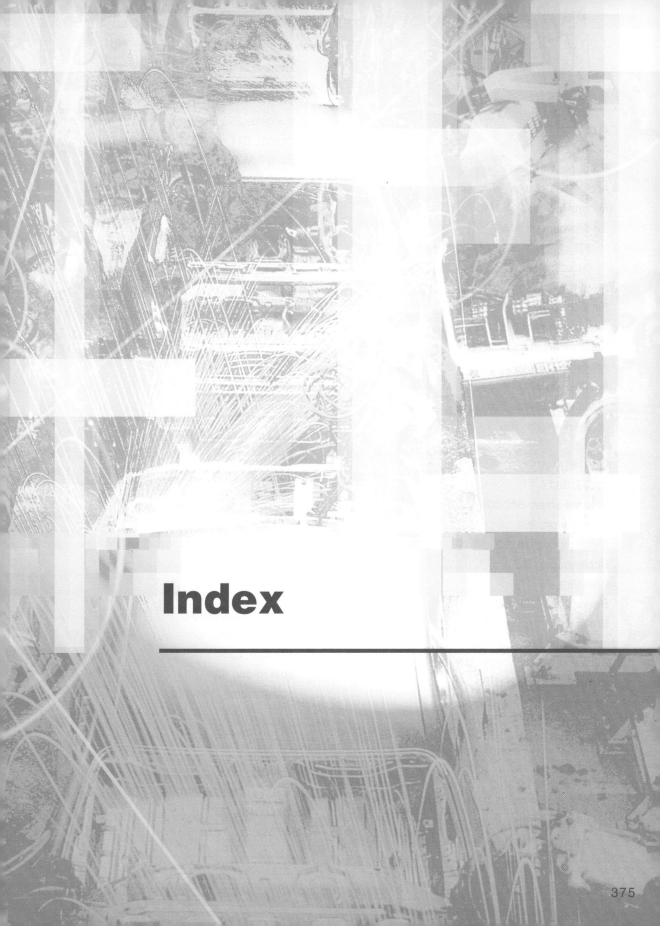

Index

notes

notes